Assembly La

Other McGraw-Hill Books of Interest

ISBN	AUTHOR	TITLE
0-07-005397-9	Birnes, Ed.	*Microcomputer Applications Handbook*
0-07-021623-1	Fortier	*Handbook of LAN Technology*
0-07-010889-7	Chorafas	*The Complete Local Area Network Reference Guide*
0-07-002394-8	Arnell	*Handbook of Disaster Recovery Planning*
0-07-005395-2	Birnes	*Online Programming Language Reference Guide*
0-07-005394-4	Birnes	*High-Level Languages and Software Applications*
0-07-067211-3	Vassilion, Orenstein	*Users Guide to Systems and Languages*
0-07-040235-3	Marca, McGowan	*SADT: Structured Analysis and Design Techniques*
0-07-043198-1	Morris	*Relational Systems Development*
0-07-036964-X	Lecarme, Gart	*Software Portability*
0-07-057299-2	Shumate	*Understanding Concurrency in Ada*
0-07-046536-3	Nielsen, Shumate	*Designing Large Real-Time Systems with Ada*
0-07-042632-5	Modell	*A Professional's Guide to Systems Analysis*
0-07-001051-X	Alford	*Requirements-Driven Software Design*
0-07-016803-2	Dickinson	*Developing Quality Systems*
0-07-065086-1	Towner (Ranade, Ed.)	*Implementing CASE*
0-07-023165-6	General Electric Company Staff	*Software Engineering Handbook*
0-07-010646-0	Wallace et al.	*A Unified Methodology for Developing Systems*
0-07-010645-2	Charette	*An Introduction to Software Engineering Environments*
0-07-067922-3	Wallace	*Practitioner's Guide to Ada*
0-07-044093-X	Musa et al.	*Software Reliability*
0-07-050783-X	Pressman	*Software Engineering: A Practitioner's Approach*
0-07-050790-2	Pressman	*Software Engineering: A Beginner's Guide*
0-07-030550-1	Howden	*Functional Program Testing and Analysis*

Computing That Works

ISBN	AUTHOR	TITLE
0-07-053923-5	Ross	*Data Exchange: PC/MS DOS*
0-07-029748-7	Hood	*Using AutoCAD with AutoLISP*
0-07-008845-4	Buerger	*LATEX for Scientists and Engineers*
0-07-029749-5	Hood	*Easy AutoCAD, 2/E*
0-07-057552-5	Simon	*How to Be a Successful Computer Consultant, 2/E*
0-07-036968-2	Lebert	*CICS for Microcomputers*
0-07-023477-9	Gliedman	*Tips and Techniques for Using Low-Cost and Public Domain Software*
0-07-056565-1	Sheldon	*Introducing PC DOS and MS DOS, 2/E*
0-07-056556-2	Sheldon	*Hard Disk Management in the PC and MS DOS Environment*
0-07-035089-2	Kliewer	*EGA/VGA: A Programmer's Reference Guide*

For more information about other McGraw-Hill materials,
call 1-800-2-MCGRAW in the United States. In other
countries, call your nearest McGraw-Hill office.

Assembly Language Programming for the 80386

Judi N. Fernandez

Ruth Ashley

McGraw-Hill Publishing Company

New York St. Louis San Francisco Auckland Bogotá
Caracas Hamburg Lisbon London Madrid Mexico
Milan Montreal New Delhi Oklahoma City
Paris San Juan São Paulo Singapore
Sydney Tokyo Toronto

IBM, IBM PC, IBM PC/AT, and IBM PS/2 are registered trademarks of International
Business Machines Corporation; Intel is a registered trademark of Intel Corporation;
Microsoft and CodeView are registered trademarks of Microsoft Corporation; Phar Lap
and 386|DOS-Extender are trademarks of Phar Lap Software, Inc.; Ventura Publisher
is a registered trademark of Ventura Software, Inc.; WordPerfect is a registered trademark of WordPerfect Corporation; WordStar is a registered trademark of MicroPro International Corporation.

1234567890   DOC/DOC   8965432109

ISBN 0-07-020575-2

The editor for this book was Theron Shreve and the production supervisor
was Dianne Walber. It was composed in Ventura Publisher by DuoTech,
Inc.

Printed and bound by R. R. Donnelley & Sons Company.

For more information about other McGraw-Hill materials,
call 1-800-2-MCGRAW in the United States. In other
countries, call your nearest McGraw-Hill office.

Contents

Preface

As more and more people use personal computers at home and on the job, software developers must learn to create useful and efficient applications for them. The newer computers in the IBM series of personal computers and their clones are built around Intel's 80286 and 80386 microprocessors. They can be programmed in high-level languages, but assembly language, which is only one step above the processor's native machine language, gives the programmer much more control over the computer's basic resources. And that results in faster programs that use less memory space and take full advantage of the microprocessor's facilities. That's the good news.

The bad news is that assembly language is much more difficult to learn and use than a high-level language. Even experienced assembly language programmers take longer to create a program in assembly language than in any high-level language. The tradeoff is worth it when a highly efficient program is needed. It might not be called for when an application or system doesn't need the increased speed, memory savings, or control assembly language provides.

Intended Audience

This book is designed to help programmers learn 80286 and/or 80386 assembly language programming. Some programming experience with other languages will help. No prior assembly language experience is needed, although it won't hurt.

Coverage

The book covers the facilities that you need to develop application programs to run under an existing operating system such as OS/2 or DOS. System programming is not covered.

The first two chapters introduce the microprocessor architecture and overview the programming process. Chapters 3 through 7 describe all the microprocessor instructions appropriate for application programs. Chapters 8 through 11 cover the most important and common assembler directives used in application programs. Finally, Chapters 12 through 14 show you how to assemble, link edit, and debug complete programs.

Two major programming systems are covered. For systems running under OS/2, we show you how to use Microsoft's program development tools, which include MASM (the macro assembler), LINK for link editing, CREF for a cross reference listing, and CodeView for debugging. You'll also learn how to bind these programs so they'll run on any microprocessor in the 8086 family operating under DOS. For 80386 machines running under DOS, you'll learn how to use the Phar Lap 386 I DOS-Extender programming system, which lets you access many of the advanced facilites of the '386 while using DOS as an operating system. The Phar Lap programs included are the 386 I ASM assembler, 386 I LINK link editor, and MINIBUG online debugger.

Both OS/2 and DOS offer myriad operating system services, mostly for input, output, and file handling. This book does not attempt to cover all the functions. You will learn enough to display messages on the monitor screen and read input from the keyboard. In the process, you will learn how to request services from each of the operating systems. After that, all you need to do is look up the service you want in the appropriate operating system reference manual and include the necessary instructions in your program.

Conventions

This sample format statement shows how instruction components are described in the book:

record-name record *field-name:width*[=*value*][,...]

Phrases in italics indicate information to be supplied by the programmer. In the **record** statement, the programmer must supply a name and at least one field-name and its width. Phrases in regular (roman) type must be included as is. The word "record" is required in the record statement. Items in square brackets ([]) are optional. In the record statement, a value may be supplied for each field, but it is not required. Ellipses (...) indicate repeated items. In the record statement, you can supply as many field descriptions (field-name:width[=value]) as necessary to define the record. Other than square brackets and ellipses, all other punctuation must be included as is. In the above example, a colon must connect each field-name with its width. If a value is included, it must be preceded by an equal sign. If additional field descriptions are included, each must be preceded by a comma. Thus, a valid record description might be:

```
date   record   month:4,day:5,year,year:7=90
```

Case does not matter in assembly language source programs. For the most part, this book uses lowercase. Mixed cases are sometimes used for clarity. Register names are lowercase in source programs but uppercase in the text so that words such as AH, AX, and ESP are clearly register names. For similar reasons, opcodes, operators, and symbols are shown in bold in the text.

Assembly Language Programming
for the 80386

The 80*xxx* Family Architecture

Intel's family of microprocessors that began with the 8086 has expanded the field of personal computing to the point where today's desktop computer has more power than a huge mainframe of just a few years ago. The earliest personal computers were built around chips such as Intel's 8080 that offered 8-bit architecture. That is, the registers, buses (the circuits that connect various parts of the computer), and instructions were designed to handle 8-bit values. Larger values had to be broken into separate 8-bit bytes for processing. The 8086 was one of the first 16-bit microprocessors—so advanced, in fact, that Intel had to develop a hybrid version, the 8088, that uses 16-bit processing internally but 8-bit buses to communicate with other chips and I/O devices for compatibility's sake. It was the 8088 that IBM chose to use in the PC computer, with all the PC compatibles following suit.

The 16-bit microprocessors offered several significant advantages over 8-bit architecture. Sixteen-bit registers allow numeric values up to 65,535 to be processed in one instruction (the 8-bit limit is 256). Sixteen-bit buses allow a complete 16-bit *word* to be fetched in one move; the 8088, with its 8-bit buses, takes twice as long to fetch or store a word.

The 16-bit architecture also influences how much memory the microprocessor can use. Every byte (8 bits) in memory has a numeric address, starting at 0 and continuing to the upper limit of memory. Since memory addresses must be stored in registers, the size of the register provides an effective limit to the amount of memory the processor can handle. With a 16-bit register, the largest memory address that can be stored is 65,535 (64 kilobytes). However, by using a combination of two registers to create a 20-bit memory address, the 8086/8088 raised their limit to 1 megabyte (1M). The 80286, also a 16-bit processor, uses two registers to create a 30-bit memory address, making it possible to address up to 1 gigabyte (one billion bytes) of memory. The 80386, which has 32-bit architecture, uses a 46-bit memory address to address up to 64 terabytes (64 trillion bytes!).

And of course, the 16-bit architecture, along with advances in microchip technology that permitted many more transistors to be included on the chip, greatly increased the number of instructions processed per second. Not only did the 8086/8088 offer greater processing power and significantly more memory than its predecessors, it was also a heck of a lot faster.

As powerful as the 8086/8088 is, it's not really a "number cruncher"; its 16-bit register size doesn't handle large enough values for scientific work, sophisticated graphics programs, and the like. Also, its built-in instructions don't go beyond addition, subtraction, multiplication, and division. The 8087 math coprocessor was designed to work with the 8086/8088 to provide advanced numeric processing. Not only does it have larger registers, it has much more mathematically sophisticated instructions along with the ability to handle real (floating point) numbers. When a math coprocessor is present, the 8086/8088 ships mathematics instructions over to it for processing; the 8087 ships answers back to the main processor. If the 8087 is not present, some programs cannot function at all, while others simulate the coprocessor functions, ver-r-r-y slowly.

The 8086/8088 chip was so successful, primarily because of its use in the PC, and so much software was developed for it, that when advances in technology permitted even more powerful chips to be developed, it was crucial that they be fully compatible with the 8086/8088. That is, any software developed for the 8086/8088 and 8087 must be capable of execution on the newer chips. And thus the 80xxx family concept was born. Figure 1-1 illustrates the growth of this family tree.

The 80186/80188 is used in some special purpose applications but never gained much acceptance as a general purpose processor. People were still concerned with using the capabilities of the 8086/8088. The 80286 and 80386 are a different story. The 80286 became the basis for

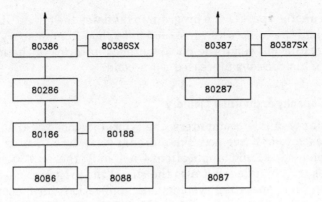

Figure 1-1   The 80*xxx* Family Tree

the IBM AT and its compatibles, while the 80386 is being used in more and more new personal computers.

80286 Features and Facilities

The 80286 offers full 16-bit architecture: registers, buses, and addresses. The chip performs at approximately three times the rate of the 8086/8088 not only because of the 16-bit design but also because it has more than three times the transistors, an on-chip Memory Management Unit, and the ability to pipeline instruction processing.

The 8086/8088 has approximately 40,000 transistors; the 80286 has more than 130,000. Many of the additional transistors are dedicated to new features, but many serve to speed up the traditional functions such as arithmetic and decision making.

The Memory Management Unit controls the use of memory, providing the basic mechanisms that make multitasking and virtual memory possible. Because this unit is built into the CPU chip instead of residing on a connected chip, access time is minimized.

To make full use of the increased speed capabilities of the chip, Intel created a pipelining scheme to speed the flow of instructions to the CPU. Traditionally, one instruction was fetched, its data fetched, the operation performed, and the output data returned to storage. Then the next instruction was fetched. The buses sat idle approximately half the time; the CPU was idle even more of the time. With the '286, when the buses are not needed by the current instruction, a separate bus management unit will automatically fetch the next instruction from memory, placing it in an on-chip queue. When the CPU is ready for another instruction, it takes one from the on-chip queue—no waiting for a fetch cycle. The slight disadvantage to this scheme is that a jump or call to another part of the program invalidates the queue. It must be emptied and the correct new instruction fetched from memory. But the advantages far outweigh the disadvantages in terms of the increased number of instructions processed per second.

Memory Capacity and Virtual Memory

In the infancy of microcomputers, the typical memory held 16K bytes. The increase to 64K seemed like a dream come true. But as memory sizes expanded, so did applications—not only the size of the data structures they handled, but also the size of the programs themselves. For a long time, operating systems and applications have been bumping up against the edges of the PC's 1M memory limit. The '286 has the capacity of 16M of physical memory, but programs are not limited to that amount. The address size of 30 bits allows programs to address up to 1 gigabyte of memory space. The Memory Management Unit provides the mechanisms for creating a virtual address space of 1G per task by transferring pages of information stored in memory between the physical memory and a mass storage unit such as a hard disk. Thus, each program appears to have 1G of memory to work with no matter how much is actually installed in the machine. However, if too little real memory is installed, system performance might degrade because too much time is being spent transferring pages between real memory and the backup device.

Protected Mode

Two operating modes are available on the '286 chip: real mode and protected virtual address mode, usually referred to as protected mode. Protected mode utilizes the full capacities of the chip: virtual memory addressing and multitasking, which allows several programs to execute at the same time.

Multitasking. With multitasking, a user can print a document from a word processor, format diskettes, ship data to the home office via telecommunications, and create a drawing on a CAD system all at the same time. Multitasking has been a feature of large-scale systems for a long time, but few microprocessors before the '286 had the speed and memory capacity necessary to make multitasking feasible.

The secret to '286 multitasking lies in the protection mechanisms that keep concurrently executing programs from accidentally or maliciously accessing each other's code or data. At the heart of the protection scheme is the concept of segmentation.

Segmentation. All information stored in memory is divided into segments, which can be up to 64K in length (the amount that can be addressed by a 16-bit address). A small program might comprise only one segment, containing both code and data. A large program, such as an operating system, might comprise multiple code segments along with many separate data segments.

Each segment is associated with a descriptor—an area of administrative information about the segment. Among other information, the descriptor contains the size of the segment, called the segment limit, and its attributes. The attributes indicate whether it can be accessed for execution only, read only, or both reading and writing. Whenever an instruction references data or another instruction, the segment limit is checked to make sure the referenced area is within the boundaries of the segment. The attributes prevent unauthorized use of segments. The execution-only attribute, which can be applied only to code segments, prevents a code segment from being read or written in; this protects code segments not only from being changed but also from being copied—if you can't read it, you can't copy it. Many code segments are marked read only, which means you can execute it or read it, but you can't write in it, so you can't change it in any way. Most data segments have the read-write attribute—you can read and change them.

Privilege Levels. Another attribute assigned to each segment is its privilege level, from 0 to 3. The privilege levels are assigned in reverse order; level 0 has the most privilege and level 3 has the least. To avoid confusion, this book always refers to the amount of privilege rather than the privilege number; thus, if segment A is "more privileged" than segment B, it has a lower privilege number. Applications operate at the least privileged level; operating system routines use the more privileged levels, with the most essential routines (the kernel) at the most privileged level (level 0).

The privilege level determines which instructions from the instruction set can be executed by the task. Instructions that affect the heart of the system, such as the system registers, are considered privileged instructions and can be executed only at privilege level 0. Thus, they can be executed only by operating systems, never by applications. The privileged instructions are listed in Appendix B but are not explained in this book, which assumes that you are not writing an operating system.

The privilege level also controls access to data segments. The privilege level of the current code segment is the privilege level of the task.

The only data segments the task can access are those in the same task that have the same privilege level. The code segment cannot access data segments outside the task, no matter what the privilege level, and it cannot access data segments at other privilege levels, whether or not they are in the same task.

Code segments frequently need to transfer execution control to other code segments either temporarily or permanently. Figure 1-2 shows the types of transfers that are permitted with the '286. The protection mechanisms allow a code segment to transfer control to any other segment in the same task at the same privilege level. The system checks the access attributes of the target segment and the referenced address within the segment against the segment limit. If those two checks are okay, the transfer is made without further fuss.

A segment can also transfer control to a more privileged code segment within the same task. This is how an application program accesses system services such as I/O routines. Only the **call** instruction, which transfers control temporarily and stores a link back to the calling program, can be used to change privilege levels like this. The **call** instruction cannot call a more privileged task directly. Instead, it references a *call gate*, a special descriptor that controls access to a higher level segment. If a more privileged routine does not have a call gate, it cannot be called by a less privileged routine. Thus the operating system can prevent unauthorized access to its routines by applications.

The call gate also has a privilege level, used to control who may access the call gate. The calling segment must be as privileged as the gate. Thus, to make a level 0 routine available to other operating

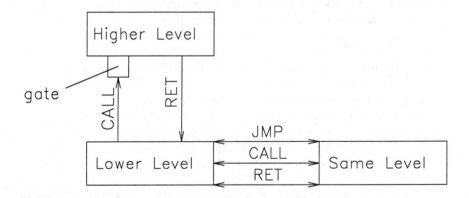

Figure 1-2   Permitted Transfers among Segments at Various Privilege Levels

system levels but not to applications, its gate is given privilege level 2 so that it cannot be accessed by level 3 segments.

A more privileged called routine returns control to a less privileged routine through the **ret** instruction, which accesses the stored back link, not a call gate, to find the return segment and address. When a **ret** instruction changes code segments, the access attributes and segment limit of the target segment are checked. The addresses of more privileged data segments are also removed from the segment address registers so that the returning segment has no opportunity to address data segments above its privilege level.

The **call** instruction cannot call a less privileged code segment; it can only call segments with the same or more privilege. On the other hand, the **ret** instruction can return to segments with either the same or less privilege—never more privilege. Thus there is no way to trick the system into illegally accessing a more privileged routine via a **ret** instruction.

A special kind of code segment, called a conforming segment, can be called from any level. It adapts its privilege level to the level of the calling segment to make calling and returning easier. This is another way for an operating system to provide services to applications with a minimum of fuss when the service routine contains no particular privileged instructions or data.

Inherent in the concept of multitasking is the need to transfer control to other tasks. To transfer control to another task, you must transfer control to either a task gate or a Task State Segment (TSS). A TSS is a data segment that stores the task's current state; that is, the current values of all its registers. When a task is suspended, its current state is stored in its own TSS. When a task is resumed, the system's registers are loaded from its TSS. This has the effect of picking the task up exactly where it left off. A task gate is similar to a call gate except that it references a TSS instead of a code segment.

Local and Global Segments. A segment can be identified as either local or global. A local segment belongs to only one task and cannot be called from other tasks without a task switch. Most application programs create only local segments. A global segment is available to all tasks; operating system services are usually contained in global segments. Two tables keep track of segment descriptors and gates: the local descriptor table (LDT) and the global descriptor table (GDT). When a program transfers control to another segment, the processor looks in either the LDT or the GDT to find the correct segment.

Real Mode

To maintain compatibility with 8086-style software, the '286 also offers another operating mode, called *real mode* because only real memory, not virtual memory, is used. Real mode simulates the functioning of the 8086/8088, at a much faster speed. Virtual memory and multitasking do not exist in real mode.

The protection mechanisms are disabled. Memory addressing is limited to 640K. This is a bit like asking Luciano Pavarotti to sing "Jingle Bells." When an IBM AT or compatible runs under DOS, it is running in real mode. DOS was developed for the 8088 and cannot use protected mode. Several operating systems have been developed to utilize the protected mode features of the '286, such as OS/2, but none of them has supplanted DOS in popularity as yet.

Exceptions and Interrupts

An *exception* is an internal event to which the system must respond before normal processing can continue, such as a protection rule violation or an attempt to divide by zero. An *interrupt* also interrupts the normal flow of processing. Hardware interrupts are demands by peripheral units such as the keyboard for attention. Each character you type at the keyboard signals an interrupt to the system, which usually reads and stores the character before returning to whatever it was doing. Some hardware interrupts, such as the keyboard input described above, are *maskable*; that is, when masking is on, the system doesn't receive the signal. Software interrupts are requested by programs when they encounter situations that warrant extra attention; for example, the **into** instruction generates an interrupt if a result has overflowed its destination field.

Both exceptions and interrupts are handled the same way and are usually referred to jointly as "interrupts." When an interrupt is detected, an interrupt code is associated with it. The processor uses the interrupt code to access the interrupt descriptor table (IDT), which contains the descriptors of the routines that handle the interrupts. The IDT contains three types of descriptors: interrupt gates and trap gates, which are very similar to call gates, and task gates for cases where the interrupt handler is in a different task. Control is transferred to the correct interrupt handler routine. What that routine does depends on the operating system; the '286 processor provides the mechanisms for sensing the interrupt and searching the IDT, but the contents of the IDT and the routines it references must be provided by the operating system. In some cases, an interrupt handler would fix the problem or service the hardware and return control to the task program that was interrupted. In other cases, the interrupt handler would issue an error message to the user and terminate the task.

80386 Features and Facilities

The 80386, with 32-bit architecture, is as advanced over the 80286 as the 80286 is over the 8086. For upward compatibility, the '386 retains all the old 16-bit registers, but extends them to 32 bits when compatibility is not needed and full advantage can be taken of the new architecture. In protected mode, a program can choose either 16-bit or 32-bit addressing mode. In 16-bit mode, the '386 acts like a very fast '286. In 32-bit mode, 64 terabytes of virtual memory can be addressed per task. This book assumes that you will be creating programs for both 16-bit and 32-bit addressing and varies examples between the two modes.

Real mode is also retained so that 8086 programs can execute. In addition, a new mode appears—virtual 8086 (V86) mode lets 8086 programs be run in a multitasking environment. In other words, on the '386 you can multitask PC-style software. (8086 programs cannot be executed in protected mode and therefore cannot be multitasked on the '286.)

Assembly Programming Resources

Assembly language is very close to the machine's own internal language and gives you much more control over the basic resources of the computer—memory, registers, and so forth—than compiler languages such as COBOL and BASIC do. It's usually harder and much more time-consuming to develop programs in assembly language, but for many programming problems, the tradeoff is worth the extra effort. Not only do you get extra control over the system, but also programs developed in assembly language tend to execute more efficiently and take up less storage space.

Assembly language programming involves developing a source program, just like you do in higher level languages, then assembling it with a program such as Microsoft's Macro Assembler (MASM). The resulting object module is then link edited to produce an executable program (an EXE file).

When working at the assembly level, the programmer's resources include the processor's registers, memory segments, and the set of instructions built into the processor.

Registers

The processor registers are small, on-chip areas for the storage and manipulation of data and addresses. Because they are built into the processor and can be accessed without using the buses, access is immediate. For example, to increment a value in memory takes 7 clock cycles ('286) or 6 clock cycles ('386), but to increment a register takes 2 clock cycles (both processors). Unfortunately, register storage space is limited, so most data must be kept in memory. Generally, the registers hold only data and addresses of immediate use to the currently executing routine.

General Purpose Registers. Most of the registers are dedicated to special system purposes and are not available for general use. However, one set of registers is provided for general program purposes. These registers, shown in Figure 1-3, are called the general purpose registers. The four registers shown at the top of the figure are generally

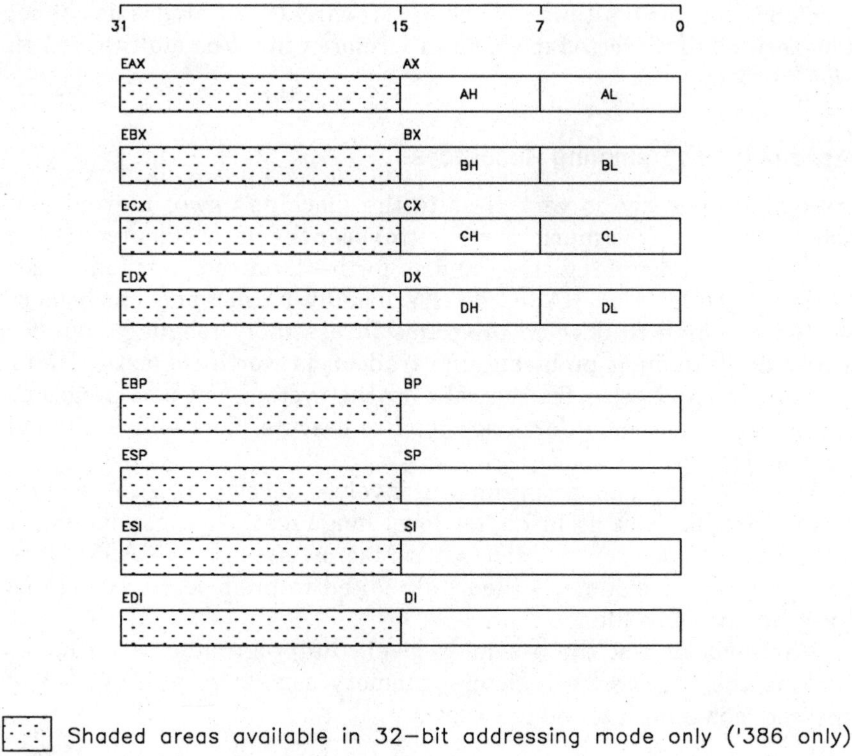

Shaded areas available in 32—bit addressing mode only ('386 only)

Figure 1-3   The General-Purpose Registers

used for data manipulation and can be accessed by byte (AL, AH, BL, BH, etc.), word (AX, BX, etc.), or in the '386, doubleword (EAX, EBX, etc.). Your programs will probably use these four registers more than any others. The four registers shown at the bottom of the figure can also be used for data manipulation but are most often used as pointers, especially SP or ESP, as you'll see shortly. A pointer is an address used to access data in memory.

The labels shown in the figure are the names you use to access these registers. For example, to increment the value in the AL register, you could use this instruction:

```
inc     al
```

The 8-bit (1-byte) registers are named *x*L for the *l*ow-order byte and *x*H for the *h*igh-order byte of the 16-bit register. The '386 versions have an extra 16 bits added to the high-order end, making them 32 bits wide. However, the low-order parts of the '386 registers are still accessible by the '286 names so that all '286 programs using those registers are executable on the '386. On the other hand, a program that references 32-bit registers such as EAX and EBP cannot be run on the '286. If you're writing a program using 16-bit addressing so that it will run on both processors, you must not use the full 32-bit registers.

This book uses "(E)AX," "(E)BX," and so forth when talking about either the 16-bit or the 32-bit version of the register. Thus, when we say "(E)SP is incremented," we mean that ESP is incremented when 32-bit addressing is being used and SP is incremented when 16-bit addressing is being used.

Although these eight registers are available for general purposes, they do have a few predefined uses—certain instructions use them automatically. It's these predefined uses that give the registers their names:

• (E)AX is used as an *a*ccumulator for arithmetic operations such as **mul** (multiply) and **div** (divide).

• (E)BX can be used as a *b*ase address register for a data structure in the '286. (In the '386, any of these registers can be used as a base register, as explained later in this chapter.)

• (E)CX is used as a *c*ount register by repetition instructions such as **rep** (repeat) and **loop**.

- (E)DX is just generally used as a *d*ata register. In arithmetic instructions requiring a double-width register, it acts as the high-order half of the accumulator.

- (E)BP is used as a *b*ase *p*ointer for data structures stored in the stack, as explained later in this chapter.

- (E)SP is used as the *s*tack *p*ointer and should not be used for any other purpose, even though it's designated as a general purpose register.

- (E)SI and (E)DI are used as the *s*ource *i*ndex and *d*estination *i*ndex for string operations such as **movs** (move string) and **cmps** (compare string). These two indexes are advanced automatically to point to successive bytes of the strings being processed.

Segment Registers. Figure 1-4 shows several system registers used by application programs. At the top are the segment registers; the '286

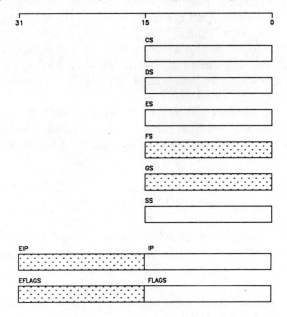

Shaded areas available with '386 only

Figure 1-4   Some Useful System Registers

has four, while the '386 has six. These 16-bit registers point to the beginning of each segment in memory and are used by the system to find instructions and data belonging to the task.

CS locates the current code segment. DS locates the main data segment. It is sometimes useful to work with two or more data segments simultaneously. ES locates an additional data segment called the extra segment. In the '386, you can also have two more data segments, located by FS and GS. A special data segment called a stack segment is located by SS. The stack segment is explained later in this chapter.

The system decides where to place the initial segments when a program is initiated and loads the initial value of the code segment into CS. If the program transfers control to another code segment, the value in CS is replaced. The initial value of the stack segment is also placed in SS so that the stack is usable as soon as the program begins. The program must load its own data segment registers (DS through GS) as needed.

In real mode, the segment register contains the actual physical address of the segment. In protected mode, the segment register value is a pointer to the segment's descriptor in one of the descriptor tables. The descriptor contains the actual base address of the segment. Actual addresses within segments are located by adding the base address to an offset, which is either 16 or 32 bits long depending on the processor and the addressing mode.

The Instruction Pointer. The (E)IP register shown in Figure 1-4 always contains the address offset of the next instruction to be executed. When a new program is invoked, (E)IP is set to point to the first instruction of the program, probably at address offset 0. When the instruction at that address offset is fetched, (E)IP is increased by the number of bytes in the instruction. For example, if the first instruction at offset 0 is 3 bytes long, (E)IP is set to 3 as soon as the instruction is fetched. When the first instruction is completed, the second instruction is fetched from address offset 3. If it is a 2-byte instruction, (E)IP is increased to 5. If control is jumped to another part of the program, (E)IP is increased, decreased, or replaced as appropriate.

The system uses CS in combination with (E)IP to find the actual memory address of the instruction. Remember that CS is pointing to the base address of the current code segment either directly (real mode) or indirectly (protected mode). The combination of CS and (E)IP, which is written as CS:(E)IP, locates the actual address.

The Flags Register. The (E)FLAGS register contains bit switches that reflect the current status of the system. Figure 1-5 shows the details of the flag bits; bits 18 through 31 are not used. The flags available in the low-order word, called FLAGS, are the same in both the '286 and '386. The flags in the extended portion of the register are available only in the '386.

Most of the flags are one-bit flags. A one-bit flag is set (value=1) when a condition is true or on; it is cleared (value=0) when the condition is false or off. For example, the zero flag (ZF) is set when a result is zero and cleared if it is anything but zero. One flag, the input/output privilege level (IOPL), is a two-bit flag so it can record the four privilege levels, 0 through 3.

Six flags reflect the status of the result field after an operation such as arithmetic or a comparison. These flags, known as the *status flags*, are used for decision-making in programs:

- Carry Flag (CF) indicates whether the high order bit of the result produced a carry that went outside the field and was lost or borrowed a 1 from outside the field. This flag is set when the high order bit produced a carry or borrow, cleared otherwise. It indicates overflow of the result field and an invalid result when unsigned values are manipulated. See the overflow flag for signed values.

- Parity Flag (PF) is set when the number of 1 bits in the result is even; cleared when the number of 1 bits is odd. Thus, PF=1 indicates even parity, PF=0 odd parity.

- Auxiliary Flag (AF) is set if a carry or borrow occurred between bits 3 and 4 of the result. This flag is used only in BCD arithmetic where it's important to identify overflow between the lower nibble and the upper nibble of a result.

17	16	15	14	13	12	11	10	9	8	7	6	5	4	3	2	1	0
VM	RF		NT	IOPL		OF	DF	IF	TF	SF	ZF		AF		PF		CF

▨ Shaded areas available with '386 only

Figure 1-5   The (E)FLAGS Register

- Zero Flag (ZF) is set if the result is zero, cleared otherwise.

- Sign Flag (SF) is set to the same value as the high order bit of the value. In signed values, the high order bit is 1 for negative values, 0 for positive values. It is meaningless for unsigned values.

- Overflow Flag (OF) indicates whether a carry or borrow occurred between the next-to-high-order bit and the high-order bit of the result. It is set to 1 if a carry or borrow occurred and cleared if not. This flag indicates whether the result overflowed the destination field and is valid for signed values only. It has no meaning for unsigned values, for which you should use the carry flag.

Some instructions affect all the status flags, some affect some, and some affect none. The instruction summary in Appendix A indicates which status flags are affected by each instruction. If a flag is not affected by an instruction, it retains its former value. However, there is a gray area. Some instructions leave some flags undefined, meaning that the former value might or might not have been changed and the current value is unreliable. This isn't as drastic as it sounds; when an instruction leaves flags undefined, those flags would probably not be useful anyway. The instruction summary in Appendix A indicates the flags affected by each instruction; undefined flags are shown in parentheses.

The remaining flags in (E)FLAGS are system and control flags. Their values affect the operation of the system. Unlike the status flags, which are set or cleared automatically according to conditions, these system and control flags can be set and cleared by program instructions to affect how processing occurs.

- Trap Flag (TF) controls step-by-step execution. When this flag is set, the processor executes only one instruction at a time, then interrupts. This "single-stepping" mode is a debugging feature and is generally used only by on-line debuggers.

- Interrupt Flag (IF) controls whether a program can be interrupted by external (maskable) interrupts. When it is set, which is most of the time, the task can be interrupted by external interrupts. When it is cleared, external interrupts are disabled. This flag should only be cleared by interrupt handling routines.

- Direction Flag (DF) controls the direction of string moves. When cleared, string instructions move forward; that is, (E)SI and (E)DI are incremented after each step. When it is set, string instructions move backward; (E)SI and (E)DI are decremented after each step. This is the only system and control flag that application programs might use. Most of the time, forward direction is desirable, but there are cases where backward direction works better, as you'll see in Chapter 3. The **std** instruction sets the direction flag, while **cld** clears it.

• Input/Output Privilege Level (IOPL) indicates the task's ability to perform system-level operations such as setting the interrupt flag and performing input and output directly; these facilities must be strictly controlled by the operating system in a multitasking environment. The IOPL is assigned to the task by the operating system and cannot be changed by any program with less than 0 privilege. Special protection checks prevent a program from attempting to insert a new value into the IOPL bits by such means as overwriting the entire (E)FLAGS register.

• Nested Task Flag (NT) indicates whether or not the current task was called by another one. It is set by the system and cannot be changed by the program.

• Resume Flag (RF) is used by on-line debuggers to resume execution after a debug exception ('386 only).

• Virtual 8086 Mode Flag (VM): This flag indicates the processor is executing an 8086 program in V86 mode ('386 only).

System Registers. All other registers are for system use only. These include registers that point at the beginning of the LDT, GDT, IDT, and the current task; testing and debugging registers in the '386; and a machine status word that uses bit flags to indicate the status of the processor. These registers are accessible by programs operating at level 0 only.

Segments

Memory segments are another important programming resource. They can be up to 64K long in 16-bit addressing mode, 4G long with 32-bit addressing.

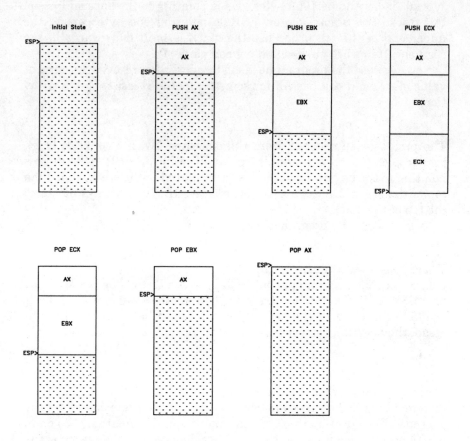

Figure 1-6   Pushing and Popping Items

The Stack Segment. A stack is a data storage area where items are stored and removed like plates in a stack—new items are placed on top of the stack, and the last item placed on the stack is the first removed. It is used primarily for temporary storage and for communicating with subroutines. When you want to preserve an item temporarily, you push it onto the top of the stack. When you want to use it again, you pop it off the top of the stack, revealing the next item in the stack.

Figure 1-6 shows how the stack operates. Thirty-two-bit addressing is shown in the figure, but the same principles apply to 16-bit addressing. The program defines a stack segment of a certain size. In the figure, a very small stack has been defined—only ten bytes. (A more typical size would be 1000 bytes.) SS is pointing to the base address of the stack. The stack pointer, ESP, is pointing one byte beyond the upper end of the stack because the stack is built downwards in the segment. Items are pushed and popped via ESP.

Now suppose the program needs to temporarily preserve the current value of AX so it can use AX for something else. It issues this instruction:

```
push    ax
```

The processor subtracts 2 from ESP (because AX is two bytes long), then copies AX to the address pointed at by SS:ESP. ESP is now pointing to the beginning of the last item placed in the stack, called the top of the stack. Unless a program misuses (E)SP, it always points to the top of the stack.

Now suppose the program needs to preserve EBX:

```
push    ebx
```

You can see the result in Figure 1-6.

Later on, the program pushes ECX onto the stack. The stack is now full; ESP=0. If the program tried to push another value, a stack fault would occur because the segment limit would be exceeded. But instead, the program removes a value from the stack:

```
pop    ecx
```

The top item on the stack (the last one pushed) is always the one popped by **pop**, which copies the item addressed by SS:(E)SP, then increments (E)SP by the number of bytes popped (determined by the operand of the **pop** instruction). In Figure 1-6, the program goes on to pop the remaining items off the stack. At the end, ESP has reached the upper segment limit. One more **pop** would cause a stack fault.

It's not necessary for a program to clear the stack. It could push three items, pop two, push four more, pop one, push two, pop three, and so forth, as long as it doesn't exceed the segment limit. It's also not necessary to pop a value back into the same field it was pushed from; not only does the processor not remember the source of items on the stack, it doesn't remember the original sizes. If you code:

```
push    eax        ; 4 bytes
pop     bx         ; 2 bytes
pop     cx         ; 2 bytes
```

you have just copied half of EAX into BX and half into CX. Be sure you know what you are doing when you manipulate the stack as it greatly increases the chance of error, not only on your part but especially on the part of someone trying to maintain or adapt your program. In general, you should pop items back to the same place they came from or to a memory area.

Sometimes you want to work on an item right in the stack without popping it, especially if it's not at the top of the stack. (E)BP was designed for that purpose. You can place the item's address offset in (E)BP, then use it as the operand of an instruction. The processor uses SS as the segment register when you use (E)BP as an operand.

Usually a task functions just fine with only one stack. But a program can create more than one stack segment if necessary. For example, a called routine might want to use its own stack to avoid exceeding the stack segment limits of the calling routine. You can switch stacks by replacing the selector in SS. Since the stack must have the same privilege level as the code segment (the stack must follow the data segment rules), if the task switches privilege levels via a call gate, the stack is switched automatically to one with the correct privilege level. A back link to the former stack is stored in the new stack. When control returns to the former level, the former stack is restored.

The Instruction Set

The assembly language instruction set, with which you write assembly language source code, has been growing since the days of the 8086. The original instruction set offered all the basic facilities of a modern-day processor—**add, mov,** and so forth. Each new processor in the family retained all the former instructions and added several more to take advantage of the improved features. The numeric coprocessor has its own instruction set, which has also grown with each new chip.

Appendix A shows the '286/'386 instructions used by application programs. Appendix B describes system programming instructions. Appendix C describes coprocessor instructions. Not all the details of these instructions are shown. In particular, we have omitted clock cycles and machine language translations. If you feel you need these items, which can help in system programming, optimizing, and debugging, they are documented in Intel's programmer reference manuals. The information contained in the instruction appendices is not repeated in the chapters. As each instruction is introduced in the text of a chapter, be sure to look up that instruction in the appropriate appendix to see the details of flags affected, operand formats, etc.

Most instructions take some form of operand that identifies the data to be worked on or the target of a control transfer. Operands take the form of immediate data, registers, or memory addresses.

Immediate Operands. An immediate operand includes the data to be operated on right in the instruction. The second operand, 5, is immediate in this instruction:

```
add     ax,5
```

The instruction causes 5 to be added to the value in AX.

Immediate operands can be signed or unsigned numbers or ASCII values. How these are expressed depends on the assembler you use, but most assemblers use the following conventions:

- A number can be expressed in binary, octal, decimal, or hexadecimal. Decimal is assumed unless a suffix indicates another radix: B for binary, O or Q for Octal, H for hexadecimal. For consistency, D can also be used for decimal. Thus, 101B = 5D; 101Q = 65D; 101H = 257D. Hexadecimal numbers must start with a digit to avoid confusion with names; 0BH is a hexadecimal number, but BH is the name of a register.

- Plus signs (+) and minus signs (–) placed before numbers indicate the sign.

- Decimal points (124.56) or scientific notation (629E–7) can be used for floating point numbers for the numeric coprocessor (the main processor cannot handle real numbers).

- ASCII values can be expressed either numerically or by placing an ASCII printable character in quotes: '1' = 31H = 49D = 00110001B.

Most assemblers also let you define a symbol that represents an immediate value. An equal sign or the **equ** directive is usually used for this purpose

```
mask        =       00FFh

tax_rate    equ     6
```

Mask and **tax_rate** can now be used as immediate operands in instructions. Wherever **mask** is used, the assembler substitutes 00FFh. Wherever **tax_rate** is used, the assembler substitutes 6.

Register Operands. Registers are referenced by their names, as shown in these instructions:

```
        add     ax,bx

        mov     eax,ecx
```

```
push    eax
```

Memory Operands. There are many ways to express memory operands, each suited to particular situations. You can specify a complete address as segment:offset, or you can specify just the offset and let the processor assume the segment.

When a memory operand is used, the processor calculates the effective address of the desired memory field by adding the segment base address plus the offset. The offset, in turn, is calculated by adding up to three elements: a displacement, a base register, and an index register, which may be scaled in the '386. All three elements are optional, but at least one must be provided. Each element is described below:

Displacement: The displacement is usually expressed as an address offset that either directly identifies the desired item, in simple cases, or locates the beginning of the data structure when a base register and/or index register is also used. The displacement is usually expressed as a symbolic address.

A symbolic address is a symbol that has an address value. In a data segment, a symbolic address is defined by attaching a label to a field definition. This directive defines a one-word field with the symbolic address **work_hours**:

```
work_hours dw     ?
```

The memory address offset of this word becomes the value of the symbol **work_hours**. Anywhere that **work_hours** is used as an address operand in the program, the assembler substitutes this operand value. Thus, the instruction below causes the value contained in this word to be moved into AX:

```
mov     ax,work_hours
```

The symbol also has a length associated with it according to the data definition it labels. **Work_hours** is one byte long because the **dw** directive defines one byte. The assembler would reject the following instruction because the two operands are different sizes:

```
mov     eax,work_hours
```

Symbolic addresses can also be defined in code sections to create target addresses for control transfers. Two common ways of defining symbolic addresses in a code segment are:

```
loop_start:
```

and

```
factorial   proc    near
```

Again, the assembler substitutes the desired address wherever it finds these symbolic addresses used as address operands, as in:

```
jmp     loop_start
call    factorial
loop    loop_start
```

Sometimes the desired address is a few bytes before or after the address pointed to by a symbolic address. You can add a base or index register to the displacement to reach the right address, or you can simply add or subtract the correct number of bytes from the displacement:

```
mov     ax,work_hours+4
mov     ax,work_hours-1
```

Even though the effective address is offset from the beginning of the **work_hours** field, the size of the operand is still determined by the definition of **work_hours**; since **work_hours** is defined as one word, two bytes will be moved into AX. In the first case, the two bytes moved are **work_hours+4** and **work_hours+5**. In the second case, the two bytes moved are **work_hours–1** and **work_hours**.

Base Register: A base register is a general purpose register that contains an address offset value or an offset from the displacement if both are used. It is placed in square brackets to differentiate it from a register operand:

```
mov     ax,[ebx]
mov     ax,work_hours[ebx]
```

In the first example, EBX contains the address offset of the desired memory word used as an *indirect address*; that is, the processor looks in the register to find the desired address. In the second example, **work_hours** is the displacement and [EBX] contains the number of bytes (signed) to add to the displacement to find the desired word. In the first example, the operation size is taken from the first operand. In the second example, **work_hours** determines the size of the second operand even though the effective address is offset from **work_hours**.

In the '286, only BX, BP, SP, DI, and SI can be used as a base register. In the '386, any general purpose register can be used.

Index Register: It's sometimes difficult to tell the difference between a base register and an index register. In the above examples, [EBX] could be an index as easily as a base register. There are some slight differences, however. In the '286, if only one register is used, it is a base register. If two registers are used, one is a base register and can

be only BX or BP, while the other is an index register and must be SI or
DI. SP cannot be used for either register when two registers are used.

In the '386, any general purpose register can be a base register, and
any general purpose register except (E)SP can be an index register. In
the '386, an index register can be scaled (multiplied) by 2, 4, or 8 as
part of the address calculation:

```
mov    ax,[esi]

mov    ax,hours_table[esi*2]

mov    ax,hours_table[ebx][esi*4]
```

In the first example, it's unclear whether [ESI] is a base or index
register, but as long as it contains the correct value, it doesn't matter.
In the second example, [ESI*2] is clearly an index register because it is
scaled by 2. This format is handy for accessing a table of words, as
you'll see later in this book. The third example uses all three addressing elements, which comes in handy primarily when accessing two-
dimensional tables. The same instructions for the '286 would probably
look like this:

```
mov    ax,[si]

mov    ax,hours_table[si]

mov    ax,hours_table[bx][si]
```

Since scaling isn't available, the value in SI must be multiplied by the
scaling factor in a separate instruction preceding the use of SI as an
index register, which takes a lot more time than the '386 version.

In all the address examples so far, the segment has been assumed.
Figure 1-7 shows the assumptions the processor makes. In general, all
indirect register addresses are presumed to be in the main data segment, addressed by DS, except [(E)SP] and [(E)BP], which are assumed to address the stack segment. (If you use a symbolic address
instead of an indirect register, the processor determines the correct
segment by the location of the instruction or directive that defines the
symbolic address.)

Base Register	Assumed Selector
Any register but (E)SP and (E)BP	DS
(E)SP or (E)BP	SS

Figure 1-7   Segment Assumptions for Base Registers

If you want to override the processor's segment assumptions, you can specify the segment address as in:

```
mov    ax,table_seg:[bx]
```

More easily, you can specify the segment selector:

```
mov    ax,es:[bx]

mov    ax,fs:[esi]

mov    ax,ds:[bp]
```

It's a lot more efficient to let the processor assume the segment, so try to work with the address registers instead of against them. That is, use (E)SP and (E)BP to access the stack, the other registers to access the main data segment. Of course, if you want to use any of the extra data segments, you'll have to use segment overrides with indirect register addresses.

Data Types

The basic data types of the '286 are the byte and the word; the '386 also offers the doubleword. The numeric coprocessors work with doublewords, quadwords (64 bits), and tenbytes (80 bits).

The contents of these fields can be in any format. The instruction set is designed to work with the formats described below:

Unsigned integers: The entire field is treated as a binary value with no sign or decimal point.

Signed integers: The high order bit represents the sign (0 for positive, 1 for negative). The rest of the field represents the value with no decimal point. Negative numbers are stored in two's complement notation.

Unpacked BCD: Each byte represents one decimal digit, from 0 to 9. Values above 9 are illegal.

Packed BCD: Each byte is treated as two nibbles. Each nibble represents one decimal digit, from 0 to 9, so each byte can hold two digits. Values above 9 are illegal.

Bit string: Each bit operates independently representing a flag, a pixel, or whatever. The (E)FLAGS register is a good example of a bit string.

Character string: A series of consecutive bytes, words, or doublewords ('386 only), containing one character per field.

Byte Reversal. When the processor stores a value longer than a byte in memory it reverses the bytes, as shown in Figure 1-8. The bits within

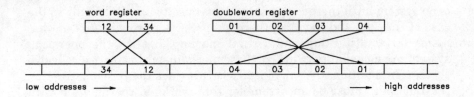

Figure 1-8   Byte Reversal from Registers to Memory (including the Stack)

the bytes are not reversed, so the value isn't completely backwards, but the low-order byte goes into the lowest memory address, the next-higher byte at the next address, and so forth. This is true whether the value is stored in a data segment or a stack. When the value is moved to a register, the bytes are straightened out again automatically.

Every instruction that handles data in memory takes the byte reversal into account. If you add 5 to a doubleword in memory, the 5 gets added to the correct byte and any carries are carried over to the correct bytes. If you shift the bits of a word in the stack to the left one position each, the result will come out correctly. For the most part, you don't need to be aware of the byte reversal, except for two situations:

- If you try to access only part of a value, you don't give the system a chance to straighten the bytes. If you push a doubleword but pop a word, for example, or treat a value that was stored as a doubleword as a 4-byte string, you're going to run into trouble unless you reverse the bytes yourself.

- When using memory dumps for debugging, you will see the reversed bytes in memory. You'll have to straighten them out manually (or at least mentally) to find out what values were in memory at the time of the dump.

Other than these two situations, you don't need to be aware of byte reversal.

The Role of the Operating System and the Assembler

The microprocessor provides the raw facilities for a system, but there is no system until there is operating system software. Especially in the case of the '286 and the '386, the microprocessor provides the mechanisms for multitasking and virtual memory, but it's the operating system's responsibility to utilize those mechanisms to create a cohesive system. In addition, the microprocessor provides the basic instruction set, but there must be an assembler that works in coordination with the operating system to translate assembly language source programs into machine language. You'll see how all three elements work together to create a working program in the next chapter.

Programming Overview

This chapter shows how to combine the features of the microprocessor and its instruction set, the services provided by the operating system, and the features of the assembler to create complete, working programs. Two programming problems are dealt with. The first is the classic "Hello, World" problem (modified in this case to say "Help! I'm being held prisoner in your microcomputer!"); that is, the program simply displays one line on the monitor and terminates itself. The second problem adds an input routine: the program asks for the user's name, then displays the message, "Hello, *name*."

Each problem is solved in three contexts: the first uses Microsoft's Macro Assembler (MASM) to create a program to run on the '286 under OS/2; the second is a variation of the same program that will run on any processor in the 80*xxx* family under either DOS or OS/2; the third uses Phar Lap's programming system to create a program that will run in '386 protected mode under a DOS extender.

Walking through several short programs like this should help to keep you from getting lost in the myriad details presented in the remainder of the book. This chapter presents the forest; the rest of the book deals with the trees. Don't worry if you don't understand every instruction presented in this chapter; each item overviewed here is covered in much more detail in upcoming chapters.

Modular Design

The benefits of modular programming have been recognized for many years now. Both assemblers used in this book make it easy to break programs into *procedures* (the same as subroutines or modules). Even these very short programs are modularized to serve as models for more complex programs. In each case, the main routine is simply a control routine that designates the order in which procedures are executed. The called procedures do all the detail work.

Directives vs. Instructions

The source programs in this chapter, like all assembler language programs, are a combination of microprocessor instructions and assembler directives. The microprocessor instructions come from the instruction set and cause the microprocessor to execute an operation such as **mov** (move data), **add**, or **call**. The assembler directives are not provided by the microprocessor instruction set; each assembler offers its own set of assembler directives, which gives orders to the assembler during the assembly process. If you peek ahead at the program figures in this chapter, you'll see many examples of assembler directives. Lines that create segments, such as **.stack** and **.data** in Figure 2-1 and the **segment** directives in Figure 2-6, are assembler directives. The lines that define data fields, such as **db** and **dw**, are also assembler directives.

A microprocessor instruction is translated by the assembler into machine language code and stored in the code segment to be executed by the microprocessor each time the program is executed. An assembler directive is not translated into machine language; it is executed on the spot by the assembler while translating the program. It does not appear in the machine language version of the program and takes up no room in memory. Its sole purpose is to tell the assembler *how* to interpret the microprocessor instructions.

Because they are associated with the microprocessor, the microprocessor instructions are standardized across all assemblers. The assembler directives, on the other hand, can vary from assembler to assembler. However, the two assemblers used in this book have very similar directives. In fact, since the MASM assembler has set the standard, most '286 and '386 assemblers offer the same directives as the MASM assembler. (You will see some exceptions later in this chapter.)

Format

Both instructions and directives take this general format:

[*label*] opcode [*operands*] [*;comments*]

The *label* creates a symbolic address at the position where the instruction appears. The function of labels in an assembler directive depends on the directive. The *opcode* is a mnemonic code for the operation to be performed, such as **mov** or **add**. "Opcode" is really the correct term for instructions only; since assembler directives also use similar-looking codes, such as **db** and **equ**, they are often called "pseudo-ops" to distinguish them from true opcodes.

In instructions, the *operands* identify the data to be operated on, as you saw in Chapter 1. In directives, the operands supply variable information about the directive. For example, in the **db** directive, the operand specifies the initial value of the byte to be defined:

```
end_code     db       '$'                  ; end-of-message code
```

This directive reserves one byte in memory and places the ASCII code for a dollar sign in it.

Comments are ignored by the assembler but can make life much easier for people who are reading and/or trying to maintain your program. In addition to adding comments to the end of instructions, you can also create longer comments on lines by themselves, as in this example:

```
; This program displays the message:
;
;        Help! I'm being held prisoner in your microcomputer!
;
; Then it terminates itself.
```

The HELP Program for MASM-OS/2

Figure 2-1 shows the source code for the MASM-OS/2 version of the HELP program. We have numbered the lines in the source code solely to facilitate this discussion. Don't number your source code or your assembler might reject it.

```
 1                      dosseg
 2                      .model small
 3                      .286
 4                      .stack 1000

 5                      .data
 6 cr                   equ    0Dh           ; ASCII return
 7 lf                   equ    0Ah           ; ASCII line feed
 8 std_device           equ    1             ; monitor handle

 9 help_msg             db     "Help! I'm being held prisoner"
10                      db     " in your microcomputer",cr,lf
11 help_msg_len         dw     $ - help_msg ; length of help_msg
12 bytes_out            dw     ?             ; needed by DosWrite

13                      .code
14                      extrn  DosWrite:far,DosExit:far
15 begin:
16                      call   write_msg_proc
17                      call   exit_proc

18 exit_proc            proc   near
19                      push   1             ; quit all threads
20                      push   0             ; return code
21                      call   DosExit       ; terminate program
22 exit_proc            endp

23 write_msg_proc proc  near
24                      push   std_device
25                      push   ds            ; address of message
26                      push   offset help_msg
27                      push   help_msg_len
28                      push   ds            ; addr. of bytes_out
29                      push   offset bytes_out
30                      call   DosWrite      ; write message
31                      ret
32 write_msg_proc endp
33                      end    begin
```

Figure 2-1   HELP Program for '286 under OS/2

Overview of OS/2

OS/2 is a full '286 operating system, offering multitasking and virtual memory in protected mode as well as the ability to switch into and out of real mode. Although OS/2 has maintained many of the features of DOS, including directory and file structures, it also offers many new features. Of major significance to the application programmer is the *Application Program Interface* (API), which provides the operating system services such as I/O to application programs. You will meet three API services in this chapter: **DosWrite**, which writes a message on the monitor; **DosRead**, which reads a line from the keyboard when the user presses Enter; and **DosExit**, which terminates a program.

DOS provides services via software interrupts, but to avoid creating havoc with other tasks executing concurrently, OS/2 applications must call API services instead. The program modules that provide the API functions are *dynamically linked* to the application. That is, the API module is not copied into the program but is brought into memory from the API library only when it is called. This saves memory and disk space.

A subset of the API, called the *family API*, can run in real mode or under DOS 3.*x*, but only if the program is *bound*. Binding inserts into the program DOS 3.*x* routines that capture family API calls and handle them appropriately. If you limit your source program to the 8086 instruction set and the family API, then bind the executable module, you can create a program that will run under either DOS 3.*x* or OS/2 on any IBM-compatible computer, thus maximizing its potential. Binding greatly increases a program's size (the tiny HELP program in Figure 2-1 is 6196 bytes bound, 1076 bytes unbound), but the result might be worth it if you want to achieve maximum portability for your software. When a bound program runs under OS/2 protected mode, OS/2 ignores the bindings (they aren't even loaded into memory) and uses the original dynamic API calls. Thus, a program's protected-mode efficiency is not hurt by binding except for the amount of storage space the program takes on disk.

One nice feature of OS/2 is the ability to establish several processing threads within a task. A *thread* is an execution path. Establishing multiple threads within a task is like multitasking within the task. A word processor task, for example, could be printing a document with one thread while the user is editing a file with another thread. The simple programs in this chapter have only one thread each.

Establishing the Processing Environment

The program in Figure 2-1 can be broken down into several main components. At the start, on lines 1 through 3, is some assembler housekeeping. Lines 4 through 12 define the data segments. Lines 13 through 32 define the code segment, which can be broken down into the mainline routine (lines 15 through 17) and two procedures (lines 18 through 22 and lines 23 through 32). Line 33 represents more assembler housekeeping.

The program starts with three MASM directives that establish the environment in which the program will be assembled. **Dosseg** tells the assembler to arrange the segments in the standard order (the same order Microsoft's higher level compilers use: code, other, data). The **.model** directive tells the assembler which memory model to use; here we've chosen the **small** model, which means the code fits in one segment and all the data segments (stack, data, and extra) should be grouped into one data segment called **dgroup**. Based on the **.model** directive, the assembler can determine the necessary offsets for each symbolic address. When the program is loaded, CS is automatically pointed to the beginning of the one and only code segment, DS is pointed to the beginning of dgroup, and SS is pointed to the end of dgroup.

The **.286** directive tells the assembler to use the '286 instruction set. Without it, MASM limits you to the 8086 instruction set. In this example, lines 19, 20, 24, 26, and 29 would be rejected because those forms of **push** were not available in the 8086 instruction set.

The **.stack** directive (line 4) is a shortcut for defining the stack segment. If we didn't use this shortcut, we'd have to code several more complicated directives to create the segment. But **.stack** lets us do it in one directive. Here we've asked for 1000 bytes, more than enough for the data we push directly and those items pushed automatically by the **call** instructions.

Data Segment

The **.data** directive (line 5) is another MASM shortcut for defining a data segment with standard characteristics. In this data segment, we place the message we want to output, plus some fields needed by the OS/2 service that writes the message.

Lines 6 through 8 establish some symbols that we want to use in this segment. We set **cr** equal to the ASCII code for a carriage return and **lf** equal to the ASCII code for a line feed. Why? Just to make the program a little easier to read. Look at the definition of **help_msg** on lines 9 and 10 to see how these two symbols are used. Isn't it clearer that the message is followed by a carriage return and line feed with the symbols **cr** and **lf** rather than the ASCII codes 0Dh and 0Ah?

The **db** (define byte) directive stores the desired message in memory, assigning the first byte the symbolic address **help_msg**. **Db** reserves one or more bytes in memory, inserting in the bytes the values contained in the directive's operand. When an ASCII string in quotes is defined, as in this example, **db** reserves one byte for each character in the string. Values separated by commas, such as **cr** and **lf**, each also reserve and initialize one byte.

The **dw** directive on line 11 defines one word with the symbolic address **help_msg_len**. This field tells the OS/2 output service the length of the message to be written. The operand in this directive looks complex, but isn't. It is an equation that the assembler solves to find the value to place in the word. The $ is a special assembler symbol that means "the current address offset." Therefore, the program is asking the assembler to subtract the address offset represented by **help_msg** from the current address offset to determine the value to place in **help_msg_len**. The result is the exact length of **help_msg**, including the space reserved by both **db** directives.

Ordinarily, instructions and directives should be as straightforward as possible, and using an equation as an operand seems out of keeping with that philosophy. Why ask the assembler to calculate the message length when it is obviously 53 bytes long? Most programmers know that a message is one of the most revisable parts of a program, and when a message changes, its length usually changes too. People invariably forget to revise the message length word when they revise the message. It has become almost a standard in the industry to calculate message lengths this way so that the length field is recalculated automatically each time the program is reassembled.

Line 12 defines a word named **bytes_out** with no initial value. **Bytes_out** is another field needed by the OS/2 output service. The ? symbol in a data definition directive means that no particular value is to be placed in the field. This will not necessarily cause the initial value to be zero or null. Previous values in the memory area might carry through.

Code Segment

Line 13 terminates the data segment and starts the code segment. Line 14 warns the assembler of any external calls the program makes. Without this **extrn** directive, the assembler would look for the OS/2 service functions, **DosWrite** and **DosExit**, within this source program file. The **extrn** directive tells the assembler to pass those calls on to the linkage editor for resolution. The label on line 15 marks the entry point of the program. This is the point where execution begins whenever the program is invoked. You can code it on its own line, as shown in this example, or put the label on the same line with the first instruction of the program (currently on line 16). It doesn't matter to the system, so it's a matter of personal preference. The **end** directive (line 33) tells the assembler which label marks the entry point.

Line 16 calls **write_message_proc**, which puts out the message. When that procedure terminates, control returns to line 17, which calls **exit_proc**. The **exit_proc** procedure terminates the program, so control does not return.

The Exit_Proc Procedure

Lines 18 through 22 define **exit_proc**, which uses OS/2's **DosExit** function to terminate the program. Like all OS/2 functions, **DosExit** requires certain information to be pushed onto the stack before it is called. This is how the calling procedure communicates with the called procedure. **DosExit** requires two words: the first contains a 0 or a 1 to indicate whether the current thread or the whole program is terminating; the second contains the return code. In this case, we're terminating the whole program (which has only one thread). There are lots of ways of pushing a word containing a 1 onto the stack; we've chosen to push it as a literal. We also push a word containing 0 as the return code (line 20). The call to **DosExit** then terminates the program (line 21).

Lines 18 and 22 are the **proc** and **endp** directives that mark the beginning and end of the procedure. Note that it's a *near* procedure, meaning it can be called only from within the same code segment. A *far* procedure can be called from other code segments. You can't have far procedures in a **small** program, since it contains only one code segment.

The Write_Msg_Proc Procedure

Now let's look at the procedure that writes the output message, shown on lines 23 through 32. The values pushed onto the stack are required by the **DosWrite** function. The first word (line 24) is the file handle (that is, the identifier of the file) where the data should be written. A 1 indicates the standard I/O device (i.e., the monitor unless the user has changed to some other device). The symbol **std_device** was equated to a 1 on line 8, so pushing **std_device** is exactly the same as pushing 1. The next two words on the stack must be the segment:offset address of the data to be written. Pushing DS followed by the offset of **help_msg** (lines 25 and 26) accomplishes that. Note the use of the **offset** operator in the **push** instruction. If we used this instruction:

```
push    help_msg
```

the microprocessor would push the *contents* of **help_msg** instead of its address offset. The **offset** operator tells the microprocessor to push the address offset, not the contents.

The next word on the stack must be the length of the message to be written. Pushing **help_msg_len**, so carefully calculated by the assembler, accomplishes this.

DosWrite also requires the address of a one-word memory area where it can record the number of bytes it actually wrote; you can use this feedback for error checking after the return. We have defined a word called **bytes_out** (line 12) and pushed its address onto the stack (lines 28 and 29). Now all the required data is in the stack and we can call **DosWrite** (line 30).

When control returns from **DosWrite**, the **write_msg_proc** procedure has finished its task and can return control to the calling procedure. The **ret** instruction (line 31) accomplishes that.

The End Directive

The **end** directive (line 33) must appear at the end of every source program file. It marks the end of the assembler's work and identifies the entry point of the program.

Preparing the Program

Figure 2-2 shows the process of preparing a program for production. The process starts with a programmer creating a source code file (such as the one in Figure 2-1), usually by typing it on a word processor or editor. If you use your word processor, be sure the file gets stored in ASCII format; lines should end in CR+LF codes and should not be justified or otherwise formatted. For example, WordPerfect should use Text Out to save the file, and WordStar should use nondocument mode. Upper- and lowercase may be used interchangeably with most assemblers, which simply ignore the case. Hard tabs may be used to align instructions, as we have done in all the figures in this book. Vertical spacing (blank lines) may also be used as you wish to make the program easier to read.

When the source code file is ready, the assembler translates it into an *object module*. An object module is in machine language except that the addresses haven't been finalized. The assembler also produces message output to the monitor and, if you request them, various listing

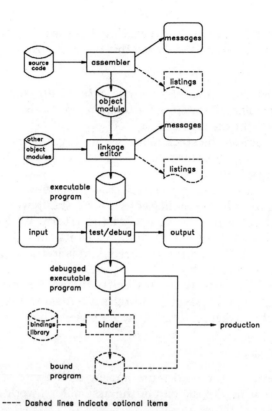

---- Dashed lines indicate optional items

Figure 2-2   Preparing a New Program for Production

files. The messages file lists any errors encountered in the source file. For the most part, the assembler can identify errors in syntax but not in logic. The listing files list the source code, the object code, error messages, symbol cross references, and other information.

You continue to revise and assemble the source code until an error-free object module is produced. Then the linkage editor is used to produce the executable program file. Linkage editing is an important step in the creation of a working program. The linkage editor's job is to bring together segments that were assembled in separate runs and finalize addresses in **call** instructions. The linkage editor resolves the external references to **DosExit** and **DosWrite**, for example. As before, any errors are listed on the monitor, and the programmer repeats whatever steps are necessary to create an executable program file. Usually, the only errors encountered by the linkage editor are missing external module and unresolved references (called "fixup errors").

Once an executable module has been produced, it can be tested and debugged. If logic errors occur, you must go back to the source code again to fix them, then assemble, link, and test again. An online debugger, such as Microsoft's CodeView or Phar Lap's Minibug, can help pinpoint and fix tricky logic errors, letting you execute the program slowly, a few instructions at a time, examining the registers, memory, and the stack in between steps. When all the logic errors are fixed, the program is ready to go into production unless you want to bind it. If you want to bind it, then you run it through the binder to produce the final, production version of the program.

Preparing the Program for OS/2. We prepared a source code file named HELP.ASM using our favorite word processor. We assembled the program under MASM using this command:

```
MASM HELP;
```

This command, in which the semicolon is very important, says to assemble HELP.ASM and produce an object file, HELP.OBJ, but no listing files. Error messages will be listed only on the monitor. The system must be able to find MASM.EXE and HELP.ASM in order to do this.

When error messages were displayed on the monitor, we went back to the source program file to fix the problems. We continued to fix and reassemble until the program assembled with no errors. (A windows program such as Windows or Presentation Manager is helpful here, as you can view the error messages in one window while you edit the program in another. Otherwise, for long programs, you might want to print the error list.)

We invoked the Microsoft's linkage editor with this command:

```
LINK HELP,,,DOSCALLS;
```

This links HELP.OBJ, using DOSCALLS.LIB for the external calls, and produces an executable program file called HELP.EXE and a map file called HELP.MAP, which you can ignore for now. The linkage editor seldom has problems with a simple, small program like this unless it can't find the object modules. If both HELP.OBJ and DOS-CALLS.LIB are present, LINK will run successfully.

To test the program, we entered the command HELP at the OS/2 command prompt and our new program was loaded and executed. It displayed the desired message on the monitor and terminated itself.

To bind the program, we used this command:

```
BIND DOSCALLS.LIB HELP
```

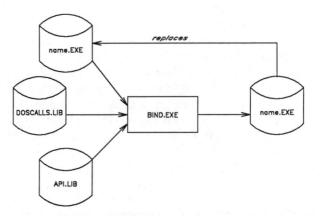

Figure 2-3   Files Required for BIND Process

Figure 2-3 diagrams the I/O files for this process. You must make sure
the system can find them by specifying the appropriate path or making
sure they're in one of the directories where OS/2 will search for them.
Both the DOSCALLS.LIB file and the API.LIB file are necessary to
convert the protected-mode calls into equivalent real mode routines.

8086 Version

Once bound, the program will run under DOS 3.*x* or OS/2 in either
mode on an AT or PS. It still won't run on a PC or XT because it
contains '286 instructions. To make it truly compatible with all Intel-
based personal computers, we must limit it to the 8086 instruction set.
Figure 2-4 shows an 8086 adaptation, in which we have removed the
.286 directive and changed the **push *immediate*** instructions to **push
*memory-address***, since **push *immediate*** isn't available with the
8086.

The beginning housekeeping that establishes the assembler environment now consists of two directives (lines 1 and 2). **Dosseg** tells the
assembler to order the segments in the standard order and **.model
small** tells the assembler to create one data segment named **dgroup**
and one code segment.

The **.stack** directive, as before, creates a stack segment 1000 bytes
long (line 3). The **.data** directive (line 4) marks the beginning of the
data segment. **Cr** and **lf** (lines 5 and 6) create names for the ASCII
codes for carriage return and line feed characters, as in the previous
version of this program. However, the **std_device** symbol (line 7) is
defined differently here than it was in the previous version. In the
previous version, an **equ** directive assigned a value to the symbol; now,

```
 1                  dosseg
 2                  .model small
 3                  .stack 1000

 4                  .data
 5 cr               equ    0Dh          ; ASCII return
 6 lf               equ    0Ah          ; ASCII line feed
 7 std_device       dw     1            ; monitor handle
 8 help_msg         db     "Help! I'm being held prisoner"
 9                  db     " in your microcomputer",cr,lf
10 help_msg_len     dw     $ - help_msg ; length of help_msg
11 bytes_out        dw     ?            ; needed by DosWrite
12 return_code      dw     0            ; for DosExit
13 all_threads      dw     1            ; for DosExit

14                  .code
15                  extrn  DosWrite:far,DosExit:far
16 begin:
17                  call   write_msg_proc
18                  call   exit_proc

19 exit_proc        proc   near
20                  push   all_threads  ; quit all threads
21                  push   return_code  ; return code
22                  call   DosExit      ; terminates program
23 exit_proc        endp

24 write_msg_proc   proc   near
25                  push   std_device
26                  push   ds           ; address
27                  lea    ax,help_msg  ;   of
28                  push   ax           ;        message
29                  push   help_msg_len
30                  push   ds           ; address
31                  lea    ax,bytes_out ;   of
32                  push   ax           ;        bytes_out
33                  call   DosWrite     ; writes message
34                  ret
35 write_msg_proc   endp
36                  end    begin
```

Figure 2-4   HELP Program for 8086 under DOS

a **dw** directive defines it. The **equ** directive merely creates a symbol that can be used instead of a value; when you use a symbol defined by **equ** as an operand, you are using an immediate operand. On the other hand, the **dw** directive reserves a memory word and places a value in it. When you use its label as an operand, you are using a memory address operand. Thus, in the 8086, you can **push** a symbol defined by **dw** but not **equ**.

Lines 8 and 9 define the output message and line 10 defines its length. These haven't changed from the previous version. Nor has line 11, which creates the one-word field needed by **DosWrite** to store the length of the message written. However, the definitions on lines 12 and 13 are new. **DosExit** needs two values pushed onto the stack: the return code and the number of threads to be terminated. The '286 version of the program pushed them as immediate values. Now they must be defined as memory words; the **exit_proc** routine pushes the memory words.

Line 14 starts the code section, and line 15 warns the assembler of external procedure names. Lines 16 through 18 represent the main routine and have not changed from the previous version. Lines 19 through 23 define **exit_proc**. Line 20 pushes onto the stack the value in **all_threads**, which is a word containing the value 1. Line 21 pushes the value in the memory field named **return_code**, which is a word containing a 0, onto the stack. Having set up the stack properly, the program calls **DosExit** on line 22.

Lines 24 through 35 define **write_msg_proc**. The first item into the stack must be the handle of the output device, which is a 1 for the monitor. Pushing the memory word named **std_device** accomplishes this (line 25). The second item in the stack must be the full address of the message. Lines 26 through 28 do this. Line 26 pushes the DS register, as in the previous version of the program. However, we are unable to push the offset of **help_msg** directly, as we did before, because that is considered an immediate value. Instead, we use the **lea** (load effective address) instruction to access the address offset of the message and load it into AX (line 27). Then we push AX (line 28).

Line 29 pushes the length of the message, as in the previous version. Lines 30 through 32 push the address of the **bytes_out** field, using the same technique that pushed the address of the message. After the stack has been completely set up, the **DosWrite** routine is called (line 33).

Lines 34 through 36 terminate the procedure and the program.

When the program in Figure 2-4 is assembled, linked, and bound under OS/2, it will run on any IBM-compatible machine.

The 386|DOS Version

Figure 2-5 shows another version of the HELP program, this time prepared for the Phar Lap programming system. This system lets you create '386 protected-mode programs that run under DOS. A special 386 | DOS-Extender module establishes a '386 protected-mode environment in which you can access the full range of virtual memory (4G)

```
 1                     assume cs:cseg,ds:dseg,ss:sseg
 2 sseg                segment stack 'data'
 3                     db     1000 dup (?)
 4 sseg                ends

 5 dseg                segment public 'data'
 6 cr                  equ    0Dh           ; ASCII return
 7 lf                  equ    0Ah           ; ASCII line feed

 8 help_msg            db     "Help! I'm being held prisoner"
 9                     db     " in your microcomputer",cr,lf,"$"
10 dseg                ends

11 cseg                segment public 'code'
12 begin:
13                     call   write_msg_proc
14                     call   exit_proc

15 exit_proc           proc   near
16                     mov    ah,4Ch         ; termination code
17                     int    21h            ; terminates program
18 exit_proc           endp

19 write_msg_procproc  near
20                     mov    ah,09h         ; code to write
21                     lea    edx,help_msg   ; address of message
22                     int    21h            ; writes message
23                     ret
24 write_msg_proc endp
25 cseg                ends
26                     end    begin
```

Figure 2-5   HELP Program for 386|DOS System

using 32-bit addressing and the extended registers. Some differences between the 386 I DOS-Extender and a full '386 operating system are:

All programs execute at privilege level 0; the privileged instructions can be executed by any program.

The linker places all program "segments" into one large physical segment, which is identified as both a readable code segment and a writable data segment.

The 386 I DOS-Extender uses up to 250 bytes of the caller's stack when a system call is made; make your stacks large enough to allow for that much usage.

System services are provided through the DOS software interrupt system.

Interrupts and system calls are captured by the 386 I DOS-Extender, which then switches to real mode and passes the call to DOS. When control returns from DOS, the extender switches back to protected mode again.

Differences in Directives

The shortcuts used with MASM—**dosseg, .model, .stack, .data,** and **.code**—aren't available with 386 I ASM, so some other directives are necessary. These directives are also used with MASM when the assumptions made by the shortcuts are not appropriate.

The Assume Directive. The **assume** directive (line 1) tells the assembler which segment registers will be pointing at which segments when the program is executed. The assembler needs to know this in order to determine addresses correctly. The **assume** directive does not actually cause the registers to be loaded with the correct addresses. Under the extender, segment selectors are fixed and all the segment selectors are automatically loaded into the segment registers when the program is loaded. (EIP is automatically pointed at the address identified in the **end** directive.)

The Segment and Ends Directives. The **segment** and **ends** (end segment) directives mark the outer limits of a segment. The directives' labels, which are required, specify the name of the segment. Everything defined between those two directives belongs to that segment. The **ends** directive is required to end the segment before starting another one; without it, the assembler assumes the next segment is nested inside the current one.

The **segment** operands identify the segment's characteristics. Several specific assumptions are made about the segment unless operands override them. The segment starts at an address divisible by 16 (this is **para** alignment). Segments having the same name cannot be combined to form a single segment (this is the **private** combine type). Thirty-two bit addressing is used (this is the **use32** use attribute). The segment is a readable code segment (this is the **er** access type). The segment has no class name; the class name determines how the segments are ordered in memory. Segments with the same name are ordered contiguously; all segments with no class name belong to the same class.

For the stack segment (lines 2 through 4 in Figure 2-5), the **stack** operand overrides the **private** combine type and tells the assembler that this is a stack segment; it also makes the segment public so it can be combined with other segments such as the data segment. When the program is loaded, SS is pointed at the base of this segment and (E)SP is pointed at the end, because the stack is built upside down in the segment. The **'data'** operand identifies the segment as belonging to the 'data' class, along with the data segment, which has the same class name (line 5). The **db** statement (line 3) is necessary to reserve room for the stack in memory, since the **.stack** shortcut is not available. The **db** statement shown here reserves 1000 uninitialized bytes.

For the data segment (lines 5 through 10), the **public** operand allows the segment to be combined with the other segments at link editing time. The **'data'** operand identifies the segment's class. Since it has the same class as the stack segment, these two segments will be combined into one in the final version of the program. The resulting segment will be large enough to incorporate both the 1000-byte stack and the fields defined in the data segment. The data fields will be located at the beginning of the segment, while the stack space will be located at the end of the segment, with DS, SS, and (E)SP initialized appropriately.

The message to be written is stored in memory by the directives on lines 8 and 9. DOS requires the message to end with a dollar sign ($), which you can see on line 9.

The code segment (lines 11 through 25) also has the **public** combine type, but it belongs to the **'code'** class. Don't worry if these operands

seem somewhat confusing at this time; they are explained more fully
later in this book.

Differences in Operating System Services

The main routine in the 386 | DOS-Extender version (lines 11 through
14) is identical to that in the previous examples. However, the called
procedures are completely different because of the different way of
communicating with DOS. Both procedures use **int 21h** to request
DOS services. This is a software-generated interrupt with a wide variety of input/output functions. The specific function is requested by a
code placed in AH. Additional operands are placed in other registers.

Terminating the Program. To terminate a program, you place the code
4Ch in AH before issuing **int 21h**. The **exit_proc** procedure (lines 15
through 18) does just that. Line 16 moves 4Ch into AH. Then line 17
invokes the interrupt.

Writing a Message. The **write_msg_proc** writes the message on the
monitor. The code 09h (line 20) requests this particular service. For
this service, the address offset of the message must be placed in (E)DX.
(DS is assumed to be the segment register.) Since this program is using
32-bit addressing, it loads the address into the 32-bit register, EDX.
The **lea** (load effective address) instruction on line 21 does this. DOS
identifies the end of the messsage to be written by a dollar sign ($)
buried in the message. Without that dollar sign, DOS would continue
writing bytes on the monitor until it reached the end of the segment
and encountered a segment limit error.

Preparing the Program

The process of preparing the program follows the same steps shown in
Figure 2-2 (type source code, assemble, link edit, test and debug, and
perhaps bind). To assemble with the 386 | ASM assembler, we used this
command:

```
386ASM HELP
```

This translates HELP.ASM into HELP.OBJ (unless errors are encountered), producing messages on the monitor and a listing file. The
system needs to find 386ASM.EXE and HELP.ASM for this step.

Once the assembler shows no errors, the object file can be linked
with this command:

```
386LINK HELP
```

This command causes HELP.OBJ module to be finalized as HELP.EXP. The necessary files are HELP.OBJ and 386LINK. The .EXP extension indicates a special program file that can be executed only under the DOS-Extender. To execute the program, this command is used:

```
RUN386 HELP
```

The RUN386 command invokes the 386|DOS-Extender, which then runs the HELP.EXP program. The .EXP file cannot be run under DOS without the extender, and it can't be run under OS/2 at all. (If you want to prepare a version of the program for distribution, you bind the program with a run-time version of the DOS extender.)

Adding an Input Step

Our next program is a little more complicated. Here we ask for the user's name, read the user's keyboard input, then say "Hello, *name*."

MASM-OS/2 Version

Figure 2-6 shows the MASM-OS/2 version of this program. The beginning housekeeping on lines 1 through 3 are the standard instructions

```
 1                  dosseg
 2                  .model small
 3                  .286

 4                  .stack 1000

 5                  .data
 6 cr               equ    0Dh              ; ASCII return
 7 lf               equ    0Ah              ; ASCII line feed
 8 std_device       equ    1                ; monitor/keyboard

 9 what_msg         db     "What is your name? "
10 what_msg_len     dw     $ - what_msg

11 hello_msg        db     "Hello, "
12 hello_name       db     20 dup (?)
13 hello_msg_len    dw     $ - hello_msg
14 io_bytes         dw     ?                ; needed by OS/2
```

Figure 2-6   HELLO Program for '286 under OS/2 (part 1 of 3)

```
15                    .code
16         extrn   DosWrite:far,DosRead:far,DosExit:far
17 begin:
18                    call   write_what_proc
19                    call   read_name_proc
20                    call   write_hello_proc
21                    call   exit_proc

22 exit_proc       proc   near
23                    push   1            ; end all threads
24                    push   0            ; return code
25                    call   DosExit      ; terminates
26 exit_proc       endp

27 write_what_proc proc   near
28                    push   std_device   ; handle for monitor
29                    push   ds           ; address of message
30                    push   offset what_msg
31                    push   what_msg_len
32                    push   ds           ; address of io area
33                    push   offset io_bytes
34                    call   DosWrite     ; writes message
35                    ret
36 write_what_proc endp

37 read_name_proc  proc   near
38                    push   std_device   ; handle of keyboard
39                    push   ds           ; address of buffer
40                    push   offset hello_name
41                    push   length hello_name
42                    push   ds           ; address of io area
43                    push   offset io_bytes
44                    call   DosRead      ; gets   input
45                    ret
46 read_name_proc  endp
```

Figure 2-6   HELLO Program for '286 under OS/2 (part 2 of 3)

```
47 write_hello_proc proc near
48                    push    std_device    ; handle for monitor
49                    push    ds            ; address of message
50                    push    offset hello_msg
51                    push    hello_msg_len
52                    push    ds            ; address of io area
53                    push    offset io_bytes
54                    call    DosWrite      ; writes the message
55                    ret
56 write_hello_proc endp
57                    end     begin
```

Figure 2-6   HELLO Program for '286 under OS/2 (part 3 of 3)

for a small program intended for the '286. Line 4 is the same stack definition we always use when the **.stack** directive is available. The data segment (lines 5 through 14) contains both output messages. It begins with several equates created to make other instructions more readable. Line 9 defines the first output message, called **what_msg**. We include a space as the last character, but no **cr** or **lf**, so that the user can enter his input on the same line as the question. Since we are going to write this message with **DosWrite**, line 10 defines the length of the message, once again using an expression that will force the assembler to calculate the length of the message by subtracting the current offset from the offset of the beginning of the message.

Lines 11 and 12 define the second message to be written, which includes the word "Hello," followed by whatever text the user enters. **Hello_name** is a 20-byte uninitialized field that receives the user's input during **DosRead**. The *n* **dup** (*i*) construction duplicates the field *n* times, initializing each element with *i*, where a question mark indicates no initialization. Thus, **20 dup (?)** defines 20 uninitialized bytes in memory.

Hello_msg_len on line 13 calculates and stores the length of the message by subtracting the offset of **Hello_msg** from the offset of **Hello_msg_len**. And once again, **io_bytes** on line 14 is a field needed by both the **DosWrite** and **DosRead** functions.

The code section is created by lines 15 through 56. The **extrn** statement on line 16 now references three OS/2 functions: **DosWrite**, **Dos-Read** (which will be used to read the user's input), and **DosExit**.

Lines 17 through 21 comprise the main routine, which first calls the procedure to write out the "What is your name" message (line 18), then calls the procedure to read the user's input (line 19), then calls the procedure to write out the "Hello" message (line 20), and finally calls the procedure to terminate the program.

The **exit_proc** procedure on lines 22 through 26, which terminates the program, is the same as the one in HELP. The **write_what_proc** procedure on lines 27 through 36 writes out the first message. First, it pushes the handle for the monitor (line 28). Then it pushes the address of the message to be written (lines 29 and 30). Then it pushes the length of the message (line 31) and the address of the I/O area (lines 32 and 33). With the stack set up, it calls the **DosWrite** function (line 34) and terminates (line 35).

The **read_name_proc** procedure (lines 37 through 46) reads the user's input from the keyboard and stores it in **hello_name**. It starts by pushing a full word containing the standard handle, which is the same for the keyboard as it is for the monitor. (When the handle is 1, an output function addresses the monitor, while an input function addresses the keyboard.) Then it pushes the starting segment:offset of the receiving field (lines 39 and 40). Line 41 pushes the length of the receiving field by using the **length** operator. This nifty way of obtaining the length of a data item is unfortunately available only when the item is defined with the **dup** operator; otherwise, we would use it for all the other messages. Finally, the program pushes the segment:offset of **io_bytes** (lines 42 and 43), calls **DosRead** (line 44), and returns control to the calling routine (line 45).

DosRead waits for the user's input. When the user presses Enter, up to the maximum number of bytes are read into **hello_name**. The maximum number of bytes are defined by the length of the receiving field, the third item pushed onto the stack. If the user enters more than the maximum number of bytes, they are truncated. The actual number of bytes read are stored in the I/O field, in this case **io_bytes**.

The **write_hello_proc** procedure (lines 47 through 56) writes the "Hello, *name*" message, displaying all 20 bytes of **hello_name** no matter how many the user entered. The program could use **io_bytes** to determine exactly how long the name is, but in such a short, meaningless program, it hardly seems worth the extra effort.

8086 Version

Figure 2-7 shows the 8086 version of the same program. The only differences have to do with pushing words instead of immediate bytes. The differences are detailed below:

Line 3: The .286 directive has been removed.

```
 1                dosseg
 2                .model small

 3                .stack 1000

 4                .data
 5 cr              equ     0Dh          ; ASCII return
 6 lf              equ     0Ah          ; ASCII line feed

 7 std_device      dw      1            ;  monitor/keyboard
 8 return_code     dw      0            ; for DosExit
 9 all_threads     dw      1            ; for DosExit

10 what_msg        db      "What is your name? "
11 what_msg_len    dw      $ - what_msg

12 hello_msg       db      "Hello, "
13 hello_name      db      20 dup (?)
14 hello_msg_len   dw      $ - hello_msg

15 hello_name_len  dw      length hello_name
16 io_bytes        dw      ?                 ; needed by OS/2

17                .code
18         extrn    DosWrite:far,DosRead:far,DosExit:far
19 begin:
20                call    write_what_proc
21                call    read_name_proc
22                call    write_hello_proc
23                call    exit_proc

24 exit_proc       proc    near
25                push    all_threads
26                push    return_code
27                call    DosExit       ; terminates program
28 exit_proc       endp
```

Figure 2-7   HELLO Program for 8086 under DOS (part 1 of 2)

```
29 write_what_proc   proc near
30                   push  std_device   ; handle for monitor
31                   push  ds           ; address of message
32                   lea   ax,what_msg
33                   push  ax
34                   push  what_msg_len
35                   push  ds           ; address of io area
36                   lea   ax,io_bytes
37                   push  ax
38                   call  DosWrite      ; writes message
39                   ret
40 write_what_proc   endp

41 read_name_proc proc   near
42                   push  std_device   ; handle of keyboard
43                   push  ds           ; address of buffer
44                   lea   ax,hello_name
45                   push  ax
46                   push  hello_name_len
47                   push  ds           ; address of io area
48                   lea   ax,io_bytes
49                   push  ax
50                   call  DosRead       ; gets input
51                   ret
52 read_name_proc endp

53 write_hello_proc        proc          near
54                   push  std_device   ; handle for monitor
55                   push  ds           ; address of message
56                   lea   ax,hello_msg
57                   push  ax
58                   push  hello_msg_len
59                   push  ds           ; address of io area
60                   lea   ax,io_bytes
61                   push  ax
62                   call  DosWrite      ; writes the message
63                   ret
64 write_hello_proc  endp
65                         end   begin
```

Figure 2-7   HELLO Program for 8086 under DOS (part 2 of 2)

Lines 7–9: Values are stored in memory words for the standard handle, the return code, and the number of threads to terminate. In the '286 version, these items are all pushed onto the stack as immediate values; in this 8086 version, they must be pushed as memory words.

Line 15: A value is stored in a memory word for the length of the input message. The **length** operator is used to obtain the length of the item. (As a reminder, this operator works only when the referenced item is defined with a **dup** operator.) In the '286 version, the **length hello_name** was used as the operand of the **push** instruction in **read_name_proc**, but that is an immediate operand and cannot be pushed with the 8086. Hence, we added the definition of **hello_name_len**.

Lines 25, 26, 42, 46, and 54: Push memory words instead of immediate values.

Lines 32 and 33, 36 and 37, 44 and 45, 48 and 49, 56 and 57, 60 and 61: Load the necessary address offset into AX and push AX instead of pushing the offset immediately.

'386 Version

Figure 2-8 shows the '386 version developed for the 386 I DOS-Extender. This version is so different from the preceding two versions that we'll walk through it line-by-line instead of highlighting the differences.

The **assume** directive on line 1 tells the assembler what segments to relate to what segment registers.

The stack segment is defined on lines 2 through 4 to contain 1000 uninitialized bytes.

The data segment is defined on lines 5 through 14. Lines 6 and 7 merely establish some equates that are used in defining the messages. Line 8 stores the "What is your name" message in memory. It terminates with the dollar sign required by the DOS **int 21h** function to identify the end of an output message. The "Hello" message is defined on lines 9 through 11. It starts with a carriage return and line feed, then the phrase "Hello, " followed by 20 uninitialized bytes to hold the user's name. And, like all output messages, it terminates with a dollar sign.

Lines 12 and 13 are set up to receive keyboard input from the DOS **int 21h** function, which requires two extra bytes appended to the

```
 1                      assume cs:cseg, ds:dseg, ss:sseg

 2 sseg                 segment stack 'data'
 3                      db      1000 dup (?)
 4 sseg                 ends

 5 dseg                 segment public 'data'
 6 cr                   equ     0Dh             ; ASCII return
 7 lf                   equ     0Ah             ; ASCII line feed

 8 what_msg             db      "What is your name? $"

 9 hello_msg            db      cr,lf,"Hello, "
10 hello_name           db      20 dup (?)
11                      db      "$"

12 input_name           db      20
13                      db      21 dup (?)
14 dseg                 ends

15 cseg                 segment public 'code'
16 begin:
17                      call    write_what_proc
18                      call    read_name_proc
19                      call    write_hello_proc
20                      call    exit_proc

21 exit_proc            proc    near
22                      mov     ah,4Ch          ; termination code
23                      int     21h             ; ends the program
24 exit_proc            endp

25 write_what_proc proc near
26                      mov     ah,09h          ; code for output
27                      lea     edx,what_msg    ; address of message
28                      int     21h             ; writes message
29                      ret
30 write_what_proc endp
```

Figure 2-8   HELLO Program for 386|DOS System (part 1 of 2)

```
31 read_name_proc proc    near
32                mov     ah,0Ah          ; code to read
33                lea     edx,input_name
34                int     21h             ; reads keyboard
35                lea     esi,input_name
36                add     esi,2
37                lea     edi,hello_name
38                sub     ecx,ecx
39                mov     cl,input_name+1
40                rep movsb               ; moves input_name
41                                        ;      to hello_name
42                ret
43 read_name_proc endp

44 write_hello_proc  proc near
45                   mov     ah,09h       ; code to write
46                   lea     edx,hello_msg; address of message
47                   int     21h          ; writes message
48                   ret
49 write_hello_proc endp
50 cseg             ends
51                  end     begin
```

Figure 2-8   HELLO Program for 386|DOS System (part 2 of 2)

beginning of the receiving field. The first byte must contain the maximum length of the user's input. This byte is defined on line 12 with an initial value of 20 (in decimal). The next byte is where DOS will place the number of bytes received. The input message starts in the third byte. The reason line 13 defines 21 uninitialized bytes is to have one byte for DOS to use and 20 bytes for the user's input.

Because of these two extra bytes in the input buffer, we can't bury the input buffer in the middle of the output message, as we did in previous versions of the program. We have to read the input into one area, then copy the user's message over to the output message.

The code section appears on lines 15 through 50. The main routine on lines 16 through 20 hasn't changed from the two previous versions. **Exit_proc** loads the termination code (4Ch) into AH (line 22) and issues **int 21h** to cause the program to terminate (line 23).

The **write_what_proc** procedure (lines 25 through 30) loads the monitor output code of 09h into AH (line 26) and the address of the message into EDX (line 27), then issues **int 21h** (line 28).

The most complicated procedure is the **read_name_proc** (lines 31 through 43), because it must not only read the user's input but also transfer it from the original input buffer to the output message. Line 32 moves the code for the keyboard input function (0Ah) into AH. Line 33 loads the address of the input buffer into EDX. Then line 34 causes the input to take place. (Control does not return to the program until the user presses Enter on the keyboard.) The remainder of the procedure is concerned with transferring the user's name over to the output message. The procedure will use the **rep movsb** (repeat move string bytes) instruction to do this, and it requires some set up. DS:ESI must be pointing at the source string, ES:EDI must be pointing at the destination area, and ECX must contain the number of bytes to be moved. Line 35 points ESI at the beginning of the input buffer, and line 36 increases it by two bytes so it points to the beginning of the user's input (recall that the first two bytes of the input buffer are used by DOS). Line 37 points EDI at the place in the output message where the user's name should appear. DS and ES are both pointing at the beginning of the data segment automatically, so we don't have to worry about setting them. Lines 38 and 39 move the length of the user's name into ECX; first, line 38 zeros ECX by subtracting it from itself; then line 39 moves one byte into CL from the second byte of the input buffer. This is the byte where DOS placed the length of the user's message. Thus, the number of bytes the user entered is the number of bytes that will be transferred by the **rep movsb** instruction on line 40. After the **rep movsb** is complete, the **read_name_proc** procedure has finished its function and it can return control to the calling procedure (line 42).

Write_hello_proc outputs the "Hello, *name*" message in the same fashion as **write_what_proc**.

Looking Ahead

Now that you're acquainted with the basics, you're ready to dive into details. The next few chapters deal primarily with the instruction set. All the examples would fit into short programs such as the ones shown in this chapter. All I/O accesses the standard devices (the monitor and keyboard) using **DosRead** and **DosWrite** or **int 21h**. Following that, you'll learn about assembler directives. The final chapters in the book deal with assembling, link editing, and online debuggers.

Before you start Chapter 3, we suggest you get your assembler set up in a subdirectory on your hard disk; enter the two programs from this chapter in the form appropriate to your assembler and operating system, then assemble, link, and test them. If appropriate, bind and test the bound version. You'll want to have this experience under your belt as you continue through the book.

Chapter

3

Basic Data Movement

One of the basic operations of any computer programming language is
moving data from one point to another. Actually, "copy" would be a
better term than "move," because the value is not removed from the
source location. Only the destination location is affected by the move.
After the move, both the source and the destination hold the same
value.

This chapter covers the move instructions that are commonly used
in application programs, which fall into five categories: basic moves,
loading and storing registers, pushing and popping the stack, conversions, and string moves. Moves restricted to system programs, mostly
because they involve system registers, are overviewed at the end of the
chapter but are not covered in detail.

Moving Data

The basic move instructions simply move a value from point A to point
B. Either point may be a register or a memory location, except that you
can't move from memory to memory. Figure 3-1 shows the instructions
that fall into this category. (Don't forget that details about each in-

mov   Move data

xchg   Exchange data

Figure 3-1   Move Instructions

struction are contained in Appendix A.) In all these instructions, as in most instructions that move data, the movement is from the second operand to the first operand. Thus the instruction **mov xcount,al** moves a value from register AL to memory area **xcount**.

The Mov Instruction

The **mov** instruction moves a value from a register, memory location, or the instruction itself (an immediate value) to a register or memory location. Suppose you want to load the immediate value 5 into the count register CL, then call the timer routine. You could use these instructions:

```
mov    cl,5
call   timer
```

Make sure that both operands are the same size. If not, the assembler will generate an error. For example, you cannot move a value from AL to DX since AL is a byte register and DX is a word (two-byte) register, but you can move from AL to DL or from AX to DX. If one of the values is a symbolic address, it will be defined as a byte, word, or doubleword. Here are some examples:

```
one_byte    db    ?          ; defines one byte
one_word    dw    ?          ; defines one word
dbl_word    dd    ?          ; defines doubleword
```

Using these definitions, the following moves are legal:

```
mov    one_byte,al       ; moves one byte
mov    bx,one_word       ; moves one word
mov    dbl_word,ecx      ; moves doubleword
```

The following moves are illegal:

```
mov    dbl_word,ch       ; byte vs. doubleword
mov    eax,one_word      ; word vs. doubleword
```

The source may be an immediate byte, but the destination may not. If the immediate value is smaller than the destination field, it is expanded to fit the size of the field. For example, if you move 25h to AX, the value stored is 0025h. Be sure an immediate source value does not exceed the size of the destination field:

```
mov    ax,5              ; moves one word to ax

mov    al,350            ; illegal—256 maximum

mov    di,10110001b      ; legal—one byte
```

You can transfer data between different size areas, but you must use conversion instructions, which are explained later in this chapter.

The Xchg Instruction

A special variation lets you exchange two values. You could write your own routine to do an exchange:

```
mov    cx,ax

mov    ax,one_word

mov    one_word,cx
```

This routine exchanges the values in AX and **one_word**. The first step copies one value from AX to CX for temporary storage. The second step copies the other value from **one_word** to AX. The third step then copies the original value from CX to **one_word** to complete the exchange. The disadvantages of this routine are the time it takes (12 clock cycles in the '286; 8 in the '386) and the possibility of being interrupted. The **xchg** instruction overcomes both those disadvantages:

```
xchg    ax,one_word
```

The system still goes through a three-step operation, using an intermediate holding area for the destination value, but only 5 clock cycles are consumed, and the instruction cannot be interrupted.

The primary application of the **xchg** instruction is to manipulate *semaphores*—flags that protect shared resources. For example, suppose you are creating a data base management system to run on a local area network. To prevent two users from accessing the same record for update at the same time, you make the first byte of each record a semaphore. When the record is not in use, the byte = 0; when it has been accessed for update, the byte = 1. The update routine accesses the semaphore this way:

```
mov     al,1             ; prepare for semaphore

xchg    al,semaphor      ; access and set it
```

Now the semaphore has been set to 1 so that no one else can access the record. At the same time, the previous value of the semaphore has been stored in AL. Testing the byte in AL determines whether or not it was already a 1.

If the byte in AL is a 1, the record is in use by someone else and cannot be updated. The program can loop back and continue testing the semaphore until the value shows up as a 0 (you might want to have a timeout escape in the loop to prevent closed loops in case some other program misuses the semaphore). When the byte in AL is a 0, you can go ahead and update the record. When the update is complete and the record is ready for use by others, free it with this instruction:

```
mov     semaphor,0
```

A semaphore works only if all programs that access the protected resource agree on and use the same conventions; in other words, there is nothing inherent in the 80xxx instruction set to prevent a program from accessing a shared resource without honoring the semaphore.

Notice how important it is to use the **xchg** instruction in accessing the semaphore. If you just tested the semaphore without setting it to 1, someone else might be testing it at the same time, both of you would receive a 0, and both would go ahead with the update simultaneously, one update overwriting the other. If you use the three-step method to access the semaphore, again someone else could access the semaphore after you access it but before you set it to 1, and two updates could occur simultaneously. Furthermore, there's a possibility of an interrupt occurring during the process, with the possibility of other processes taking place, possibly on the data base, before you can complete the semaphore exchange.

Loading Registers

The **mov** instruction moves data from one point to another, but cannot figure out the address of a memory field and load that into an address register. Figure 3-2 shows the load instructions that are commonly used in application programs to place addresses in registers. Also shown is the **lahf** instruction, which loads selected flags from the (E)FLAGS register into AX.

Loading the Effective Address

You can access the address offset of a memory field by loading it into a register using the **lea** (load effective address) instruction. Suppose **tax_table** is defined this way:

lea	Load effective address
lds	Load DS
les	Load ES
lfs	Load FS ('386 only)
lgs	Load GS ('386 only)
lss	Load SS
lahf	Load AH from flags

Figure 3-2   Load Instructions

```
tax_table    db      1,5,12,17,26,34,42,50,58
```

This definition creates a string of nine bytes; the first contains the value 1, the second contains the value 5, the third 12, etc. To point SI at the beginning of **tax_table**, you would issue this instruction:

```
lea    si,tax_table
```

What is placed in SI is the address offset of **tax_table**. In the '286, this is always a one-word value. In the '386, the size of the offset is determined by the size of the destination register. The above instruction would move a one-word offset. A doubleword offset would be stored by the following instruction:

```
lea    esi,tax_table    ; 32-bit version
```

In '386 programs, each memory segment also has an offset size associated with it. In the '386 programs presented in Chapter 2, the size was allowed to default to 32 bits. You'll learn in a later chapter how to change the size. Unlike the **mov** instructions, the two **lea** operands do not have to represent the same size offset. If you load a doubleword offset into a word register such as SI, the upper 16 bits of the offset are truncated. If you load a one-word offset into a doubleword register such as ESI, the upper word of the destination register is set to 0. In general, however, there's little reason to manipulate conflicting sizes. If you are working with 16-bit offsets, use a one-word destination register; 32-bit offsets should go to doubleword registers.

Loading Pointer Registers

The **lds**, **les**, **lfs**, **lgs**, and **lss** instructions all do essentially the same thing using different registers. When you are manipulating addresses, these instructions will load an address stored in memory into a pair of registers: the segment portion of the address goes into the segment register that is part of the opcode, and the offset portion of the address goes into whatever general register you specify as an operand. Suppose you want to load the segment:offset stored in **seg_pointer** into DS and SI. **Seg_pointer** is defined as a memory pointer:

```
seg_pointer    df    ?                    ; define full pointer

                                          ; in seg:offset format
```

A memory segment:offset address must have been stored in it by some previous operation.To load the address back into DS and SI, you would code:

```
              lds    si,seg_pointer
```

Loading Flags

The **lahf** (load AH from flags) instruction loads five of the flags from the flag register into AH. You can't manipulate the flags in the flag register, but you can manipulate them in AH, then store them back in the flag register again using a corresponding store instruction (discussed below). The flags that are loaded into AH are sign (bit 7), zero (bit 6), auxiliary (bit 4), parity (bit 2), and carry (bit 0). They maintain their same position in AH as in flag; the other bits in AH (bits 5, 3, and 1) are undefined and should not be used. Once they are loaded into AH, you can use bit manipulation instructions (discussed in a later chapter) to turn them on or off. The other flags are not loaded because they cannot be manipulated by an application; they are for system manipulation only. (The direction flag, bit 10, can be manipulated by an application using the **std** (set direction) and **cld** (clear direction) instructions discussed in a later chapter.)

Storing Registers

Once you have loaded the flags into AH and manipulated them as desired, you store them back into the flag register using **sahf** (store AH into flag), shown in Figure 3-3. This is the only store instruction commonly used by application programs.

sahf   Store AH in flags

Figure 3-3   The Store Instruction

Suppose you are getting ready to enter an arithmetic loop that requires the sign flag to be on at the outset. To turn the sign flag on, you could use these instructions:

```
lahf

or      ah,10000000b    ; turns on bit 7 of ah

sahf
```

This routine loads the eligible flags into AH, turns on bit 7 without affecting any of the other bits (the **or** instruction is explained in a later chapter), then stores the new set of flags back in the flag register, overlaying the previous flags in bits 7, 6, 4, 2, and 0. The remaining bits in (E)FLAGS are unaffected by this operation.

Pushing and Popping Data

The **push** instructions are used to place data in the stack and the **pop** instructions are used to retrieve data from the stack. You can push and pop between the stack and memory, the general registers, and the flag register. Figure 3-4 lists the various forms of **push** and **pop** instructions.

push	Push value onto top of stack
pusha	Push all one-word general registers
pushad	Push all doubleword general registers
	('386 only)
pushf	Push FLAGS
pushfd	Push EFLAGS ('386 only)

pop	Pop value from top of stack
popa	Pop all one-word general registers
popad	Pop all doubleword general registers
	('386 only)
popf	Pop FLAGS
popfd	Pop EFLAGS ('386 only)

Figure 3-4   Push and Pop Instructions

The Push and Pop Instructions

The basic instructions are **push** and **pop**, which push a word or a doubleword onto the top of the stack. In the '286, a word is pushed; in the '386, the operand size determines the number of bytes pushed. You can push a memory area, a general purpose register, or a segment register. In the '386, you can also push an immediate byte. Here are some legitimate **push** instructions:

```
push    memword        ; pushes a word
push    ax             ; pushes word register
push    "stop"         ; immediate doubleword
                       ;    386 only
push    cs             ; pushes code segment
                       ;    register
```

The **pop** instruction retrieves data from the top of the stack into memory, a general purpose register, or a segment register, as in these examples:

```
pop     memword        ; pops word into memory
pop     eax            ; doubleword into eax
pop     ds             ; pops word into ds
```

Notice that the last instruction changes the value of DS, thus pointing to a different data segment. This is one way of repointing a segment register. Since the code segment register can be controlled only by jump instructions, you cannot pop a value into CS.

Suppose a called routine must use the **work_field** segment as the data segment. At the beginning of the routine, you must preserve the current value of DS so it can be restored before terminating the routine:

```
push    ds                  ; preserve ds
mov     ds,work_field       ; repoint ds
; processing instructions
; (must balance push and pop)
pop     ds                  ; restore ds
```

The first instruction pushes the current value of DS onto the stack. The next instructions can then change DS without jeopardizing the calling routine. The final instruction restores the original value of DS from the stack.

Managing the Stack. The above routine won't work properly if the unseen processing instructions push any data onto the stack that isn't popped again. For example, suppose the routine contains these instructions:

```
push    ds                  ; preserve ds
mov     ds,work_field       ; repoint ds
; processing instructions
push    ah
; more processing
push    250
; more processing
pop     ah                  ; restore ah from stack
pop     ds                  ; restore ds
```

Figure 3-5 shows the condition of the stack after the **push 250** instruction. Notice what gets popped from the stack into AH. It's not the former value of AH but the immediate value 250. Therefore, the calling routine's AH value has been damaged, which will probably lead to serious problems somewhere along the way. (With luck, the program will abort before it damages any files or data bases.) In addition, the last **pop** instruction retrieves not the saved DS value but the saved AH value; still more damage can result from that.

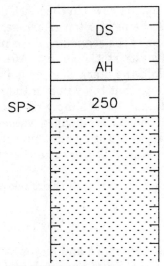

Figure 3-5   Stack Example

Be careful always to balance **push** and **pop** instructions. Keep careful track of the values that you push, and pop them in reverse order. Here's an example of the correct way to do it:

```
push    ax

push    250

push    memword

. . .

pop     memword

pop     ax

pop     ax
```

Since AX is the first value onto the stack, it is the last one off. The next value onto the stack is immediate; to get it off, we pop it into AX since we're going to change the value of AX again in the next instruction. We could have popped it into any place where it doesn't do any harm; alternatively, we could manipulate the stack pointer to bypass it (explained in a later chapter). Since **memword** is the last value onto the stack, it is the first one off.

When a program is loaded, the stack pointer is initialized to the end of the stack; that is, it is given the highest address in the stack. Each **push** decrements the stack pointer by 2 if the operand size is 16 bits or four if the operand size is 32 bits ('386 only). The new value of the stack pointer is then used to place the pushed value on the stack. Thus, the stack hangs upside down in the stack segment (if you visualize the highest address being the top of the segment and the lowest address being the bottom of the segment). Each **pop** accesses the value currently pointed to by the stack pointer. After the value has been copied to the destination, the stack pointer is incremented by two or four, as appropriate. Note that the value in the stack is not erased by being popped; the stack pointer is simply moved to the previous item. Thus, you can continue to access popped values in the stack either through other pointer registers or by adjusting the stack pointer. However, the next pushed value will overwrite the previous popped value in the stack.

A special case exists when you push the stack pointer itself, as in:

```
push    sp

push    esp                  ;'386 only
```

This is a perfectly legitimate move and might be handy in some situations, but a dilemma arises. Since the **push** instruction itself changes the value of the stack pointer, which value will be pushed—the value at the beginning of the instruction, before it is decremented, or the decremented value? Intel started off pushing the decremented value but changed their minds with the '286 and now the undecremented value is pushed. This is a slight difference between the behavior of the 8086 and the later microprocessors which can prevent a program from being upwardly compatible. If you intend to write a program to run on all models, avoid pushing the stack pointer. If you are upgrading an existing program written for the 8086, watch out for the **push sp** instruction.

If you pop the top of the stack into the SS register, all interrupts are inhibited until after the next instruction is processed. The system assumes you are restoring a former stack, that the next instruction pops (E)SP, and that an interrupt before the complete SS:(E)SP has been restored would be disastrous.

A stack fault occurs if a push or a pop exceeds the stack segment limits. The microprocessor signals a stack fault exception to the operating system, which probably aborts the program with an appropriate message. Stack faults are easy to run into since called subroutines frequently use the calling routine's stack. Nested routines can really eat up stack space. Therefore, you might need much more stack space than you can estimate from your own routines. If your program experiences stack faults, try using a larger stack or establishing separate stack segments for subroutines.

Pushing All the General Registers

Every called routine should preserve the registers of the calling routine except for those registers that are used to pass data back and forth (which is usually done in the stack instead). Suppose you are writing a routine that will use AX, BX, CX, SI, DI, and BP. Before beginning the routine, push those registers. Pop them at the end of the routine, just before you return control to the calling routine:

```
        push    ax

        push    bx

        push    cx

        push    si

        push    di

        push    bp

        ...     ...              ; remainder of routine

        pop     bp
```

```
pop     di

pop     si

pop     cx

pop     bx

pop     ax

ret                           ; return control
```

If you're going to preserve this many registers, you can save time with the **pusha, pushad, popa,** and **popad** instructions. **Pusha** (push all) pushes all the one-word general registers in this order: AX, CX, DX, BX, SP (as it was before the **pusha** instruction began), BP, SI, and DI. **Popa** (pop all) pops the same registers in reverse order, discarding the value of SP. **Pushad** (push all doubleword) pushes all the doubleword general registers in this order: EAX, ECX, EDX, EBX, ESP (as it was before the **pushad** instruction began), EBP, ESI, and EDI. **Popad** (pop all doubleword) pops them in reverse order, discarding the value of ESP. The number of clock cycles saved over pushing and popping all eight registers individually depends on which microprocessor is involved.

Is it better to push and pop the registers individually or to take advantage of **pusha(d)** and **popa(d)**? If you're writing a routine that could be called many times per second, where a few machine cycles will build up to a slower processing time, the answer depends on how many registers you need to push and pop and which processor is involved. If you're writing a routine that uses the registers to pass values back and forth—for example, the calling routine passes input values in CX and DX and expects to receive the result value in CX—obviously you don't want to restore the original value of CX at the end of the routine; either push and pop individually or place the result value in CX after **popa(d)** is complete.

The Pushf, Pushfd, Popf, and Popfd Instructions

A called routine might also need to preserve the calling routine's flag register. **Pushf** (push flags) and **pushfd** (push flags doubleword) push the flag register onto the stack, and **popf** (pop flags) and **popfd** (pop flags doubleword) pop it back into the flag register again. If the called routine executes any instructions that affect the flag register, these instructions might be advisable. (In practice, however, many called routines do not preserve the calling routine's flags. When calling routines that you have not created yourself, don't depend on your flags being preserved.)

Pushf and **popf** are different from **sahf** and **lahf** in that the store and load instructions manipulate only some of the flags, protecting the system flags from application manipulation. **Pushf** and **popf** push and pop the entire flag register, except that **popf** cannot overwrite **vm**, **rf**, **iopl**, or **if** unless the privilege level is high enough. Thus, one way to change the values of certain flags is to push them into the stack, set or clear the desired flags in the stack, then pop them back in the flag register again. You could also push an immediate word or doubleword onto the stack that represents the desired setting of all the flag bits, then pop that value into the flag register.

Conversions

You saw earlier that the **mov** instructions require both operands to be the same size. To move a value between two operands that are different sizes, you must use one of the conversion instructions. The conversion instructions expand a value, giving you control over what gets placed in the upper bits of the larger value. Figure 3-6 summarizes the conversion instructions.

movsx	Move with sign-extend ('386 only)
movzx	Move with zero-extend ('386 only)
cbw	Convert byte (AL) to word (AX)
cwd	Convert word (AX) to doubleword (DX:AX)
cwde	Convert word (AX) to doubleword extended (EAX) ('386 only)
cdq	Convert doubleword (EAX) to quadword (EDX:EAX) ('386 only)
xlat	Translate
xlatb	Translate bytes

Figure 3-6   Conversion Instructions

The Movsx and Movzx Instructions

Unlike a regular **mov** instruction, which requires that both operands be the same size, **movsx** and **movzx** let you expand the size of a value while moving it. You can move a byte or word to a word or doubleword. **Movsx** (move with sign-extend) propagates the high order bit (the sign bit) of the source value throughout all the high order bits of the destination. This makes a signed binary number keep its value as it is extended into a larger destination area. **Movzx** (move with zero-extend) turns all the high order bits of the destination area into zeros. This makes an unsigned binary number keep its value as it is extended into the larger area.

The Cbw, Cwd, Cwde, and Cdq Instructions

Cbw, cwd, cwde, and **cdq** convert signed binary values contained in the accumulator into larger values by extending the sign bit throughout the upper bits of the larger value. **Cbw** (convert byte into word) converts the byte in AL into a word in AX. **Cwd** (convert word into doubleword) converts the word in AX into a doubleword in DX:AX, perfectly set up to act as a dividend for a single-word **idiv** (integer divide) operation (which is explained in a later chapter). **Cwde** (convert word into doubleword extended) converts the word in AX into a doubleword in EAX, which can happen only with the '386. **Cdq** converts the doubleword in EAX into a quadword in EDX:EAX; this instruction is available only for the '386 and sets up a dividend for a doubleword **idiv** operation. None of these instructions have operands because both the source and the destination are implied by the instruction itself.

Suppose you have a one-byte signed value in AL that you want to use as the dividend in a doubleword division; the byte must be converted to a quadword in EDX:EAX in preparation for the division instruction:

```
cbw            ; from al to ax
cwde           ; from ax to eax
cdq            ; from eax to edx:eax
```

Now the value is ready to be used as a dividend in a doubleword division instruction.

Don't use these conversion instructions on unsigned values. If the value happens to have a 1 in the high-order bit, it will be propagated throughout the upper half of the expanded result, yielding an incorrect value. Use **movzx** instead to expand the size of an unsigned value. To expand a value into DX:AX or EDX:EAX for a **div** (unsigned division) instruction, move the value into (E)AX and clear (E)DX.

The difference between the **movsx** and these **cxx** instructions is in the location of the operands. With **movsx** you can specify the operands; with **cxx** they are assumed to be in the accumulator. Furthermore, **movsx** is available only on the '386.

The Xlat Instruction

One more conversion instruction translates values from one code system to another. For example, if you are receiving character values from a mainframe IBM system in EBCDIC (extended binary coded decimal interchange code) and must translate them into ASCII, **xlat** (translate) is the instruction to use. First, you must set up a table showing the ASCII equivalent for EBCDIC 00, 01, 02, ...:

```
ascii_table db      00,01,02,03,0Eh,09,etc.
```

You point (E)BX at the beginning of this table:

```
        lea     ebx,ascii_table  ; 32-bit version
```

Now you read the EBCDIC value into AL and issue the **xlat** instruction:

```
        call    get_ebcdic_char  ; stores char in al
        xlat    ascii_table
```

The **xlat** instruction uses the unsigned value in AL as an index into the table pointed to by EBX. It retrieves the value pointed to by DS:[EBX][AL] into AL. (The expression DS:[EBX][AL] means that the segment register is DS, and the offset is calculated by adding the value contained in EBX with the value contained in AL.) If the incoming value is 05, the result placed in AL (overlaying the incoming value) will be 09.

The intention of **xlat** is in making character code translations such as this. The key is in the setup of the table, arranging the target codes so they will be indexed properly by the incoming source codes.

There are two forms of the **xlat** instruction: **xlat** and **xlatb**. **Xlat**, as shown above, takes an operand that is meaningless except to indicate the segment containing the desired table. In the above example, if **ascii_table** is not in the segment currently pointed to by DS, an exception would occur. You could override the segment:

```
        xlat    es:ascii_table
```

or

```
        xlat    tableseg:ascii_table
```

Don't forget that the operand identifies only the segment; the actual operands of the instruction are assumed: [(E)BX][AL] for the source, AL for the destination. You don't even have to use the table's symbolic address as the operand; any symbolic address in the correct segment would do.

Xlatb takes no operand; the desired table must be in the current DS segment, at DS:[(E)BX]. If you are sure that the desired table will always be in the current DS segment, then the **xlatb** form of the instruction is a little easier to code. If you want the system to make an extra check of the segment, then use the **xlat** form of the instruction, and specify the table's symbolic address as the operand.

In either case, the values in (E)BX and AL are crucial to locating the correct item in the table. Be sure to load the correct values into these two registers before issuing the **xlat** or **xlatb** instruction.

String Moves

Moving character strings from one part of memory to another is a common operation. Since no instruction can have two memory operands, if you use the **mov** instruction, it takes two steps:

```
mov    al,input_name[si]    ; 16-bit version
mov    output_name[si],al
```

In this routine, the SI register is used as an index to the desired byte. It contains the offset to the desired character within **input_name** and **output_name**. The first time the routine is executed, SI would be set to 0, thus moving a byte from **input_name+0** to **output_name+0**. Then SI would be incremented to 1 and the routine would be repeated. If the operands are 25 bytes long, the routine would be repeated 25 times, with SI set to 0, 1, ... 24. Each time the routine is repeated, it takes two steps to move the character from one memory location to the other. That's a lot of extra steps in a loop to move a 25-character string.

A special set of string instructions get around this problem by assuming the operands. The string instructions are shown in Figure 3-7. All the string move instructions assume DS:(E)SI is pointing to the source operand and ES:(E)DI is pointing to the destination. To make the move shown above using **movsb**:

```
lea    esi,input_name    ; 32-bit version
lea    edi,output_name
movsb
```

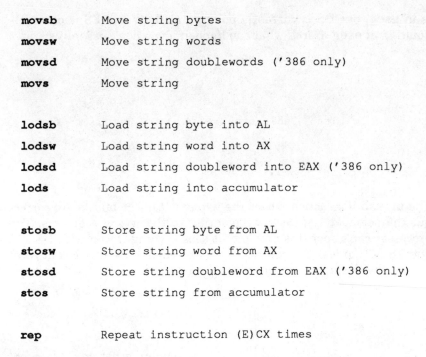

movsb	Move string bytes
movsw	Move string words
movsd	Move string doublewords ('386 only)
movs	Move string
lodsb	Load string byte into AL
lodsw	Load string word into AX
lodsd	Load string doubleword into EAX ('386 only)
lods	Load string into accumulator
stosb	Store string byte from AL
stosw	Store string word from AX
stosd	Store string doubleword from EAX ('386 only)
stos	Store string from accumulator
rep	Repeat instruction (E)CX times

Figure 3-7   String Move Instructions

The **movsb** instruction moves the byte at DS:(E)SI to the byte at
ES:(E)DI. Then it automatically advances both (E)SI and (E)DI by 1 so
the instruction can be repeated in a loop to move an entire string. In a
similar manner, **movsw** moves the word at DS:(E)SI to the word at
ES:(E)DI, advancing both indexes by 2. **Movsd**, available only on the
'386, moves the doubleword at DS:(E)SI to the doubleword at ES:(E)DI
and advances the indexes by 4.

The **movs** instruction without the **b, w,** or **d** is the basic form of the
instruction. It requires two operands that look like the source and
destination operands but in fact merely dictate the size of the move:
byte, word, or doubleword. Any symbolic addresses with the correct
length definition and in the correct segments can be used. The advantage of using this form of the instruction is that, when you specify
the real operands' symbolic addresses as the fake operands, then the
defined size of the symbolic addresses becomes the size of the operation. This prevents you from accidentally treating byte-defined fields
as words or doublewords, and vice versa, or from mixing sizes. In
addition, using the symbolic addresses forces the fields to be in the
correct segments. Suppose **input_name** is in **fseg** and **output_name**

is in **gseg**, but DS is currently pointing at **dseg** and ES is currently pointing at **eseg**. Here's what can happen if you don't use **movs**:

```
lea    esi,input_name   ; loads offset of
                        ;    fs:input_name
                        ;    into esi
lea    edi,output_name  ; loads offset of
                        ;    gs:output_name
                        ;    into edi
movsb                   ; moves ds:esi to es:edi
```

The **movsb** instruction moves the wrong data! The offsets are correct but the segment registers are pointing to the wrong segments. The processor can't spot this problem; it sees nothing wrong with DS:ESI and ES:EDI unless a segment limit is exceeded. Now let's look at what happens with the **movs** form of the instruction:

```
lea    esi,input_name   ; loads offset of
                        ; fs:input_name into esi
lea    edi,output_name  ; loads offset of
                        ; gs:output_name into edi
movs   output_name,input_name   ; exception!
```

The **movs** instruction results in an exception since the processor knows that **output_name** is not in ES and **input_name** is not in DS.

Which form is better? That's up to you. Some programmers prefer the shorter instruction and the greater control they get with **movsb**, **movsw**, and **movsd**. Others prefer the extra measure of protection they get with **movs**.

You also can't override the segment assumptions unless you use the **movs** form of the instruction, and even then you're not permitted to override the extra segment for the destination operand. In the small program model we've used so far in this book, the extra segment coincides with the data segment, so you don't need to define a separate segment. However, MASM-OS/2 doesn't automatically load ES, so it's necessary to copy DS to ES sometime before the first string instruction appears. It takes two **mov** instructions:

```
mov    ax,ds
mov    es,ax
```

This isn't necessary with 386 I ASM and the 386 I DOS-Extender, which loads ES automatically.

To make string moves even more efficient, you can prefix string move instructions with a **rep** (repeat) instruction. **Rep** causes the string instruction to be repeated until (E)CX is 0; each time the string instruction is executed, (E)CX is decremented. To move 25 bytes, you would code:

```
mov     cx,25           ; 16-bit version

rep movsb
```

A complete routine to move input_name (which contains 20 bytes) to **output_name** might look like this:

```
mov     es,ds           ; 32-bit version

lea     esi,input_name

lea     edi,output_name

mov     ecx,20

rep movsb
```

You'll see more about **rep** in Chapter 4.

So far in this discussion, we've been assuming that the direction flag (DF) is cleared. But when it's set, then the move works backwards. That is, the indexes are decreased after each step instead of increased. Thus, the move starts at the end of the string and works toward the beginning. (Be sure to point the indexes at the end of each string, not the beginning, before starting the move.)

Why would you do this? The most common application is an overlapping move in a forward direction (from lower addresses to higher addresses). Figure 3-8 diagrams the problem. The top part of the drawing shows the problem itself. The center part shows what happens in a forward move: the first byte moved overlays a byte further on in the source string. When the move terminates, the string has been destroyed. The bottom part of Figure 3-8 shows how a backward move solves the problem. The overlapped bytes are moved before they can be overlaid.

You set the direction flag with the **std** instruction. You'll have to clear it after the move with the **cld** instruction or later string operations will be affected. (Even if you know that all the string operations in your program will use **std**, don't leave the direction flag set; you might affect a called routine such as an operating system service.)

A complete routine to do a backward move might look like this:

```
std                     ; backward move

mov     es,ds           ; 16-bit version

lea     si,input_name   ; source field
```

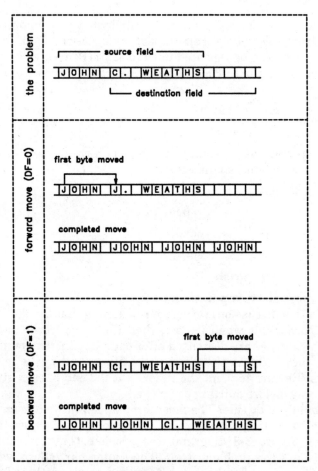

Figure 3-8   Overlapping String Moves

```
        add     si,19           ; point to end of string

        lea     di,output_name  ; destination field

        add     di,19           ; point to end of string

        mov     cx,20           ; number of bytes to move

        rep movsb               ; moves 20 bytes

        cld
```

A backward move is not the appropriate solution to all overlapping moves. If the direction of the move is backward in memory (from higher addresses to lower addresses), then a forward move avoids overlaying the source string.

The Load and Store String Instructions

Another set of instructions lets you load and store strings. **Lods** and **stos** each require a fake operand to identify the size of the move; the actual operands are always the accumulator and the memory area pointed to by (E)SI. **Lodsb, lodsw,** and **lodsd** move one byte, word, or doubleword from DS:[(E)SI] to AL, AX, or EAX. **Stosb, stosw,** and **stosd** use ES:[(E)DI] instead of DS:[(E)SI]. After the byte, word, or doubleword is moved, the index is advanced by 1, 2, or 4, as appropriate, in the direction indicated by DF.

You can use **rep** with these instructions; it is more useful with the store string instructions than the load string instructions. Suppose you want to clear a string in memory by setting it to all blanks:

```
lea     esi,user_id      ; 32-bit version

mov     al,' '           ; ascii space character

mov     ecx,5            ; length of user_id

rep stosb
```

This routine points ESI at the beginning of the field to be cleared, loads an ASCII space into AL, and loads the length of the move into ECX. The **rep movsb** instruction then stores the ASCII space in **user_id, user_id+1, ... user_id+4.** You can use a similar routine to initialize a character string with nulls (00), high values (0FFh), zeros ('0'), or whatever value is needed. **Rep** makes little sense with **lods** as it gives you no chance to process each character placed in the accumulator before it is overwritten with the next one. However, **lods** can be very useful in a loop containing other instructions:

```
lea     si,user_id       ; 16-bit version

mov     cx,5             ; length of user_id

check_loop:

lodsb

call    check_bits

loop    check_loop
```

This routine points SI at **user_id** and sets the loop counter to 5 (the **loop** instruction uses this value just like **rep** does). Then the loop starts. **Lodsb** loads the first character into AL. The **call** to **check_bits** causes the character to be processed as appropriate to the application. Then the **loop** instruction decrements CX by 1 and branches back to **check_loop** if the result isn't 0. When CX is 0, the loop terminates.

If you use the **lods** form of the instruction, you can override the source segment, as in:

```
lods    fs:user_id
```

However, you can never override the destination segment for **stos**; it must be ES. As with the **movs** instruction, the real advantage of **lods** and **stos** lies in forcing the system to do a segment check and type check on the operand, assuming you use the real operand as the fake operand:

```
lea     di,user_id      ; 16-bit version

mov     ax,' '          ; ascii spaces

mov     cx,5

rep stos user_id
```

This routine loads a space into AX and stores it in all five bytes of **user_id**, thus clearing the field. This is a good way to clear a string field to spaces. Because the routine uses **stos** with **user_id** as the operand, it forces **user_id** to be in the extra segment, or an exception will occur. Furthermore, it uses the defined size of **user_id**, whatever that is.

String Instruction Exceptions

Since the string instructions advance the indexes automatically and are used in loops that depend on (E)CX being set correctly, an undebugged program can easily experience a runaway index that eventually exceeds the segment limit and causes a general protection exception. **Stosx** can also cause a general protection exception by attempting to write in a read-only segment.

System Instructions

Figure 3-9 lists the system programming instructions that move data. If you want to know more details about these instructions, you can look them up in Appendix B or your Intel manual.

in	Input value from port
ins	Input string character from port
insb	Input string byte from port
insw	Input string word from port
insd	Input string doubleword from port
out	Output value to port
outs	Output string character to port
outsb	Output string byte to port
outsw	Output string word to port
outsd	Output string doubleword to port
lar	Load access rights byte
lgdt	Load global descriptor table
lidt	Load interrupt descriptor table
lldt	Load local descriptor table
lmsw	Load machine status word
lsl	Load segment limit
ltr	Load task register
sgdt	Store global descriptor table
sidt	Store interrupt descriptor table
sldt	Store local descriptor table
smsw	Store machine status word
str	Store task register

Figure 3-9   System-Level Move, Load, and Store Instructions

Program Flow

Ordinarily, control flows from instruction to instruction in a program in sequential order. However, you need the ability to interrupt the sequential order to create decision structures such as branches and loops. This chapter describes the instructions used to control program flow, including instructions to jump, call, loop, and interrupt, as well as the comparison instructions that many decisions are based on. You will also learn more about using the stack for passing variables to subroutines, including instructions to create and use stack frames.

Using (E)IP

The instruction pointer register always indicates the address offset of the next instruction to be executed in the task. When a task is initialized, (E)IP is loaded with the offset of the instruction identified as the entry point of the program. As soon as the first instruction is fetched, and before it is executed, (E)IP is incremented to point to the next instruction. Thus, as each instruction is executed, (E)IP is pointing at the next instruction in sequence. If the current instruction changes the program flow via a jump, call, or interrupt, then it changes the value in

(E)IP. When the current instruction completes execution, the changed (E)IP is used to access the next instruction.

Near and Far Transfers

Whenever the assembler and linkage editor are translating an instruction that transfers control to another point in the program, they must decide whether to use an address offset within the same code segment (a *near* transfer) or a segment:offset form of address to reach a point in another code segment (a *far* transfer). A near transfer is encoded in machine language as a one- or two-byte displacement to be added to the current (E)IP to reach the desired new location. A far transfer is encoded in machine language as a complete segment:offset to replace the values in CS:(E)IP.

The type of transfer is determined by examining the target address. In nearly all cases, a symbolic label is coded as the target address in the source code. It's the definition of that label, not its location, that determines whether a near or far transfer is encoded. Labels that are defined with a colon represent near labels, as in this example:

```
sum_loop:
```

They can only be jumped to or called from other locations within the same code segment, not from other code segments. Other ways to define near labels are with the **label** directive:

```
sum_loop    label near
```

and the **proc** directive:

```
sum_loop    proc  near
```

Far labels cannot be created by the colon shortcut, but they can be created by **label** and **proc**:

```
handle_err label  far
error_proc proc   far
```

Gates and TSS names are always far labels. Far labels can receive control from any point in the program. If you transfer control to a far label from within the same code section, a far type of transfer is still encoded even though a near transfer would be possible from that location.

When you create a label, you must decide whether it is a near label only or whether the program will address it from other segments. If you need to be able to transfer control to a label from other segments, give it the **far** characteristic. If it will receive control only from its own segment, give it the more efficient **near** characteristic.

The label itself must be unique within the program (or within the module if multiple-modules are being combined to create one program).

Jumps

A jump transfers control to another part of the program. A *conditional* jump transfers control only if a condition is true; for example, after a mathematical operation, you might want to jump to an error routine if the result overflowed the destination field. An *unconditional* jump always transfers control; no condition is involved. For example, after completing an error routine, you might want to jump to the end of the program.

A jump can be far, near, or short. A *short* jump transfers control within the range of −128 bytes to +127 bytes from the current instruction, which is always the instruction following the jump instruction since the (E)IP is updated as soon as the jump instruction is fetched and before it is executed. Unconditional jumps can be far or near. Conditional jumps must be short for the '286, short or near for the '386. The concept of short, as opposed to near, applies to jumps only. There are no short calls or returns.

A jump occurs when the value in CS:(E)IP is changed. For far jumps, the entire address is replaced. For near jumps, CS stays the same but the machine instruction contains a two-byte signed operand that is added to (E)IP. For short jumps, a one-byte signed operand is added to (E)IP (thus the −128 to +127 range limit). Far jump instructions take up the most bytes in machine language and take the longest to execute. Near and short instructions take about the same time to execute, but near jumps take up more machine language bytes than short jumps since near jumps have two-byte operands and short jumps have one-byte operands.

Figure 4-1 lists the jump instructions. (Refer to Appendix A for detailed information about each instruction as you read this chapter.)

Unconditional Jumps

The **jmp** instruction causes an unconditional jump. All you need to code is **jmp** followed by the target address, which is usually a symbolic

```
jmp        Unconditional jump
jcond      Conditional jump
```

Figure 4-1   Jump Instructions

address. For example, to jump to the address represented by the symbol ending, you could code:

```
jmp     ending
```

The assembler decides whether this is a near or far jump depending on the location and definition of the label. Remember that each label must be unique within the program module; therefore, the assembler can find the label you are referring to, even if it's in another segment. To jump forward to another segment, you need to tell the assembler that a far jump is wanted using the **far ptr** operator, as in this example:

```
jmp     far ptr sort_proc
```

If the target label is in another module, then you must use a global symbol (covered in Chapter 9).

Forward jumps can create difficulty for the assembler, which processes each line in the source program in sequential order. A forward jump is one in which the destination address follows the jump instruction. Therefore, when the assembler is translating the jump instruction, it has not yet encountered the referenced label and does not know whether it is a short, near, or far label. It cannot complete the translation during the first pass through the assembly job; it must make a second pass to finalize the addresses in all forward references. However, on the first pass, it must decide how much room to leave for the instruction; otherwise, it couldn't determine the address of the next instruction and all subsequent instructions. When they encounter a forward jump, both the MASM assembler and the Phar Lap assembler assume that the target address is a near address. Each assembler leaves three bytes for the instruction if 16-bit addressing is being used (one byte for the instruction code and two for the address operand), five bytes if 32-bit addressing is being used.

On the second pass, if the address for a jump turns out to be a short address, little harm is done; a little extra room has been left in the program, creating a minor inefficiency. The assembler fills any extra bytes with **nop** instructions; **nop** (no operation) is a one-byte instruction that does absolutely nothing. The assembler might issue a warning message (non-fatal) advising you of the **nop** solution. You can avoid this slight problem by using the **short** operator to advise the assembler that the jump is a short one, as in this example:

```
jmp     short bad_check
```

With the **short** operator, the assembler leaves the correct amount of space for the instruction on the first pass.

If the assembler assumes that a forward reference is a near reference and it turns out to be far, there's not enough room to store the
needed address in the machine language instruction. This problem
cannot be resolved, and the program cannot be assembled. The Phar
Lap fatal error message is: "Illegal forward reference to symbol." The
MASM fatal error message is: "Near JMP/CALL to different CS." To
avoid this problem, you must warn the assembler that a far reference
is needed with a **far ptr** operator, as shown in this example:

```
jmp    far ptr sort_proc
```

The expression **far ptr** tells the assembler to leave room for a far
pointer in the instruction.

Jump targets can be coded as register names or data variables, in
which case the assembler assumes that the register or variable holds
the address to be jumped to. In this example, we use a register as an
indirect jump target:

```
lea    bx,phase_error

. . .

jmp    bx
```

The first instruction loads the address-offset of **phase_error** (which
must be a label somewhere in the same code segment) into BX. The
second instruction uses the value in BX to identify the target of the
jump. You might use this technique to determine the target address at
execution time.

Conditional Jumps

A conditional jump transfers control only if a condition is true. If the
condition is false, control falls through to the next instruction. Figure
4-2 lists the 32 conditional jump mnemonics and the conditions they
test. All the conditions test the status flags except **jcxz** and **jecxz**,
which test the value in (E)CX. We'll explain the use of **jcxz** and **jecxz**
later in this chapter. The other conditional jumps are meant to be used
following instructions that affect the status flags, such as arithmetic
and comparison instructions, although other instructions (that don't
affect the flags) might intervene. A simple subtraction routine will
serve as an example:

```
sub    cx,dx           ; cx = cx - dx
mov    balance,cx
jz     paid_off
js     overpaid
```

GENERAL USE

mnemonic	meaning	condition for jump
je	jump if equal	ZF=1
jne	jump if not equal	ZF=0
jc	jump if carry	CF=1
jnc	jump if not carry	CF=0
jo	jump if overflow	OF=1
jno	jump if not overflow	OF=0
jp	jump if parity	PF=1
jpe	jump if parity even	PF=1
jnp	jump if not parity	PF=0
jpo	jump if parity odd	PF=0
js	jump if sign	SF=1
jns	jump if not sign	SF=0
jz	jump if zero	ZF=1
jnz	jump if not zero	ZF=0
jcxz	jump if CX is zero	CX=0
jecxz	jump if ECX is zero	ECX=0 ('386 only)

FOLLOWING SIGNED COMPARISONS

mnemonic	meaning	condition for jump
jg	jump if greater	ZF=0 and SF=OF
jng	jump if not greater	ZF=1 or SF≠OF
jge	jump if greater or equal	ZF=OF
jnge	if not greater or equal	SF≠OF
jl	jump if less	SF≠OF
jnl	jump if not less	SF=OF
jle	jump if less or equal	ZF=1 and SF≠OF
jnle	jump if not less or equal	ZF=0 or SF=OF

Figure 4-2   Conditional Jump Instructions (part 1 of 2)

FOLLOWING UNSIGNED COMPARISONS

mnemonic	meaning	condition for jump
ja	jump if above	CF=0 and ZF=0
jna	jump if not above	CF=1 or ZF=1
jae	jump if above or equal	CF=0
jnae	jump if not above or equal	CF=1
jb	jump if below	CF=1
jnb	jump if not below	CF=0
jbe	jump if below or equal	CF=1 or ZF=1
jnbe	jump if not below or equal	CF=0 and ZF=0

Figure 4-2   Conditional Jump Instructions (part 2 of 2)

Here the subtraction affects all the status flags, indicating whether the result is positive, negative, zero, and so forth. The **mov** instruction doesn't affect the flags so they retain their values for the **jz** instruction. **Jz** jumps to **paid_off** if the zero flag is set—that is, if the subtraction produced a zero result. For a nonzero result, control falls through to the **js** instruction. The flags still haven't changed, so **js** also tests the result of the **sub** instruction. **Js** jumps to **overpaid** if the sign flag is set—that is, if the subtraction produced a negative result.

As you can see in Figure 4-2 and Appendix A, several jump instructions are logically identical. For example, **jz** and **je** both jump if the zero flag is set; **jc**, **jnae**, and **jb** all jump if the carry flag is set; **jp** and **jpe** both jump if the parity flag is set. Logically identical instructions are actually synonyms, producing the same machine-language code. The different assembler language mnemonics simply provide you with more meaningful opcodes to use in various contexts. For example, **jz** is meaningful after subtraction, but **je** would be more meaningful after comparing two values even though **jz** would have the same effect:

```
cmp    cx,dx            ; compare cx to dx
je     no_diff          ; jump if they're equal
```

Several differences exist between '286 and '386 conditional jump instructions. First, the '386 instruction set includes **jecxz** to test the ECX register, which isn't available on the '286. In addition, with the '286, all conditional jumps must be short jumps; with the '386, they can be short or near, except that **jcxz** and **jecxz** must be short. If you code a target address too far away, the assembler will reject the instruction.

(If you don't want to count bytes for a short jump, about 40 instructions in either direction is usually safe.) If you need to jump farther than the allowed range, combine conditional and unconditional jump instructions to achieve the desired result. These two routines are logically identical:

```
        jz      none_left
```

and:

```
        jnz     some_left
        jmp     none_left

some_left:
```

The shorter routine simply jumps to **none_left** if the zero flag is set, but if **none_left** is out of the range of a short jump and the '286 processor is being used, then it is illegal. The longer routine uses **jnz** to jump around the **jmp** instruction if the zero flag is cleared; if the zero flag is set, control falls through to the **jmp** instruction, which has no range limitations. You could also use this technique to accomplish a far conditional jump.

You might be wondering about the differences between the above/below instructions (**ja, jb, jae,** etc.) and the greater/less instructions (**jg, jl, jge,** etc.). They are not logically identical as you can see from examining the flags they test. The above/below instructions are appropriate after comparing or manipulating two unsigned values:

```
        cmp     income,outgo
        ja      profit
```

This routine jumps to **profit** if the value in **income** is greater than the value in **outgo** as determined by the carry flag and the zero flag. The greater/less instructions have meaning after comparing or manipulating two signed values:

```
        cmp     score,-10
        jl      unqualified
```

Here we compare the signed value in **score** to −10. If it's less than −10, we jump to **unqualified**. If it's greater than or equal to −10, we fall through to the next instruction. It's important to use the **jl** instruction rather than **jb**, because **jb** could produce the wrong results. By comparing the sign bit to the overflow bit, as the greater/less instructions do, the system can accurately determine which value was higher.

Jump Tables

A jump table is a list of target addresses used to select a particular branch from a large set of possibilities. A short example will illustrate. Suppose your database program offers these menu choices:

```
1  Browse

2  Add new records

3  Delete records

4  Update records

5  Extract records

6  Quit
```

You want to jump to **browse_proc**, **add_proc**, **delete_proc**, etc., accordingly. Figure 4-3 shows the relevant portions of a program to handle this type of problem using a jump table. Lines 2 through 11 show the directives that create the jump table itself in the data section. Ten entries are created, one for each possible digit the user might enter, from 0 through 9. Each entry is the address offset of a procedure in the code section; if you don't care to work with procedures, any code section labels can be used. Since the '286 uses two-byte address offsets, each entry is defined as one word; the value is supplied by the assembler in response to the **offset** operator. There are other ways to get the address-offset values into the jump table, but this is the easiest and clearest. Notice that several entries use the same target address offset, **error_proc**. Those entries reflect incorrect input by the user: 0, 7, 8, or 9. **Error_proc** can issue a message to try again and jump back to the top of the routine.

```
1               .data
                ...
2   jump_table  dw      offset error_proc
3               dw      offset browse_proc
4               dw      offset add_proc
5               dw      offset delete_proc
6               dw      offset update_proc
7               dw      offset extract_proc
8               dw      offset quit_proc
9               dw      offset error_proc
10              dw      offset error_proc
11              dw      offset error_proc
```

Figure 4-3   Using a Jump Table—'286 Version (part 1 of 2)

```
12                    .code
                      ...
13   next_action:
14                    call   get_user_choice
                  ; get_user_choice gets one digit into AX
15                    and    ax,00001111b  ; ascii to binary
16                    shift  ax,1           ; multiply ax by 2
17                    mov    si,ax
18                    jmp    jump_table[si]
                      ...
19   browse_proc      proc   near
                      ...
20                    jmp    next_action
21   browse_proc      endp
22   add_proc         proc   near
                      ...
23                    jmp    next_action
24   add_proc         endp
25   delete_proc      proc   near
                      ...
26                    jmp    next_action
27   delete_proc      endp
28   update_proc      proc   near
                      ...
29                    jmp    next_action
30   update_proc      endp
31   extract_proc     proc   near
                      ...
32                    jmp    next_action
33   extract_proc     endp
34   quit_proc        proc   near
                      ...
35   quit_proc        endp
36   error_proc       proc   near
                      ...
37                    jmp    next_action
38   error_proc       endp
```

Figure 4-3   Using a Jump Table—'286 Version (part 2 of 2)

Now let's look at the code that uses the jump table. Lines 14 through 17 get a single ASCII digit from the user, convert it to binary, multiply it by 2 because each entry in the table is two bytes long, and move it to SI. Now the value in SI is an index into the jump table. If the user entered 0, the index is 0, so **jump_table[si]** points to the first entry in the table. If the user entered 1, the index is 2 and **jump_table[si]** points to the second entry in the table. And so forth.

Line 18 is the **jmp** instruction that actually uses the jump table to get to the desired procedure. The secret to its operation is this: if the target address of a jump instruction is in the data section, not a code section, the system treats it as an *indirect* address. In other words, the system doesn't try to jump to the address but instead uses its value as the target address. Thus if you jump to **jump_table[8]**, the system picks up the value from the fifth table entry and ends up jumping to **update_proc**.

Lines 19 through 39 show the framework of the procedures that are jump targets. Each procedure begins with a **proc** directive and ends with an **endp** directive. Since the procedures are jumped to, each procedure ends with a **jmp** instruction that returns control to the beginning of the entire routine at **next_action**. If you didn't include the **jmp next_action** instruction, control would fall through to the next procedure. **Quit_proc** doesn't need a **jmp next_action** instruction because it terminates the program.

Figure 4-4 shows how the jump table concept can be made even more efficient with the '386 processor where you can use a scale value with your index. First of all, notice that the jump table uses doubleword entries since the '386 address-offsets need four bytes instead of two. Second, notice that two lines have been eliminated between lines 14 and 15. Since the '386 can use any general-purpose register except ESP for indexing, it's not necessary to move the value to SI. And since we can scale the index in the jump instruction, it's not necessary to have a separate **shift** instruction to multiply the input value. Therefore, we get the value from the user (line 14) in AX, convert it to binary (line 15) in EAX, then use EAX scaled (multiplied) by 4 to access the jump table (line 16).

The example in Figure 4-4 is a perfect application of the '386 scaling feature, which was designed to make it easy and more efficient to access tables composed of words, doubleword, or quadwords. That's why you can scale by 2, 4, or 8. Using the scaling factor in the **jmp** instruction saves several machine cycles over multiplying the index in a separate instruction.

If you're used to thinking of programs in terms of structures, the jump table (along with the call table discussed in the next section) is

```
1                    .data
                     ...
2   jump_table  dd      offset error_proc
3               dd      offset browse_proc
4               dd      offset add_proc
5               dd      offset delete_proc
6               dd      offset update_proc
7               dd      offset extract_proc
8               dd      offset quit_proc
9               dd      offset error_proc
10              dd      offset error_proc
11              dd      offset error_proc

12                   .code
                     ...
13  next_action:
14                   call    get_user_choice
                ; get_user_choice gets one digit into AX
15                   and     eax,0000000000001111b
16                   jmp     jump_table[eax*4]
                     ...
```

Figure 4-4   Using a Jump Table—'386 Version

the best solution to the case structure. Whenever three or more equivalent branches are involved in a decision, the jump table can efficiently route control to the desired branch.

Calls

A call also transfers control to another part of the program, but it stores return information so that when the called routine terminates, control can be transferred back to the instruction following **call**. A jump is a permanent transfer of control, but a call is a temporary transfer. The **call** instruction makes a call; the **ret** instruction terminates a called routine and returns control to the calling instruction, as illustrated in Figure 4-5. Calls can be near or far; there are no short calls.

CALLING ROUTINE

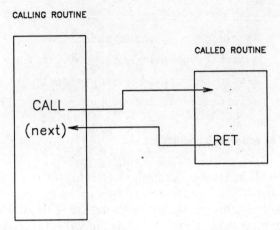

Figure 4-5   Calling and Returning

Mechanics

The success of a call and return operation depends on the mechanics for storing the return link. When a task transfer is not involved, the mechanics are fairly simple. If the transfer stays within the same segment (a near call), the value in (E)IP is pushed onto the stack. Remember that (E)IP is incremented as soon as an instruction is fetched, so the preserved value is the address-offset of the instruction following the **call** instruction. After the push, the transfer takes place exactly as if it were a jump. That is, it adjusts the value in (E)IP to point to the desired instruction. All the **ret** instruction does is pop the top of the stack into (E)IP. Assuming that the former value of (E)IP is still on the top of the stack, the effect is to cause a return to the previous position in the program, the instruction following the **call**. If an intersegment (far) transfer is involved, CS:(E)IP is pushed by **call** and popped by **ret**.

As you can see, it's vital that the called routine not destroy the return address stored at the top of the stack. Anything the called routine pushes onto the stack must be popped again before the **ret** instruction. If **ret** pops the wrong values into CS and/or (E)IP, the result can be unpredictable and disastrous. Later in this chapter, we'll show you some methods for using the stack in a called routine without damaging the integrity of the return link.

If the target of the call is a TSS (task state segment) or a task gate, then the current task is suspended and the called task installed. In these cases, the system preserves the current task's status by recording all its registers in its own TSS, then loads the new task from its TSS. A return link to the calling TSS is stored in the called TSS. When

call	Call
ret	Return from a called procedure
retf	Return by popping a far pointer into CS:(E)IP
retn	Return by popping a near pointer into (E)IP
iret	Return from an interrupt or task call

Figure 4-6   Call and Return Instructions

the **ret** instruction is encountered, the status of the called task is stored in its own TSS, then the return link to the previous TSS is used to get back to the calling task. By restoring CS:(E)IP, the status flags, the general registers, and so forth from the values stored in the TSS, the calling task can be resumed exactly where it left off at the instruction following the **call** instruction.

Figure 4-6 lists the instructions used to create calls and returns.

The Call Instruction

No matter what type of target you are calling, the format of the **call** instruction is the same: **call *address***. Here are some examples:

```
call    change_page     ; near label
call    error_proc      ; far label
call    quit_gate       ; call gate
call    excel_task      ; task gate
call    word_tss        ; tss
```

All the above examples use code section labels. Other forms of memory direct address could be used, but the symbolic label is usually the clearest. You can also use indirect addressing:

```
call    edx             ; address in edx
call    call_table[si]  ; address in call table
```

This last example should look familiar to you, as it implements a call-table structure similar to the jump tables discussed earlier. Figure 4-7 is a revision of Figure 4-4 using calls and returns rather than jumps. The difference between the two routines lies in the **call** instruction on line 16 and the **ret** instructions on lines 18, 21, 24, and so forth. With this revised structure, each subroutine returns control to the line following the **call** (except **quit_proc** which terminates the program).

```
1                    .data
                     ...
2    call_table     dd      offset error_proc
3                    dd      offset browse_proc
4                    dd      offset add_proc
5                    dd      offset delete_proc
6                    dd      offset update_proc
7                    dd      offset extract_proc
8                    dd      offset quit_proc
9                    dd      offset error_proc
10                   dd      offset error_proc
11                   dd      offset error_proc

12                   .code
                     ...
13   next_action:
14                   call    get_user_choice
          ; get_user_choice gets one digit into AX
15                   and     eax,0000000000001111b
16                   call    call_table[eax*4]
                     ...
17   browse_proc     proc    near
                     ...
18                   ret
19   browse_proc     endp
20   add_proc        proc    near
                     ...
21                   ret
22   add_proc        endp
23   delete_proc     proc    near
                     ...
24                   ret
25   delete_proc     endp
26   update_proc     proc    near
                     ...
27                   ret
28   update_proc     endp
```

Figure 4-7   Using a Call Table—'386 Version (part 1 of 2)

```
29    extract_proc    proc    near
                       . . .
30                     ret
31    extract_proc    endp
32    quit_proc       proc    near
                       . . .
33    quit_proc       endp
34    error_proc      proc    near
                       . . .
35                     ret
36    error_proc      endp
```

Figure 4-7   Using a Call Table—'386 Version (part 2 of 2)

You can use the **far ptr** operand to override the assembler's **near** assumption for forward references to far labels, as in this example:

```
call    far ptr revise
```

The **short** operator does not pertain to calls since there is no such thing as a short call.

The Ret Instructions (2)

When a called routine is ready to terminate, the **ret** instruction returns control to the calling routine by popping the return address off the stack into (E)IP or CS:(E)IP. Ordinarily, **ret** appears inside a **proc** structure, as shown in Figure 4-7, and it pops (E)IP or CS:(E)IP as specified by the parameter **near** or **far** on the **proc** directive. If you are coding a **ret** outside a **proc** structure or need to override the **near** or **far** declaration (be sure you know exactly what you are doing), you can use **retn** to pop (E)IP only and **retf** to pop CS:(E)IP.

Ret can specify a numeric parameter indicating how many bytes should be removed from the stack after the return address has been popped. This feature makes it easy to pop variables that were passed between the two routines. You'll see how to use it later in this section.

If task switching is necessary to return to the calling routine, use **iret** instead of **ret**. **Iret** causes the state of the current task to be stored in its TSS, then the calling TSS is loaded and its task restored and given control.

Passing Data in the Stack

Most programs use the stack to pass variables back and forth between the calling procedure and the called procedure. The calling procedure pushes input variables into the stack. The called procedure can't pop the input variables because the return address is in the way. The most common solution is to use (E)BP to access the variables buried in the stack without disturbing the return address. The called procedure places return variables in the stack in spaces left by the calling routine. After returning, the calling routine can pop the return variables from the stack.

Figure 4-8 shows how the stack is used to pass parameters to a subroutine that converts Fahrenheit to Centigrade temperature. The top row in the figure shows the preparation of the stack before the call.

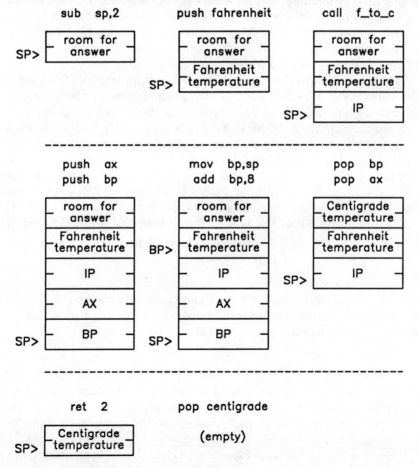

Figure 4-8   Passing Parameters to a Subroutine

First the calling routine adjusts the stack pointer to make room for the answer from the subroutine. As you'll see when we get to the end of the routine, it's important that the answer space go into the stack first so that it can be the last thing out. There are several possible ways to leave answer room in the stack. You could, for instance, push zeros or some other value onto the stack. However, manipulating the stack pointer itself is a simple and efficient means of accomplishing the objective. Since the stack is built upside down in the address space, from high to low addresses, you must subtract to advance (E)SP. Subtracting two bytes makes room for one word in the stack. If the subroutine needs more room, you would subtract more bytes.

The next step pushes the input variables onto the stack. In this case, the Fahrenheit temperature, which is one word, is pushed. Other cases might involve pushing several words or doublewords. Finally, the **call** instruction pushes the return address onto the stack. In the example shown, a near call using 16-bit addressing causes one word to be pushed onto the stack, the IP. Far calls and 32-bit addressing would cause more words to be pushed.

The middle row in the figure shows the manipulation of the stack by the subroutine. First AX and BP are pushed because the subroutine uses those registers. Then BP is pointed at the passed variable. This is accomplished by copying SP to BP, then adjusting BP up eight bytes. Why eight bytes? Because we know in this particular example that the passed variable, the return address, and the two preserved registers are taking up four words in the stack. For each subroutine you prepare, you must figure out how many bytes to adjust BP based on your knowledge of what's in the stack at that time.

After pointing BP at the passed parameter, the subroutine can access the parameter using indirect addressing, as in:

```
mov    ax,[bp]
```

The portion of the routine that calculates the Centigrade temperature is not shown in the figure. As you can see in the last diagram in the middle row, the Centigrade temperature has been placed in the stack, probably using this instruction:

```
mov    [bp+2],ax
```

Since BP is pointing at the Fahrenheit temperature, BP+2 points to the word above that in the stack. The final step the subroutine takes is to pop the preserved registers out of the stack again.

The bottom row of the figure shows how the stack is treated upon returning to the calling routine. First of all, look at the **ret** instruction. It pops IP from the stack automatically. Next, because an operand of 2 is specified, it adds 2 to SP, thus moving the stack pointer up one word in the stack and eliminating the input variable. By the time the **ret** is completed, the only thing left in the stack is the return variable. SP is perfectly set up to access this variable with a simple POP instruction. That is why you place the room for the return variables in the stack first, so the **ret** instruction can eliminate the input variables and leave only the answers in the stack, ready to be popped.

In preparing the stack for a call, keep these points in mind:

- Make room for the answers first; that way you can use the **ret** instruction to remove the input variables from the stack and all you have to do is pop the answers when control returns.

- In making room for the answers, subtract 2 bytes from (E)SP for each word of answer space you need.

- Push the input variables next.

In using the stack in a called procedure, keep these points in mind:

- Make sure you know exactly how many bytes have been pushed onto the stack by the call and any registers you pushed. In the '286, a near call pushes 2 bytes onto the stack while a far call pushes 4 bytes onto the stack. When 32-bit addresses are being used, a near call pushes 4 bytes onto the stack while a far call pushes 8 bytes onto the stack. Each 16-bit register you push adds 2 bytes to the stack. Each 32-bit register you push adds 4 bytes to the stack.

- Be sure to preserve (E)BP before you point it at the input variables.

- Move (E)SP to (E)BP, then add as many bytes as needed to (E)BP to point it at the last input variable in the stack. Use indirect addressing via (E)BP to access the variables in the stack ([EBP], [EBP+2], [EBP+4], etc.).

If the called procedure calls another, SP is still positioned correctly to create input and return variables and store the return address. Thus, there is no problem with nesting except the possibility of running out of stack space if you don't know how much space your called procedures and their called procedures use.

Enter and Leave. Two special instructions were added to the instruction set after the 8086 instruction set to accommodate high-level languages that require a stack frame when calling subroutines. A stack frame is a structure in the stack similar to the one created in Figure 4-8, but more formalized. If you're not writing a high-level language translator, then you probably don't need **enter** and **leave**.

Enter creates the stack frame. Its first operand specifies the number of bytes of variable space, and its second operand specifies the level of nesting. If the level of nesting is 0, **enter** creates a stack frame following these steps:

1. Push (E)BP
2. (E)BP = (E)SP
3. (E)SP = (E)SP – first operand

Level 0 is used in cases where nesting is not anticipated. If nesting is intended, then the main routine should use level 1, with subroutines using higher levels. At each level above 0, the system stores the parent level's (E)BP first, as a back link to the parent's stack frame, then all the higher levels' (E)BP's in order, ending with the current (E)BP, as shown in Figure 4-9. Thus, the parent (E)BP is pushed twice, once at the beginning of the frame and once in the "display" of base pointers.

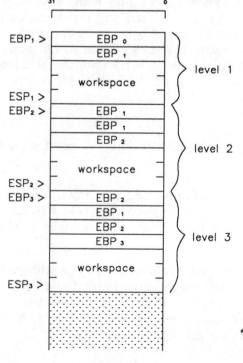

Figure 4-9   Stack Frames Created by Enter

These stored pointers give the current routine access to all the higher routine's stack variables. (E)BP is always left pointing at the beginning of the stack frame so that the entire stack frame can be accessed by indirect addressing. The following example would address the first variable at level 3, 16 bytes beyond the base pointer:

```
mov     eax,[ebp-16]
```

Figure 4-9 shows each stack frame using six words of work space, but in reality one subroutine might use two words while another uses 1000.

Leave eliminates the current stack frame from the stack, restoring the previous settings for (E)BP and (E)SP.

The current value of (E)BP is crucial to the successful operation of **enter** and **leave**. If you're going to use them, make sure that none of the enclosed routines alter (E)BP. Use displacements to reach other values in the stack, as shown in the example above. If you want to use a preserved (E)BP to reach a higher level routine's workspace, copy it to another pointer register, remembering that other registers must be prefixed with SS to access the stack. Suppose your stack looks like Figure 4-9 and you want to access the first variable in the level 1 workspace; here's one way:

```
mov     esi,[ebp-4]
mov     eax,ss:[esi-8]
```

The first instruction loads level 1's base pointer into ESI. The second instruction uses SS:ESI to reach indirectly the desired variable, which is 8 bytes down from the position of that frame's EBP.

Comparisons

Comparisons compare two operands and manipulate the flags to indicate whether the first operand is greater, equal, or less than the second operand. You can then use a conditional jump instruction to make a decision based on the result of the comparison. Figure 4-10 lists the comparison instructions.

The system performs the comparison by setting the flags as if the second operand was subtracted from the first operand. In fact, the subtraction does not take place, and neither operand is affected. Only the flags are affected.

```
cmp          compare

cmps         compare string
cmpsb        compare string bytes
cmpsw        compare string words
cmpsd        compare string doublewords ('386 only)


scas         scan string
scasb        scan string bytes
scasw        scan string words
scasd        scan string doublewords ('386 only)
```

Figure 4-10   Comparison Instructions

The Cmp Instruction

Cmp makes a straightforward comparison between two operands of
the same size. Suppose you input a signed number from the keyboard
into AX. You want to jump to **more_proc** if the input is greater than 0,
zero_proc if it's 0, and **less_proc** if it's less than zero:

```
          cmp     ax,0

          jg      more_proc

          je      zero_proc

less_proc etc.
```

The **cmp** instruction sets the flags as if 0 was subtracted from AX. **Jg**
jumps if the flags indicate that AX is greater than zero. **Je** jumps if the
flags indicate that AX equals 0 (**jz** would do as well here). If control
falls through those two jumps, AX must be less than 0.

We used **jg** in this case because the value in AX is a signed number,
and the greater/less conditional jumps are the only correct tests for
signed comparisons. Suppose we want to test the unsigned value in AX
against 3000:

```
          cmp     ax,3000

          ja      master_class

journey_class:
```

Here we jump to **master_class** if the value is higher than 3000; otherwise we fall through into **journey_class**. Since the value in AX is unsigned, the above/below conditions are correct and the greater/less tests incorrect. Thus we use **ja** instead of **jg**.

The Cmps Instructions

The **cmps** instructions compare two string bytes, words, or double-words, setting the flags accordingly. As with all string instructions, they assume a source operand at [(E)SI] and a destination operand at ES:[(E)DI]. They also adjust both index registers, incrementing if DF is cleared, decrementing if DF is set.

The comparison is made exactly as with the **cmp** instruction: the flags are set as if the second operand was subtracted from the first. After a string comparison, the above/below set of conditional jumps are appropriate, as are **je** and **jne**.

Cmps without any suffixes requires two fake operands to identify the size and segments of the operation. The operands coded in the source instruction are not the actual operands of the operation, which are always identified by (E)SI and (E)DI. The two fake operands can reference any defined symbols of the correct size in the correct segment. The source segment register is assumed to be DS unless you override it. The destination segment register cannot be overridden.

Cmpsb, cmpsw, and **cmpsd** take no operands. The source and destination and the size of the operation are all implied by the opcode.

The Scas Instructions

The **scas** instructions compare the value in AL, AX, or EAX to the byte, word, or doubleword at ES:[(E)DI] and set the flags accordingly. Then (E)DI is automatically advanced. The flags are set as if the value at ES:[(E)DI] was subtracted from the accumulator.

Scas without any suffix requires a false operand to identify the size and segment of the operation. **Scasb, scasw**, and **scasd** take no operands. The following routine examines the byte at **ds:in_byte** for a 'Y.'

```
lea     esi,in_byte        ; '386 version

mov     ax,'y'

scasb

jne     not_yes
```

If it is 'Y,' control falls through to the next instruction; if not, it jumps to **not_yes**.

Both **cmps** and **scas** were designed to be used in loops. That's why the indexes are advanced automatically. When used in a loop, **cmps** compares two strings for equality/inequality. **Scas** scans a string for a specific character, contained in the accumulator. You will see how to use **cmps** and **scas** in loops later in this chapter.

Bit Comparisons

The comparisons discussed in this chapter operate on bytes, words, doublewords, and strings. You can also test individual bits and jump accordingly. Bit operations are discussed in Chapter 7.

Preserving a Condition

Sometimes you need to preserve a condition while executing other instructions that might change the flags. The **set*cond*** instruction sets a destination byte to either 1 or 0 depending on the specified condition. The 30 possible conditions should all be very familiar to you, as they are the same as the jump conditions except for **jcxz** and **jecxz**.

Loops

A loop is a routine that is executed repeatedly. Usually, one or more items are varied in the loop, causing each iteration to affect a different item. A loop might be executed a specific number of times or until a condition becomes true. A malfunctioning loop in an untested program might become closed; that is, there is no way out of the loop and it executes repeatedly until something external interrupts it (such as the user rebooting). Figure 4-11 shows the instructions used for creating loops.

The Loop Instruction

The **loop** instruction causes a routine to be repeated until (E)CX is 0. The structure of a routine using **loop** looks like this:

```
            mov     cx,count          ; 16-bit version
    loop_start:

                . . .

            loop    loop_start
```

Before entering the loop, (E)CX must be set to the number of iterations to be executed, which must be greater than 0. The label at the beginning of the loop provides the target of the **loop** instruction that ends

loop	Loop (repeat until (E)CX=0)
loope	Loop while equal (until ZF=0 or (E)CX=0)
loopz	Loop while zero (same as loope)
loopne	Loop while not equal (until ZF=1 or (E)CX=0)
loopnz	Loop while not zero (same as loopne)
rep	Repeat string instruction (until (E)CX=0)
repe	Repeat while equal (until ZF=0 or (E)CX=O)
repz	Repeat while zero (same as repe)
repne	Repeat while not equal (until ZF=1 or (E)CX=0)
repnz	Repeat while not zero (same as repne)
set*cond*	Set destination byte if condition is true

Figure 4-11   Loop and Set*cond* Instructions

the loop. In between, of course, come the processing instructions of the loop.

The **loop** instruction works by subtracting 1 from (E)CX without affecting any of the flags; if the result is not zero, control jumps back to the referenced label. If the result is zero, the jump is not taken; control falls through to the instruction following the loop, thus ending the loop. It's important that the processing instructions do not change the value in (E)CX; only **loop** should manipulate (E)CX during a loop. If the routine needs to use (E)CX for its own purposes, it should push the register at the beginning of the loop and restore it before reaching the **loop** instruction.

Suppose you want to perform the **get_digit** procedure five times in succession. Here's a routine to do it:

```
            mov     ecx,5              ; 32-bit version
get_loop:
            call    get_digit
            loop    loop_start
```

Since we move 5 into ECX before starting the loop, the loop will be executed exactly five times (unless **get_digit** changes the value in ECX). After the fifth time, ECX reaches 0 and the loop terminates with control falling through to the instruction following the **loop** instruction.

If (E)CX is set from a variable rather than an immediate value, the chance of creating a nearly closed loop exists. If (E)CX gets initialized to 0, then the first loop will cause it to be decremented to 0FFFFh if CX is being used or 0FFFFFFFFh if ECX is being used. Thus, the loop will be repeated 64K times for 16-bit addressing or 4G times for 32-bit addressing. The **jcxz** and **jecxz** instructions can be used to avoid this possibility by testing the loop counter and bypassing the loop if it equals zero. Here is an example of how you would apply the bypass:

```
            mov     cx,file_size      ; 16-bit version
            jcxz    file_empty
load_file:
            call    load_record_proc
            loop    load_file
            . . .
file_empty:
```

After loading the loop counter, the program tests it for zero. If it is zero, a forward jump to **file_empty** bypasses the loop. Otherwise, control falls into the loop.

The Loop*cond* Instructions

Many loops are terminated not by the number of iterations but by some condition coming true within the loop. For example, you might want to read user input until the user enters a 'Q.' Or you might want to shift a value to the left until the first digit is not a zero. The **loop*cond*** instructions let you create conditional loops. To avoid the possibility of closed loops, (E)CX is also manipulated as with the **loop** instruction. The loop is terminated if the condition comes true or (E)CX reaches zero, whichever happens first. Thus, you can set a limit to the number of times the loop is executed without the condition coming true.

Loope and **loopz**, which are synonymous, test the zero flag. If it's 0, the loop terminates; if not, and (E)CX is also not 0, control returns to the target address. Suppose you want to perform **get_input** as long as the user enters a 'Y,' with a limit of 500 iterations. As soon as the user enters any character other than a 'Y,' the loop should terminate. The following routine will work:

```
            mov     ecx,500
```

```
get_loop:
                call    get_input
                cmp     al,'Y'
                loope   get_loop
```

Loopne and **loopnz**, which are synonymous, do the opposite of the above. That is, they terminate the loop if ZF becomes 1. As long as ZF is 0, the loop is repeated. (Assuming that (E)CX is not 0.)

The **loop***cond* instructions are useful in cases where the repeated routine manipulates some variables such as an index. Suppose you want to perform the **shift_left** procedure until the character in AL is a period. The following routine will do it:

```
                mov     ecx,0FFFFFFFFh    ; '386 version
shift_loop:
                call    shift_left
                cmp     al,'.'
                loopne  shift_loop
```

Here we set ECX to its maximum value so it won't end the loop prematurely. Within the loop, we execute **shift_left**, then use **cmp** to set the flags. **Cmp** will set ZF if the value in AL equals '.' and clear ZF if it doesn't. Thus the **loopne** instruction will restart the loop if AL does not equal a period; when AL does contain a period, it terminates the loop by falling through to the next instruction.

Figure 4-12 shows one way to do a sequential table search. Line 1 defines a table of 300 words. We treat this as a table of 100 entries, each entry comprising 3 words. Line 2 calls a procedure that loads values into the table from a disk file. Line 3 calls a procedure that

```
1   wave_table      dw      300 dup (?)
                    . . .
2                   call    load_proc     ; loads table
3                   call    key_proc      ; gets search key
4                   mov     ecx,100
5                   mov     si,-6
6   search_loop:
7                   add     si,6
8                   cmp     wave_table,ax
9                   loopne  search_loop
10                  jne     not_found
```

Figure 4-12   Sample Sequential Search Routine

places a search key in AX. The search key is a value that identifies the desired table entry. The job is to search the table for an entry with the same value in the first word.

Lines 4 and 5 set up the search parameters. Line 4 sets ECX to 100. If ECX reaches 0, we have reached the end of the table and want to terminate the loop even if a match has not been found. Line 5 sets SI to –6 because the loop begins by adding 6 to SI and we want SI to be 0 the first time the **cmp** instruction is executed.

Lines 6 through 9 comprise the search loop. Line 7 advances the index by 6 bytes to point to the beginning of the next table entry. You might be wondering why we don't adjust the index after the **cmp** instruction, avoiding the awkwardness of presetting the index to –6 with code like this:

```
            mov     di,0
search_loop:
            cmp     wave_table[si],ax
            add     si,6
            loopne search_loop
```

The **add** instruction affects the zero flag, which invalidates the interaction between **cmp** and **loopne**. Therefore it must not be permitted to intervene between **cmp** and **loopne**.

When we fall out of the search loop to line 10, we don't know whether the loop terminated because a matching entry was found or because the end of the table was reached. The **jne** instruction on line 10 tells us. The flags are still valid from the **cmp** instruction, so if **cmp** didn't set the zero flag, we know that the routine terminated because ECX reached zero without finding a matching entry.

The Rep Instructions

Rep is a prefix you can place before certain string instructions to repeat them until the entire string is processed. **Rep** without any conditional suffix repeats the string instruction until (E)CX is 0. To move a 20-byte employee name from an input buffer to an output buffer:

```
            lea     si,in_name      ; '286 version
            lea     di,out_name
            mov     cx,20
            rep movsb
```

In this example, the two **lea** instructions point SI and DI for the **movsb** instruction. The **mov** instruction prepares CX with the desired count for the **rep** prefix. The **rep movsb** instruction then moves **in_name[0]** to **out_name[0]**, **in_name[1]** to **out_name[1]**, and so forth through **in_name[19]** to **out_name[19]**. (If DF is set, the bytes moved would be **in_name[0]** through **in_name[-19]**. Some experts recommend always inserting a **cld** instruction before a **rep** string instruction just to make sure that some other routine didn't leave the direction flag set.) **Rep** without a conditional suffix can be prefixed to **movsx**, **insx**, **outsx**, and **stos**. You don't need **j(e)cxz** before **rep** since it tests the condition before it decrements (E)CX.

The **repe** and **repz** prefixes, which are synonymous, repeat a string instruction until a nonmatch is found by a string comparison or (E)CX equals 0, whichever comes first. When used with **cmps,** it compares the two strings until it finds a nonmatching byte, word, or doubleword (depending on the size of the operands). Look carefully at the order of processing shown in Appendix A. After making the comparison, the indexes are advanced and (E)CX is decremented before the processor checks to see if a terminating condition has been found. Therefore, when the instruction terminates, the indexes always need to be adjusted to locate the nonmatching byte. Incrementing CX will tell you how many bytes are left in the string. To compare **in_password** to **file_password** (5 bytes) use code like this:

```
lea     esi,in_password  ; '386 version
lea     edi,file_password
mov     ecx,5
repe cmpsb
jne     reject_password
```

The **lea** instructions prepare the required indexes for the **cmpsb** instruction; the **mov** instruction prepares ECX for the maximum number of repetitions. When control reaches the **jne** instruction, you don't know which condition terminated the **rep cmpsb** instruction: a mismatch or the end of the string. The **jne** instruction tells you if a mismatch was found. If so, ESI and EDI are pointing to the bytes following the mismatching bytes. Decrement them to access the mismatching bytes.

The **repne** and **repnz** instructions, which are synonymous, repeat until a match is found or (E)CX is 0. Suppose you wanted to scan **in_amount** (7 bytes) for a '$'. You could use this code:

```
lea     di,in_amount     ; 16-bit version
```

```
        mov    al,'$'
        mov    cx,7
        repne scasb
        jne    no_dollar_sign
```

The **lea** and **mov** instructions set up the **repne scasb** instruction. The **jne** identifies whether the repetition ended because a '$' was found or because the seven bytes were exhausted. If a match was found, DI is pointing at the byte after the $ and CX indicates its position minus one.

Here's how you might eliminate the leading zeros from a string and display the rest of the string:

```
              lea    di,population    ; 16-bit version
              mov    cx,11
              mov    al,'0'           ; ascii zero
              repe scasb
              je     zero_value
              inc    cx               ; number of bytes to write
              dec    di               ; di — first byte
write_loop:
              mov    al,[di]
              call   write_byte       ; write one byte
              inc    di
              loop   write_loop
```

This routine starts by pointing DI at the beginning of the **population** field. The field is 11 bytes long so CX is set to 11 to prevent DI from getting out of the field if the value is zero. AL is loaded with a 0 for comparison purposes. Then the **repe scasb** instruction scans **population** for the first byte that doesn't contain a 0. When it terminates, the **je** instruction jumps to a routine that handles an all-zero value. Assuming that a non-zero byte was found, **repe scasb** increments DI and decrements CX once more before terminating. Therefore, it is necessary to increment CX to indicate the number of bytes to be written and decrement DI to point at the first non-zero byte. Then **write_loop** writes each byte.

The conditional forms of **rep** can be used only with **cmps** and **scas** instructions. It doesn't make sense with any other string instructions because they don't set the zero flag.

Rep tests (E)CX before decrementing, so you don't need to test with **j(e)cxz** before a rep instruction.

Interrupts

Another way to transfer control is the software-generated interrupt: **int, bound,** and **into** (see Figure 4-13). **Int** is followed by a one-byte immediate unsigned integer indicating which interrupt is desired, as in:

```
int     21h
```

Int pushes the flags and CS:(E)IP, then picks up the new CS:(E)IP from the interrupt table (which must be created by the operating system). In protected mode, the call might go through an interrupt gate, a trap gate, or a task gate. Many protection checks are applied to prevent illegal access to protected segments.

Intel has provided a number of interrupts for exceptions, software-generated interrupts, and hardware-generated interrupts. For example, **int 0** is generated when a divide error exception is recognized; **int 6** is generated when an invalid opcode is encountered. Your operating system provides routines that handle these interrupts. It probably also provides a number of additional interrupts and handlers. You've already seen, for example, how DOS uses **int 21h** to provide I/O services. See your operating system manual for details of what's available and how to use it.

The Bound Instruction

Whenever you're looping while varying an index, you stand the chance of a *runaway index*; that is, an index that reaches beyond the limits of the table. The routine in Figure 4-12 uses ECX to prevent this. But in cases where you are not searching the table sequentially, you don't know the maximum number of searches, so you don't know what value to set ECX to. Then the **bound** instruction becomes useful for preventing runaway indexes.

Bound causes an interrupt (code 5) if the value of a register is below a lower limit or above an upper limit. Although this facility might be

```
int         Interrupt
into        Interrupt on overflow (OF=1)
bound       Interrupt if bounds exceeded
```

Figure 4-13   Interrupt Instructions

useful in other situations, it was designed to prevent an index from getting outside a table. To use **bound,** you must set up the lower and upper limits as adjacent items in memory. If 16-bit addressing is being used, set them up as adjacent words:

```
table_limits        dw              0,100
```

For 32-bit addressing, set them up as doublewords:

```
table_limits        dd              0,100
```

In the search routine, use the **bound** instruction after manipulating the index and before accessing the table:

```
        dec     esi                 ; '386 version

        bound   esi,table_limits

        cmp     wave_table[esi],ax
```

If you don't want to interrupt the program in case of a boundary violation, then don't use **bound.** Write your own boundary checking routine instead by comparing the computed address to predetermined limits and jumping to an error routine if either limit is exceeded.

Into interrupts if the overflow flag is set. It is designed to follow arithmetic instructions where the possibility of the result overflowing the destination field occurs. Alternatively, you can use **jo** to jump to an overflow handling routine without interrupting.

Summary Program

A password processing routine can be used to summarize the program flow instructions presented in this chapter. This procedure acts as a subroutine to any calling program. It gives the user three chances to enter the correct password. It returns a code in the stack indicating whether the user entered the correct password (0) or failed to do so (1). The calling routine must leave an empty word in the stack to receive the answer and then must push the correct password (four bytes) onto the stack.

This procedure needs some variables of its own in the data segment. Only those portions of the data segment used by the procedure are shown. You can assume that the calling procedure also defines fields in the data segment.

Figure 4-14 shows the OS/2 version of the procedure. The data used by the procedure is shown on lines 1 through 6. This includes the fields needed to write the output message and receive the user's input.

```
1                       .data
2 std_handle           equ     1
3 pass_msg             db      'enter password: '
4 msg_len              dw      $ - pass_msg
5 bytes_out            dw      ?
6 user_pass            db      4 dup (?)

7                       .code
8                       extrn DosWrite:far,DosRead:far
9 pass_proc            proc    near
10                      push    bp
11                      push    cx
12                      mov     bp,sp
13                      add     bp,6
14                      mov     cx,3
15 pass_loop:
16                      call    getit_proc
17                      mov     si,bp
18                      lea     di,user_pass
19                      push    cx
20                      mov     cx,4
21                      repe cmpsb
22                      pop     cx
23                      loopne pass_loop
24                      jne     short bad_pass
25 good_pass:
26                      mov     word ptr [bp+4],0
27                      jmp     exit
28 bad_pass:
29                      mov     word ptr [bp+4],1
30 exit:
31                      pop     cx
32                      pop     bp
33                      ret     4
34 pass_proc            endp
```

Figure 4-14   Sample Password Procedure (part 1 of 2)

```
35 getit_proc        proc   near
36                   push   ax
37                   push   std_handle
38                   push   ds
39                   push   offset pass_msg
40                   push   msg_len
41                   push   ds
42                   push   offset bytes_out
43                   call   DosWrite
44                   push   std_handle
45                   push   ds
46                   push   offset user_pass
47                   push   length user_pass
48                   push   ds
49                   push   offset bytes_out
50                   call   DosRead
51                   pop    ax
52                   ret
53 getit_proc        endp
```

Figure 4-14   Sample Password Procedure (part 2 of 2)

Lines 7 through 13 do the housekeeping for the rest of the procedure. Among other things, they point BP at the variable passed from the calling program. Line 14 sets up CX for three loops.

Lines 15 through 23 execute the loop that gets the password (up to three times) from the user. Line 16 calls a subroutine that actually displays the password message and reads the user's input. That's a very standard routine like those you have seen in earlier chapters (lines 35 through 53).

Lines 17 and 18 set up the index registers for the upcoming **cmpsb** instruction. Lines 19 and 20 set up CX for the **repe** prefix. It is necessary to preserve and restore the current value of CX because the **repe cmpsb** loop falls in the middle of another loop controlled by CX. Line 21 does the comparison.

When control reaches line 22, the zero flag has been either set or cleared, indicating whether or not the user's password matches the desired password. Line 22 restores CX, a necessary step before the **loopne** instruction. Then line 23 makes a two-pronged decision. First, it decrements CX. Then, if CX is not zero and the zero flag is cleared, it loops back to **pass_loop** for another attempt at getting the correct password from the user. However, if either CX is zero or the zero flag is set (indicating a good password from the user), then control will fall through to line 24.

Line 24 jumps to **bad_pass** if the zero flag is not set; in other words, if the loop terminated because CX reached zero indicating that the user did not enter a correct password in three tries. Note the use of the **short** operator to advise the assembler that a short jump is correct.

Lines 25 through 27 are executed when the zero flag is set (the user entered a good password). Line 26 moves 0 to the return variable in the stack, using the indirect address **[bp+4]**. The BP register is pointing at the passed variable (see lines 12 and 13), which is four bytes long. Therefore, BP+4 bypasses the passed variable and points to the return variable. Line 27 jumps around the **bad_pass** branch.

The **bad_pass** branch sets the return variable to 1. Once the return variable has been set, CX and BP can be restored and control returned to the calling routine. The **ret 4** instruction (line 33) removes the passed variable from the stack so that the calling routine can pop the return variable without any further stack manipulation.

This procedure does not apply all the program control instructions you have seen in this chapter, but it demonstrates the ones you'll use most of the time. It also includes a branching structure and two loops (one nested inside the other).

Arithmetic without the Coprocessor

Simple arithmetic operations, such as the addition of two integers, can be done in the CPU, without the numeric coprocessor. This offers two advantages: you don't have to transfer values back and forth between the two processors and you need not worry about timing between the two processors. However, the CPU offers only the four basic arithmetic operations (addition, subtraction, multiplication, and division) whereas the coprocessor instruction set includes dozens of operations, including square roots, trigonometric functions, and logarithmic functions. CPU arithmetic can be performed only on integers while the coprocessor can handle real numbers. The CPU operands must be bytes, words, or doublewords ('386 only), but the coprocessor can handle quadwords and tenbytes. However, the CPU instruction set is designed to develop loops to handle values as long as needed in the form of byte, word, or doubleword ('386 only) strings. Furthermore, only the CPU instruction set can handle values stored in unpacked BCD format.

This chapter shows you how to use the CPU arithmetic instructions. Chapter 6 shows you how to use the numeric coprocessor.

Increments and Decrements

The simplest arithmetic instructions are **inc** and **dec**, which add 1 to and subtract 1 from the destination value. Figure 5-1 shows all the addition and subtraction instructions, including **inc** and **dec**. The most common use of **inc** and **dec** is to vary indexes in a loop. For example, suppose you are summing the values in an array. You might do it this way:

```
score_array db    100 db (?)        ; 16-bit version

            ...

            mov   si,0              ; array index

            mov   cx,100            ; to count loops

            mov   dx,0              ; to hold sum

sum_loop:

            add   dx,score_array[si]

            inc   si

            loop  sum_loop
```

The above routine uses SI as an index to access each byte in the array. The **inc** instruction increments SI each time the loop is performed. When CX reaches zero, the loop terminates and DX holds the sum.

Neither **inc** nor **dec** affects the carry flag, an important feature when doing long addition and subtraction loops, as you will see later in this chapter. They do affect the zero flag, so be careful how you use

```
inc         Increment

dec         Decrement


add         Add (without carry)

sub         Subtract (without borrow)


adc         Add with the carry flag

sbb         Subtract with the carry (borrow) flag
```

Figure 5-1   Addition and Subtraction Instructions

them in loops controlled by **loop**cond. Because they don't affect the carry flag, they should not be used except for their intended purpose of incrementing or decrementing indexes in loops controlled by **loop**. In other situations, where overflow is possible, the other addition and subtraction instructions are better.

Addition and Subtraction without Carrying or Borrowing

The **add** and **sub** instructions add and subtract integers. Each instruction specifies both a destination and a source operand. The source is added to or subtracted from the destination, with the result replacing the destination. Both operands can be of any size and type, except that the destination cannot be immediate (or where would the result be stored?). You can even add an immediate byte to or subtract an immediate byte from a larger size destination, one of the few instances where different-size operands are permitted.

To increment or decrement an unsigned value and branch based on overflow, you could use a routine like this:

```
add     cx,1                ; 16-bit version
jc      too_big
...
sub     cx,1
jc      too_small
```

Adding 1 to CX is the same as incrementing it (notice that you're adding an immediate *byte* to a destination *word*), except that the carry flag will be set if the value overflows the destination field, allowing you to use **jc** afterwards.

Of course, **add** and **sub** can be used for adding and subtracting values other than 1. If you've ever used a word processor, you know that you can insert a large block of text (by copying or unerasing a block or inserting a file) and you can also delete a block. Suppose you are keeping track of the file size in CX and the size of a block in DX. To adjust the file size after insertions or deletions, you could use these instructions:

```
add     cx,dx               ; 16-bit version
jc      too_big
..
sub     cx,dx
```

```
          jc      too_small
```

You might keep the file size in ECX and the block size in memory:

```
block_size dd      ?                      ; 32-bit version

          . . .

          add     ecx,block_size
          jc      too_big

          . . .

          sub     ecx,block_size
          jc      too_small
```

What you can't do is add or subtract different size fields:

```
block_size dw      ?

          . . .

          add     block_size,cl   ; error

          . . .

          sub     ecx,block_size  ; error
```

Carrying and Borrowing

Sometimes you need to add and subtract values larger than a word ('286) or a doubleword ('386) without using the coprocessor. **Adc** and **sbb** let you create addition and subtraction routines that handle a string of bytes, words, or doublewords, accounting for a possible carry or borrow from one operand to the next. For example, suppose two values in memory are defined this way:

```
sub_total   db      5 dup (?)
grand_total db      7 dup (?)
```

Sub_total is five bytes long and **grand_total** is seven bytes long. To add these two values together, you would start with the least significant bytes, which can be accessed by the names **sub_total+4** and **grand_total+6**. Since no carry can possibly be involved with the first step, you can use this instruction:

```
          add     grand_total+6,sub_total+4
```

If this operation results in a carry, the carry flag is set to 1; if not, the carry flag is cleared to 0. Therefore, by adding the carry flag itself to the next bytes, any carry from the previous step is accounted for. This is easily done by using **adc** instead of **add**. **Adc** adds the source *and the carry flag* to the destination:

```
        adc     grand_total+5,sub_total+3
```

This pattern can now be continued to complete the addition:

```
        adc     grand_total+4,sub_total+2
        adc     grand_total+3,sub_total+1
        adc     grand_total+2,sub_total
```

You must continue the process all the way through **grand_total** to handle any leftover carries:

```
        adc     grand_total+1,0
        adc     grand_total,0
        jc      total_too_big
```

Creating an Addition Loop

You can turn the middle part of the previous routine into a loop:

```
        add     grand_total+6,sub_total+4
        mov     cx,4
        mov     di,5
        mov     si,3
add_loop:
        adc     grand_total[di],sub_total[si]
        dec     si
        dec     di
        loop    add_loop
end_loop:
        adc     grand_total+1,0
        adc     grand_total,0
        jc      total_too_big
```

If you know that CF equals 0 at the beginning of the routine, you can include the first addition operation in the loop. The **clc** instruction clears the carry flag:

```
set_up_loop:                        ; 16-bit version
        mov     si,6
```

```
            mov    di,4
            mov    cx,6
            clc                          ; clear the carry flag
add_loop:
            adc    grand_total[di],sub_total[si]
            dec    si
            dec    di
            loop   add_loop
end_loop:
            adc    grand_total+1,0
            adc    grand_total,0
            jc     total_too_big
```

Finally, if you define the two operands as the same size, you can perform the entire operation as a loop:

```
grand_total db    7 dup (?)            ; 16-bit version
Sub_total   db    7 dup (?)
            . . .
set_up_loop:
            mov    di,6
            mov    cx,7
            clc
add_loop:
            adc    grand_total[di],sub_total[di]
            dec    di
            loop   add_loop
end_loop:
            jc     total_too_big
```

This routine wouldn't work if either **dec** or **loop** affected the carry flag. Both the **adc** instruction at the beginning of the loop and the **jc** instruction following the loop depend on the carry flag from the previous execution of **adc**.

Generalized Long Addition Procedure

This routine could be turned into a generalized subroutine that will add together two memory operands of any size, where the beginning addresses of the operands and the number of bytes to be added are passed in the stack from the calling routine. The procedure places a return code in the stack indicating whether an overflow occurred.

```
ladd_proc   proc    near                ; 16-bit version
            push    bp
            push    ax
            push    cx
            push    di
            push    si
            mov     bp,sp
            add     bp,12
            mov     cx,[bp]             ; size of operands
            mov     si,[bp+2]           ; source address
            add     si,cx               ; point to last
            dec     si                  ;      byte in source
            mov     di,[bp+4]           ; destination address
            add     di,cx               ; point to last
            dec     di                  ;      byte in destination
            clc
add_loop:
            mov     al,[si]
            adc     [di],al
            dec     si
            dec     di
            loop    add_loop
end_loop:
            jc      short overflow
            mov     word ptr [bp+6],0   ; good return code
            jmp     short ladd_end
overflow:
```

```
            mov     word ptr [bp+6],1   ; bad return code
ladd_end:
            pop     si
            pop     di
            pip     cx
            pop     ax
            pop     bp
            ret     6
ladd_proc   endp
```

Creating a Long Subtraction Procedure

Subtracting two operands is nearly identical to adding them. Again,
you start with the least significant bytes. The carry flag indicates
whether or not a 1 needs to be borrowed from the neighboring byte. By
subtracting it in each operation (after making sure it is 0 for the first
operation), all borrowed digits are properly accounted for. **Sbb** automatically subtracts the value of the carry flag along with the source
value:

```
lsub_proc   proc    near               ; 16-bit version
            push    bp
            push    ax
            push    cx
            push    di
            push    si
            mov     bp,sp
            add     bp,12
            mov     cx,[bp]            ; size of operands
            mov     si,[bp+2]          ; source address
            add     si,cx              ; point to last
            dec     si                 ;      byte in source
            mov     di,[bp+4]          ; destination address
            add     di,cx              ; point to last
            dec     di                 ;   byte in destination
            clc
```

```
sub_loop:
            mov     al,[si]
            sbb     [di],al
            dec     si
            dec     di
            loop    sub_loop
end_loop:
            jc      short overflow
            mov     word ptr [bp+6],0  ; good return code
            jmp     short lsub_end
overflow:
            mov     word ptr [bp+6],1  ; bad return code
lsub_end:
            pop     si
            pop     di
            pip     cx
            pop     ax
            pop     bp
            ret     6
lsub_proc   endp
```

Multiplication

The difference between signed and unsigned values is even more important in multiplication than it is in addition and subtraction. If you need to multiply unsigned values, use **mul**; for unsigned values, use **imul**. Both instructions are shown in Figure 5-2. **Mul** uses all bits of the source operands as multipliers and sets unused leading digits of the result to zero. **Imul** uses the high-order bits of the source operands as sign bits only and stores negative results in correct two's complement notation. That is, if the product is +6d and the result field is one word, the result is stored as 00000000 00000110b; if the product is –6d and the result field is one word, the result is stored as 11111111 11111010b. (Notice that, in both cases, since the result value fits completely in the low-order byte, the high-order byte is simply an extension of the low-order byte's sign bit. This is called *propagating* the sign bit throughout the high-order byte.)

mul   Unsigned multiplication

div   Unsigned division

imul   Signed multiplication

idiv   Signed division

Figure 5-2   Multiplication and Division Instructions

Mul is a simple instruction with little variation in format, whereas **imul** is very flexible, allowing 1, 2, or 3 operands and a wide choice of result fields. You can also multiply by immediate values with **imul**, but not with **mul**.

Unsigned Multiplication

With **mul**, you specify only one operand. The other multiplier is assumed to be the accumulator, and the result field is assumed to be an extension of the accumulator, twice as large as the multipliers. If you specify a byte operand, the other multiplier is assumed to be in AL, and the result is placed in AX. If you specify a word operand, the other multiplier is assumed to be in AX, and the result is placed in DX:AX. For the '386, you might think that EAX would be a more logical choice, but since the '286 and earlier chips use DX:AX, that system was retained in the interest of upward compatibility. If the source operand is a doubleword ('386 only), the other operand is assumed to be in EAX, and the result is placed in EDX:EAX. In all cases, the carry flag and the overflow flag, whose functions are identical for this instruction, indicate whether or not the extension of the accumulator contains any significant digits. For example, if you multiply two words, OF and CF are set if DX contains any significant digits, and cleared if DX contains only zeros. There is no possibility of the product overflowing the extended accumulator, so you don't need to test for that. All the other flags are undefined after **mul**.

Suppose you need to multiply **length** by **width**, storing the result in **area**. If **length** and **width** are bytes and **area** is a word, you could use this code:

```
length     db     ?                  ; 16-bit version
width      db     ?
area       dw     ?
           ...
```

```
        mov     al,length

        mul     width

        mov     area,ax
```

You must move one of the multipliers into AL before you can use **mul**. The other multiplier can remain in memory, since **mul** can reference memory directly. There is no problem with storing the result since **area** is big enough to hold the entire result field. However, suppose **area** is only a byte. Then the routine might look like this:

```
length      db      ?                    ; 16-bit version

width       db      ?

area        db      ?

            . . .

        mov     al,length

        mul     width

        jo      product_too_big

        mov     area,al
```

The **jo** instruction identifies those cases where the product of the multiplication won't fit into a byte. If you fall through the **jo** instruction, the product is completely contained in AL and will fit into a byte-sized field.

When you multiply words or doublewords, you run into additional storage problems because your result is contained in two registers. If you want to store only the accumulator portion of the result, there's no problem:

```
length      dw      ?                    ; 16-bit version

width       dw      ?

area        dw      ?

            . . .

        mov     ax,length

        mul     width

        jo      product_too_big

        mov     area,ax
```

In this example, the **jo** instruction identifies cases where the product overflowed into DX. In other cases, it's safe to store only AX in **area**. The same principle holds true for doublewords, as in this example:

```
length      dd      ?                       ; 32-bit version
width       dd      ?
area        dd      ?

            ...

            mov     eax,length
            mul     width
            jo      product_too_big
            mov     area,eax
```

The product in EAX can be safely moved to **area** if there are no significant digits in EDX. But what if you want to store the extended result? You can't use AX:DX or EAX:EDX as an operand of a **mov** instruction. The solution is to move each register separately into one-half of the result field. The **ptr** operator, which is explained in detail in Chapter 8, overrides the defined size of a field for one instruction. After the instruction, the field goes back to its defined size. Here's how it works:

```
length      dd      ?                       ; 32-bit version
width       dd      ?
area        dq      ?

            ...

            mov     eax,length
            mul     width
            mov     dword ptr area,eax
            mov     dword ptr area+4,edx
```

Figure 5-3 shows how the final two **mov** instructions function. The first one says to consider the destination to be a doubleword starting at **area**. The second one says to consider the destination to be a doubleword starting at **area+4**. Notice that these instructions are careful to reverse the bytes of the result. Each **mov** instruction automatically reverses the four bytes of the doubleword contained within the move, but it's up to the programmer to reverse the two doublewords, moving the low-order bytes in EAX into the leftmost bytes of the result field and the high-order bytes in EDX into the rightmost bytes of the result field.

This same technique can be used when multiplying two words and storing the result in a doubleword:

```
length      dw      ?                       ; 16-bit version
```

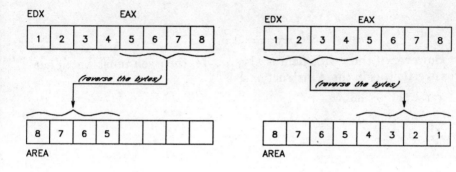

Figure 5-3   Storing a Quadword

```
width       dw      ?
area        dd      ?
            . . .
            mov     ax,length
            mul     width
            mov     word ptr area,ax
            mov     word ptr area+2,dx
```

While there are other solutions to this storage problem, this one is clearcut and efficient.

Signed Multiplication

The most basic form of **imul** looks similar to **mul**: only one operand is coded and the other multiplier is assumed to be in AL, AX, or EAX. The result is placed in AX, DX:AX, or EDX:EAX. Suppose you want to multiply **x_factor** by **y_factor**, placing the result in **xy_product**. If the operands are bytes and the result is a word, you could use these instructions:

```
x_factor    db      ?                       ; 16-bit version
```

```
y_factor    db      ?
xy_product  dw      ?

            . . .

            mov     al,x_factor
            imul    y_factor
            mov     xy_product,ax
```

However, if the result field is also a byte, then you must watch out for overflow as in these instructions:

```
x_factor    db      ?
y_factor    db      ?
Xy_product  db      ?

            . . .

            mov     al,x_factor
            imul    y_factor
            jo      product_too_big
            mov     xy_product,al
```

Similar techniques can be used if all three products are words or doublewords. The routine below handles words:

```
x_factor    dw      ?                       ; 16-bit version
y_factor    dw      ?
xy_product  dw      ?

            . . .

            mov     ax,x_factor
            imul    y_factor
            jo      product_too_big
            mov     xy_product,ax
```

The following routine handles doublewords:

```
x_factor    dd      ?                       ; 32-bit version
y_factor    dd      ?
xy_product  dd      ?

            . . .

            mov     eax,x_factor
            imul    y_factor
```

```
        jo      product_too_big
        mov     xy_product,eax
```

If you need to store a double-register product, you can use the same technique illustrated in Figure 5-3.

With **imul**, the other operand need not be the accumulator. If you specify two operands, the first operand identifies the result field as well as one of the multipliers. You can select any 16- or 32-bit register as the result field (only registers can be used here). The second operand can be a register, memory field, or immediate value of the same size as the result field, or an 8-bit immediate value. Notice that this means you can multiply a 32-bit register by an 8-bit immediate value but not a 16-bit immediate value. Given these definitions:

```
mword       dw      ?
mdouble     dd      ?
```

These instructions are all valid:

```
        imul    cx,mword        ; word by word
        imul    cx,500d         ; word by word
        imul    cx,dx           ; word by word
        imul    cx,5            ; word by imm byte
        imul    ecx,mdouble     ; dword by dword
        imul    ecx,50000d      ; dword by dword
        imul    ecx,edx         ; dword by dword
        imul    ecx,5           ; dword by imm byte
```

These instructions are all invalid:

```
        imul    cl,5            ; must be word or dword
        imul    mword,cx        ; dest must be register
        imul    cx,dl           ; word by byte
        imul    cx,mdouble      ; word by dword
        imul    ecx,500d        ; dword by word
        imul    ecx,mword       ; dword by word
        imul    ecx,dx          ; dword by word
```

When you specify the destination, it is not extended and the possibility of overflow exists. The carry flag and the overflow flag, continuing to have identical functions, are set if the product does not completely fit in the destination field. If the product fits, CF and OF are cleared.

Suppose you need to multiply the value in CX by **accum_rate**, storing the result in **cutoff**. You could use the following routine:

```
accum_rate  dw      ?                      ; 16-bit version
cutoff      dw      ?

            . . .

            imul    cx,accum_rate
            jo      product_too_big
            mov     cutoff,cx
```

After the multiplication, the product appears in CX and the overflow flag indicates whether any significant digits have been lost. The **jo** instruction handles any overflow, and the **mov** instruction stores the product that didn't overflow.

In some cases, you can specify a destination that is not one of the multiplication factors. If you multiply an immediate value by a register or memory location, you can specify another register as the destination. This is one of the few cases where you code three operands in an assembler instruction. The first operand represents the destination register, the second is the source register, and the third is source immediate value. All three operands must be the same size, except that the immediate value can be a byte. All the following are valid instructions:

```
imul    dx,cx,5                 ; dx = cx times 5
imul    dx,cx,500d              ; dx = cx times 500d
imul    dx,mword,10             ; dx = mword times 10
imul    edx,eax,5               ; edx = eax times 5
imul    edx,mdouble,50000d      ; edx = mdouble
                                ;times 50,000
```

The following instructions are invalid for the reasons indicated:

```
imul    mword,cx,5              ; dest must be register
imul    ecx,mword,5             ; mismatched sizes
imul    ecx,mdouble,500d ;      immediate must be same
                                ; size or byte
```

When you specify three operands, you must take care that the result doesn't overflow the destination. Once again, CF and OF are set if the result doesn't fit and cleared if it does.

Division

Div does unsigned division, while **idiv** does signed division. The only operand specifies the divisor, the dividend is assumed to be in the extended accumulator, the quotient is placed in the lower half of the extended accumulator, and the remainder is placed in the upper half of the extended accumulator. Thus, if the source operand (the divisor) is a byte, the dividend must be in AX, the quotient appears in AL, and the remainder appears in AH. If the source operand is a word, the dividend must be in DX:AX, the quotient appears in AX, and the remainder appears in DX. If the source operand is a doubleword, the dividend must be in EDX:EAX, the quotient appears in EAX, and the remainder appears in EDX. Notice that the two result fields, the quotient and the remainder, are the same size as the original divisor, while the dividend is always twice that size.

Both **div** and **idiv** do integer division, so no fractional digits are generated for the quotient. If you divide 4 by 8, the quotient will be 0 and the remainder will be 4. Real division is done with the coprocessor instructions; or you could devise your own means of accomplishing real division with these integer instructions.

Both **div** and **idiv** leave all flags undefined. An interrupt occurs if the quotient overflows the result field or if division by zero is attempted. To avoid overflow, make sure the dividend value fits in the quotient field; that way, even if the divisor is 1, the result won't overflow. Avoid dividing by zero by checking the divisor before executing the divide instruction.

Unsigned Division

Suppose you want to divide the unsigned value in CX by 7 and round off the result:

```
days_in_week  dw   7                    ; 16-bit version
        . . .
        mov    ax,cx
        sub    dx,dx              ; clears dx
        div    days_in_week
        cmp    dx,4
```

```
        jb      dont_round
        inc     ax                    ; round up quotient
dont_round:
        mov     cx,ax
```

Since the dividend value is word-sized, we chose to use a doubleword dividend field and a word divisor so there's no possibility of quotient overflow. You can't divide by an immediate value so the constant 7 must be placed either in memory or a register. The first instruction in our example defines a word with the constant value of 7; this will be the divisor. The next two instructions (**mov** and **sub**) prepare the dividend. (Since we're doing unsigned division, we don't have to worry about propagating the sign bit in DX.) After the division, we need to determine whether or not to round up the quotient. The general rule is: if the remainder is more than half the divisor, round up; otherwise, don't. Our divisor is 7, so our routine rounds up if the remainder is 4 or greater. If the remainder is less than 4, we skip the rounding step. The last step stores the result back in CX.

Signed Division

If you're not worried about rounding, signed division is fairly straight-forward. To divide the signed value in CX by 7, you could code:

```
days_in_week  dw   7                  ; 16-bit version
        ...
        mov     ax,cx
        cwd                           ; sign -> dx
        idiv    days_in_week
        mov     cx,ax
```

Once the dividend value has been moved into AX, the **cwd** instruction propagates the sign throughout DX; the **cwd** instruction was designed expressly for the purpose of preparing a doubleword dividend for **idiv**. (Likewise, **cbw** and **cdq** perfectly position the dividend for byte and doubleword signed division, respectively.) After the division, the integer quotient can be moved from AX back to CX.

Rounding becomes a problem with signed division because both the quotient and the remainder have signs. The remainder always takes the sign of the dividend, while the quotient's sign is determined by the signs of both operands. Negative quotients should be rounded down, not up, if the absolute value of the remainder is more than half the divisor.

```
days_in_week  dw   7                    ; 16-bit version
              ...
              mov   ax,cx
              cwd
              idiv  days_in_week
              cmp   dx,0                 ; obtain absolute
              jge   round_quotient  ;     value of
              neg   dx               ;          remainder
round_quotient:
              cmp   dx,4
              jl    store_quotient
              cmp   ax,0
              jl    neg_quotient
              inc   ax
              jmp   store_quotient
neg_quotient:
              dec   ax
store_quotient:
              mov   cx,ax
```

The first thing we do after the division is get the absolute value of the remainder. If the remainder is positive, it can be used as is. If it's negative, the **neg** instruction converts it to positive. The first two instructions after **round_quotient** determine whether or not the quotient needs to be adjusted. If so, the sign of the quotient is determined, and it is incremented or decremented accordingly.

The examples so far have used a known value for the divisor. If the divisor is a variable, then you must be sure to test for a zero divisor before dividing:

```
days          dw    ?                    ; 16-bit version
hours         dw    ?
hours_per_day dw                   ?
              ...
              cmp   days,0
```

```
            je      zero_days
            mov     ax,hours
            cwd
            idiv    days
            ...
```

The **zero_days** routine could set **hours/day** to zero and let it go at that. When the divisor is unknown, rounding becomes a little bit more difficult, too. You have to figure out what half the divisor is to find the rounding point. When a remainder is above that figure, round the quotient; otherwise, don't. The following routine divides **hours** by **days** where both values are variables:

```
two         dw      2
            ...
            idiv    days                ; 16-bit version
            mov     hours_per_day,ax
            mov     bx,dx               ; temp store remainder
            cmp     bx,0                ; get absolute
            jge     halve_divisor       ;     value of
            neg     bx                  ;           remainder
halve_divisor:
            move    ax,days
            cwd
            idiv    two
            cmp     ax,0                ; get absolute
            jge     comp_remainder      ;   value of
            neg     ax                  ;         result
comp_remainder:
            cmp     ax,bx
            jge     ending
            cmp     hours_per_day,0
            jge     round_up
            sub     hours_per_day,1
            jo      result_overflow
            jmp     ending
```

```
round_up:
            add     hours_per_day,1
            jo      result_overflow
ending:
            . . .
```

Immediately following the first division, you store the result and the remainder, converting the remainder to a positive value if necessary. Then you divide the divisor by 2 and get the absolute value of the result, which remains in AX. You can ignore the remainder of this operation, since you want this number to be either half or slightly less than half the original divisor. At **comp_remainder**, you compare the halved divisor with the original remainder, now preserved in BX. If it's equal to or greater than the original remainder, no rounding is needed. If it is less than the original remainder, then the value needs to be rounded up if it's positive, down if it's negative. (The decision to not round when the remainder is exactly half the divisor is arbitrary; you could choose to round in this case.)

Decimal Arithmetic

The arithmetic instructions do binary arithmetic. If you do binary arithmetic on values stored in decimal format, the results will be invalid. For example, if you add BCD 5 to BCD 7, the result is 0Ch, not a legitimate BCD value. Rather than create completely different sets of instructions for BCD and packed BCD arithmetic, Intel gives you instructions to adjust decimal values after binary arithmetic. One set of adjustments, called the decimal adjustments, converts a binary result into packed BCD format after addition or subtraction. The other set, called the ASCII adjustments, converts a binary value to unpacked BCD format after addition, subtraction, or multiplication, and converts a packed BCD value to a pure binary value in preparation for division. Figure 5-4 shows the adjustment instructions.

Packed BCD Adjustments

Daa and **das** adjust packed decimal values after addition and subtraction. Adjustments are necessary if either nibble is greater than 9 or if carrying or borrowing occurred between nibbles. Figure 5-5 illustrates how these two adjustment operations work. The low-order nibble is examined first. If the auxiliary flag indicates a carry to or borrow from the high-order nibble, or if the value in the nibble is greater than 9, then it is adjusted by 6. The high-order nibble is examined next. If the

daa	Decimal adjustment after addition
das	Decimal adjustment after subtraction
aaa	ASCII adjustment after addition
aas	ASCII adjustment after subtraction
aam	ASCII adjustment after multiplication
aad	ASCII adjustment before division

Figure 5-4   Adjustment Instructions

carry flag indicates a carry to or borrow from outside the byte, or if the value is greater than 9, then it is adjusted by 6. At the end of the adjustment operation, the byte contains the correct packed BCD value and the carry flag indicates whether a 1 should be carried to or borrowed from the next byte. (The AF can be ignored after the adjustment.)

Both **daa** and **das** assume the byte to be adjusted is in AL. A complete routine to subtract two three-byte values might look like this:

```
daa logic
    If low order nibble of AL is above 9 or AF is set add 6 to AL
    If high order nibble of AL is above 9 or CF is set add 60h to AL

examples
    before      after       before      after
    AL=C2h      AL=28       AL=2Dh      AL=33
    CF=0        CF=1        CF=0        CF=0
    AF=1        AF=1        AF=0        AF=1


das logic
    If low order nibble of AL is above 9 or AF is set subtract 6
    from AL
    If high order nibble of AL is above 9 or CF is set subtract 60h
    from AL

examples
    before      after       before      after
    AL=F2h      AL=92       AL=2Eh      AL=28
    CF=1        CF=1        CF=0        CF=0
    AF=0        AF=0        AF=1        AF=1
```

Figure 5-5   Logic of Decimal Adjustments

```
total_due    db      3 dup (?)              ; 16-bit version
paid         db      3 dup (?)

     ...

             mov     di,2
             mov     cx,3
             clc
sub_loop:
             mov     al,total_due[di]
             sbb     al,paid[di]
             das
             mov     total_sale[di],al
             dec     di
             loop    sub_loop
             jc      overpaid
             jz      paid_off
```

You can't do the subtraction in memory because **das** operates only on
AL. So you must place each byte of the destination operand in AL,
subtract the corresponding source byte from it, adjust the result, then
store it back in memory. Notice that you can test the zero flag after the
adjustment because DAA and DAS affect ZF, PF, and SF as well as CF
and AF. An addition loop would look practically identical to this.

ASCII Adjustments

The ASCII adjustments, which operate on unpacked BCD values, are
simpler than the packed decimal adjustments because they need to
work with only one nibble per byte. Figure 5-6 illustrates how the
addition and subtraction adjustments work. The value is adjusted by 6
if AF is set or the result is greater than 9. Then the upper nibble is
cleared and the carry flag is set. If no adjustment is necessary, none of
these operations takes place.

Like **daa** and **das**, **aaa** and **aas** assume the result to be adjusted is
in AL. A routine to add or subtract a series of unpacked bytes must
move each byte to AL for processing:

```
total        db      5 dup (?)
item         db      5 dup (?)

      ...
```

aaa logic
    If low order nibble of AL is greater than 9 or AF is set
        add 6 to AL
        add 1 to AH
        zero high order nibble of AL
        set CF

examples

before	*after*	*before*	*after*
AX=0511	AX=0607	AX=000D	AX=0103
CF=0	CF=1	CF=0	CF=1
AF=1	AF=1	AF=0	AF=0

aas logic
    If low order nibble of AL is above 9 or AF is set
        subtract 6 from AL
        subtract 1 from AH
        zero high order nibble of AL
        set carry flag

example

before	*after*
AX=02FD	AX=0108
CF=1	CF=1
AF=1	AF=1

Figure 5-6   Logic of ASCII Adjustments after Addition and Subtraction

```
              mov    di,4
              mov    cx,5
              clc
add_loop:
              mov    al,total[di]
              adc    al,item[di]
              aaa
              mov    total[di],al
              dec    di
              loop   add_loop
              jc     total_too_big
```

ASCII Adjustments with Multiplication and Division

The ASCII multiplication and division adjustment instructions pertain to unsigned multiplication and division (**mul** and **div**) only. A multi-

aam logic
    Divide AL by 10d

example

    before   *after*
    AX=0025h   AX=0307

Figure 5-7   Logic of ASCII Adjustment after Multiplication

plication product is adjusted after the fact, just as addition and subtraction are. Since **mul** extends the accumulator when it stores the
result, **aam** works on AX, placing the adjusted result in AH and AL.
With division, you adjust the dividend in AH and AL *before* division,
not afterwards. The resulting binary dividend resides in AX, correctly
located for the **div** instruction.

The multiplication adjustment is completely different from addition
and subtraction adjustments. Figure 5-7 illustrates how it works. The
value in AX is divided by 10d. The quotient is placed in AH, the
remainder in AL. These two digits are the correct BCD equivalents of
the original binary value in AX as long as it did not exceed 99, which it
shouldn't if it was the product of two unpacked BCD digits.

The division adjustment is the opposite of the multiplication adjustment; it converts a two-byte BCD value to a binary value by multiplying the byte in AH by 10d and adding the byte in AL to the result. The
result fills AX, although the value itself easily fits in AL; AH ends up
containing zeros.

A routine to multiply two BCD bytes and store the answer is fairly
simple:

```
bcd_days     db      ?                      ; unpacked

bcd_hours    db      ?                      ; unpacked

bcd_time     db      2 dup (?)              ; unpacked

             . . .

             mov     al,bcd_days            ; 16-bit versions

             mul     bcd_hours

             aam

             mov     bcd_time,ah

             mov     bcd_time+1,al

             jz      no_time
```

A routine to divide two BCD bytes turns out to be a little more complicated, even without rounding:

```
bcd_days    db    ?                 ; unpacked
bcd_time    db    2 dup (?)         ; unpacked
bcd_rate    db    2 dup (?)         ; unpacked
            ...
            mov   ah,bcd_time
            mov   al,bcd_time+1
            aad
            div   bcd_days
            sub   ah,ah             ; drop remainder
            aam
            mov   bcd_rate,ah
            mov   bcd_rate+1,al
```

The two digits making up **bcd_time** are loaded into AH:AL and converted into one binary value, which is divided by the single-byte **bcd_days**. Since you're not rounding, you can ignore the remainder in AH and deal only with the quotient in AL. However, this is still a binary value and needs to be converted back to BCD. And that brings up an interesting point. Unlike the addition and subtraction adjustments, which depend on the value of AF and CF after the arithmetic, **aam** can be used at any time to convert an unsigned binary value less than 100d in AL to an unpacked BCD value in AH:AL. It doesn't need to follow a **mul** instruction. Likewise, **aad** can be used at any time to convert two unpacked, unsigned BCD bytes in AH:AL to one binary value in AL. Thus, after the **div** instruction, you can clear the remainder out of AH, then use **aam** to convert the quotient in AL to unpacked BCD format in AH:AL.

More Complex Decimal Arithmetic Procedures

The multiplication and division routines we have shown you in this chapter have dealt with single-byte operands. You can build routines for multibyte values based on the operations here. For packed decimal values, where no multiplication or division adjustments are available, you can build a multiplication routine by adding the multiplicand to itself multiplier times, and you can build a division routine by counting the number of times the divisor can be subtracted from the dividend.

You can handle decimal points in decimal arithmetic. All you need to do is store the location of each decimal point in a separate byte. Be sure to align the operands at their decimal points before adding or subtracting. Multiplication and division operands don't need to be aligned, but you need to calculate the position of the decimal point in the answer.

You can also handle signs in decimal arithmetic. As with decimal points, store each sign in a separate byte, using whatever code you want to indicate positive and negative. With addition and subtraction, the signs tell you whether to add or subtract the operands. With multiplication and division, you can examine the operand signs to determine the sign of the result.

Math with the Coprocessor

In this chapter, you will learn how to use the coprocessor for faster and more complex numeric processing than is possible in the CPU. The coprocessor handles larger fields (80 bits) and real numbers. Its instruction set includes many operations above and beyond the basic arithmetic operations.

This chapter describes the advanced functions but doesn't try to explain how to apply them. It assumes that you will recognize the functions that fulfill your application needs. If a function has no meaning to you, you probably don't need it in your work.

The numeric coprocessor is a separate chip with its own architecture. It has a different register structure, different data types, and a different instruction set. This chapter begins with an explanation of the coprocessor architecture. The bulk of the chapter is devoted to the instruction set.

The numeric coprocessor and its functions have been designed in accordance with the IEEE Standard 754 for Binary Floating-Point Arithmetic. This standard has been under development over the years but has now been finalized. The '287 was designed to meet a draft version of the standard, while the '387 meets the final standard. Because of this, the '387 is not completely upwardly compatible from the '287 (which in turn is not completely upwardly compatible from the earlier numeric coprocessors). You will see references throughout the chapter to minor differences between the '287 and the '387. The chapter winds up by summarizing the differences and telling you where you can find detailed information.

You can safely include the numeric coprocessor instructions in your programs without knowing whether or not the coprocessor will be present at run time. The CPU includes a set of routines that emulate the coprocessor functions when the coprocessor is not present, but much, much more slowly.

Data Types

You've already seen that the CPU can handle bytes and words and the '386 can also handle doublewords. The numeric coprocessors don't deal with bytes, but in addition to words and doublewords, they handle quadwords and tenbytes. Figure 6-1 shows the formats available for each data type, which are explained in this section.

Binary Integers

The format of binary integers in the numeric coprocessor is the same as the CPU's signed binary integers. The leftmost bit is the sign bit, and the remaining bits represent the value. Two's complement notation is used for negative numbers. Words, doublewords, and quadwords can store values in binary integer foi ̄.ut, called word integers, short integers, and long integers, respectively. Neither the CPU nor the coprocessor can handle tenbyte integers.

Real Numbers

Real numbers are stored as a sign bit, exponent, and significand. (The exponent and significand are often called the characteristic and mantissa.) Figure 6-2 shows the characteristics of the subfields for each of the real formats. Unlike binary integers, negative real numbers are

	integer	real	packed BCD
word	word integer	NA	NA
doubleword	short integer	single precision	NA
quadword	long integer	double precision	NA
tenbyte	NA	extended precision	packed BCD

Figure 6-1   Coprocessor Data Types

	single precision	double precision	extended precision
exponent:			
size	8 bits	11 bits	15 bits
bias	127	1023	16383
range	-127 to +128	-1022 to +1023	-16382 to +16383
significand:			
bits	23 bits*	52 bits*	64 bits**
decimal	6-7 digits	15-16 digits	19 digits
value range:			
low	$.18 \times 10^{-38}$	2.23×10^{-308}	3.30×10^{-4932}
high	3.40×10^{38}	1.80×10^{308}	1.21×10^{4932}

* Leading 1 of normalized value not stored
** Leading 1 of normalized value stored

Figure 6-2   Characteristics of Real Data Types

not stored in two's complement notation; only the sign bit indicates the negativity of the number.

The exponent indicates the position of the binary point in the significand. The exponent is *biased*; that is, a fixed number has been added to it so that all exponents are positive. For example, an exponent of –03 in a double-precision real number is stored as 1020.

The significand represents the significant digits of the value. The significand is normalized. That is, it is shifted to the left so that it always takes the form 1.nnn...nnnb, with the exponent adjusted to indicate the true position of the binary point. This eliminates the need to store leading zeros and allows the maximum possible precision in the significand. In single and double precision formats, the leading 1 is assumed; the only part of the significand stored are the digits following the binary point. This frees up another bit for significant digit storage. In extended precision format, the only format used for 80-bit real values, the leading 1 is stored.

Packed BCD

The coprocessor can handle packed BCD values only in tenbytes. The sign bit is in the leftmost bit, making the remainder of the high-order byte unusable. (The system ignores bits 72 through 78.) The other nine bytes contain two decimal digits each, for a total of 18 decimal digits.

Special Numeric Formats

In some situations, the coprocessor is unable to generate a result in one of the formats described above. Then it stores the result in one of the special formats. The special data types result from exceptions that are handled by the coprocessor. If you are not writing exception handlers for the coprocessor, you need never handle them. But you might see them when debugging so you should be aware of their existence.

Denormal Number. Some extremely small numbers, called *tiny* numbers, have so many leading zeros that they cannot be completely normalized because the resulting exponent would underflow its subfield. (That is, it would be less than the minimum possible value.) Such numbers are stored in denormal format, with a zero exponent and the necessary number of leading zeros in the significand to match that exponent.

Infinity. Certain operations can result in infinity. Infinity is stored with all ones in the exponent and all zeros in the significand.

NaN (Not-a-Number). A NaN is simply a collection of bits that does not represent any other number, not even a denormal or infinity. NaNs result from certain operations and can also be created by the programmer. If a NaN is used as the operand of an operation, the result is a NaN.

Unsupported Data Types. Several data types in the extended real format are available for the '287 but not the '387 because of changes in the finalized version of the IEEE standard. These are pseudozeros, pseudo-NaNs, pseudoindefinites, pseudonormals, and unnormal numbers.

Registers

Figure 6-3 shows the '287/'387 registers.

The Register Stack

The processing is done in the register stack, a set of eight 80-bit (tenbyte) registers that are accessed like a memory stack, using the

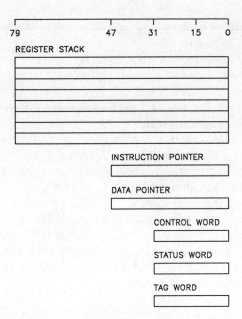

79   47   31   15   0

REGISTER STACK

INSTRUCTION POINTER

DATA POINTER

CONTROL WORD

STATUS WORD

TAG WORD

Figure 6-3 Numeric Coprocessor Registers

register name ST for the current top of the stack, ST(1) for the first register below the current top, ST(2) for the next register down, and so forth through ST(7). All data is processed in extended-precision real format, the only format that can exist in the register stack (except for the special formats). Numbers are converted into extended real format, if necessary, when they are loaded onto the stack.

We can't label ST through ST(7) in Figure 6-3 because their positions change each time you push an item onto the stack or pop it off. The register name ST always refers to the current top of stack, whether that's the first or the eighth register. ST(1) through ST(7) are always relative to ST.

The Control Word Register

The control word register contains a collection of flags that control the behavior of the coprocessor. These flags are set by the operating system. You can change them for an application, but in most cases you probably shouldn't.

An infinity control bit selects between affine and projective closures for the '287; the '387 recognizes only affine closures. Projective closure means there is only one infinity, which has no sign. Affine closure means there are a positive and a negative infinity.

A rounding control field selects from four types of rounding:
round to nearest
always round up (toward + infinity)
always round down (toward − infinity)
chop (round toward zero)

Precision control bits can be used to select less than the full 64 bits of precision in the register stack.

Six exception masking bits can be used to mask out any of the six types of exceptions the coprocessor recognizes: precision, overflow, zero divide, denormalized operand, and invalid operation. When an exception is unmasked, it is signalled back to the CPU on an error line, and the CPU triggers the appropriate interrupt procedures. When an exception is masked, the coprocessor handles it locally, usually by generating one of the special values described earlier. For example, the coprocessor response to a masked zero divide exception is to return a result of infinity. The coprocessor masked exception responses should suffice in most applications.

The Status Word

The coprocessor status word register, which is detailed in Figure 6-4, indicates the current status of the system.

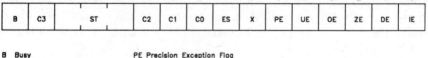

15	14	13	12	11	10	9	8	7	6	5	4	3	2	1	0
B	C3	ST			C2	C1	C0	ES	X	PE	UE	OE	ZE	DE	IE

B Busy

ST Stack Top Pointer

C3 − C0 Condition Code

ES Error Summary

X Reserved

PE Precision Exception Flag

UE Underflow Exception Flag

OE Overflow Exception Flag

ZE Zero Divide Exception Flag

DE Denormalized Operand Exception Flag

IE Invalid Operation Exception Flag

Figure 6-4   The Status Word Register

Exception Flags and Error Summary. The exception flags are automatically set when masked or unmasked exceptions are detected. Unlike the status flags of the CPU, these are *sticky* bits, meaning that once set, they remain set until a specific instruction clears them again. The error summary bit is set if any unmasked exception is encountered.

Condition Code. The condition code bits are set to reflect the outcome of numeric operations. The meaning of the bits depends on the operation performed. For example, after a comparison operation, C0 and C3 indicate the result of the comparison (greater than, less than, or equal) but after an arithmetic operation, these same bits are undefined.

Top of Stack. Bits 11-13 of the status word contain a 3-bit number indicating which physical register is the current top of stack, from 0 (000b) to 7 (111b). The stack is built upside down in the set of registers, so the stack pointer starts at 0 when the stack is empty, is decremented each time a value is pushed onto the stack, and is incremented each time a value is popped from the stack.

Busy Bit. The 8087 tested the busy bit to find out whether or not the coprocessor was busy. The '287 and '387 use a busy signal instead, so this bit isn't used.

The Tag Word

The tag word indicates the condition of each register in the stack, indicating whether it is valid, zero, special, or empty.

The Instruction and Data Pointers

The instruction and data pointers are actually in the CPU, but they are considered to be functionally part of the coprocessor because they are accessible by some of the coprocessor instruction set. Whenever the system executes a coprocessor instruction, it saves the address of the instruction, the memory address of the operand (if any), and the instruction opcode in these registers. Exception handlers might need to access these values; ordinary applications won't.

Defining Fields for Coprocessor Data

To create memory fields for the coprocessor, you need some different directives and operands. The **dq** directive defines a quadword; **dt** defines a tenbyte. To assign a real value to a doubleword, quadword, or tenbyte, express it in decimal with a decimal point and perhaps an exponent (expressed as E±*n*). All of the following instructions create real values:

```
reald      dd    -1.5            ; Real doubleword

realq      dq    5.25E-3         ; Real quadword

realt      dt    0.2357431E200   ; Real tenbyte
```

To define a packed BCD tenbyte, simply express a decimal integer value as the operand of the **dt** directive. The assembler assumes packed decimal format for a tenbyte when a decimal integer is provided, as in these examples:

```
long_int   dt    1234567890      ; Packed BCD tenbyte

constant   dt    7               ; Packed BCD tenbyte
```

The Instruction Set

The full coprocessor instruction set is listed in Appendix C, divided into six groups: data transfer, nontranscendental, comparisons, transcendental, constant, and processor control. All coprocessor instruction opcodes begin with the letter F to distinguish them from CPU instructions. In the following discussion, the "stack" refers to the coprocessor register stack, not the stack segment in memory.

Data Transfer Instructions

Figure 6-5 summarizes the data transfer instructions. The load instructions (**fld**, **fild**, and **fbld**) push a value onto the top of the stack. First the stack pointer (in the status register) is decremented, then the contents of the source is copied to the new top register. Unlike data transfer instructions in the CPU, the operands may be different sizes, and in fact frequently are. Values are converted into extended real format, the only format used for stack storage and processing.

The source may be a memory field or another stack register. Suppose these values are defined in the data segment:

```
pop_change  dd    1.E0

growth_rate dq    5

population  dt    350000
```

fld	Load real
fst	Store real
fstp	Store real and pop
fxch	Exchange registers
fild	Integer load
fist	Integer store
fistp	Integer store and pop
fbld	Packed decimal load
fbstp	Packed decimal store and pop

Figure 6-5   The Data Transfer Instructions

To load the three values into the stack, you could code these instructions:

```
fld     pop_change
fild    growth_rate
fbld    population
```

Be careful to select the correct opcode to load the value; the coprocessor converts the source value to the extended real value based on the opcode you use, not on the value that was originally defined for the field or that was moved into the field. If you use the wrong opcode, the number will be converted incorrectly and the result will be invalid.

To copy a value from another stack register to the top of the stack, use **fld** with the ST(n) operand, where n indicates the source register's position relative to the top of the stack *before* the instruction is executed. For example, to copy the value that is currently next to the top of the stack, you would code:

```
fld     st(1)
```

Fbld does not check the source value for valid decimal digits before converting and loading it. If the source contains invalid digits, the result is undefined. A value of negative zero is possible with packed BCD format, and it will be converted to negative zero in extended real format.

The store instructions (**fst** and **fist**) store a value from the top of the stack into memory or another stack register, converting the value from the extended real format to the specified storage format. If the value is a normal, nonzero value, rounding is executed according to the rounding control bits, and overflow and underflow are checked for and handled. Zero values and special values (infinity, NaNs, and so on) are always chopped so that they do not lose their special properties via rounding. If the value is negative zero, **fst** will convert it to negative zero in the word or short real format, but **fist** converts it to positive zero.

There are several differences between the simple store instructions (**fst** and **fist**) and the store and pop instructions (**fstp, fistp,** and **fbstp**). The standard store instructions do not change the stack; the same register continues to be the top of the stack. The store and pop instructions pop the top value from the stack after storing the result.

There are also some differences in the data types that can be stored by the various instructions. The integer store instruction, **fist**, cannot store a value to a long (quadword) integer field. The integer store and pop instruction, **fistp**, can.

Fstp can store to a real tenbyte; **fst** cannot. There is no simple store instruction for BCD conversion, but the **fbstp** instruction stores and pops a BCD value.

Suppose you want to store the top three stack items into each of the three fields defined earlier. To pop each value from the top of the stack, you would use these instructions:

```
fstp    pop_change

fistp   growth_rate

fbldp   population
```

If you don't want to pop the top of the stack, you could only store to **pop_change**. You cannot copy without popping into **growth_rate** because it is an integer quadword, and you cannot copy without popping into **population** because it is a tenbyte in BCD format. To copy the top of the stack into **pop_change** without affecting the top of the stack, you could code this instruction:

```
fst     pop_change
```

You can also copy the top of the stack to another register on the stack, with or without popping it. You must use the real form to do the copying, as in these two examples:

```
fst     st(3)

fstp    st(2)
```

The first instruction copies the top of the stack to the third register down from the top without changing the top. The second instruction

copies the top of the stack to the second register down from the top,
then increments the stack pointer and tags the former top as empty. To
remove the top value on the stack, pop it to nowhere with this instruction:

```
fstp    st
```

This copies the top of the stack to itself, then adjusts the stack
pointer and tags the former top empty.

The Nontranscendental Operations

The nontranscendental operations include the four basic arithmetic
operations (addition, subtraction, multiplication, and division) as well
as a collection of other standard arithmetic functions such as square
root, partial remainder, and absolute value. Figure 6-6 lists the nontranscendental instructions.

fadd	Add real
fsub	Subtract real
fmul	Multiply real
fdiv	Divide real
faddp	Add real and pop
fsubp	Subtract real and pop
fmulp	Multiply real and pop
fdivp	Divide real and pop
fsubr	Subtract real reversed
fsubrp	Subtract real reversed and pop
fdivr	Divide real reversed
fdivrp	Divide real reversed and pop
fiadd	Add integer
fisub	Subtract integer
fisubr	Subtract integer reversed

Figure 6-6   The Nontranscendental Instructions (part 1 of 2)

fimul	Multiply integer
fidiv	Divide integer
fidivr	Divide integer reversed
fsqrt	Square root
fscale	Scale
fprem	Partial remainder
fprem1	IEEE standard partial remainder ('387 only)
frndint	Round to integer
fxtract	Extract exponent and significand
fabs	Absolute value
fchs	Change sign

Figure 6-6   The Nontranscendental Instructions (part 2 of 2)

Arithmetic Operands

Three different styles of operands can be used with the nontranscendental instructions:

    no operands
    one memory operand
    two stack operands

If no operands are specified, ST is the implied source and ST(1) is the implied destination. That is, the operation is performed on the top two items on the stack, with the result replacing the second item. After the operation is performed, ST is popped so that the result is returned to the top of the stack. Since all items in the stack are in extended real format, no matter what format they were in before they were pushed onto the stack, this form of operand cannot be used with the integer instructions.

The following instruction multiplies ST by ST(1), stores the product at ST(1), then pops the source operand off the stack:

    fmul

Figure 6-7 shows the result of this operation. By the time the instruction is finished, the original operands have disappeared and the product is available at ST.

If the instruction includes one operand, it must be a memory operand that represents the source. The implied destination is ST. The

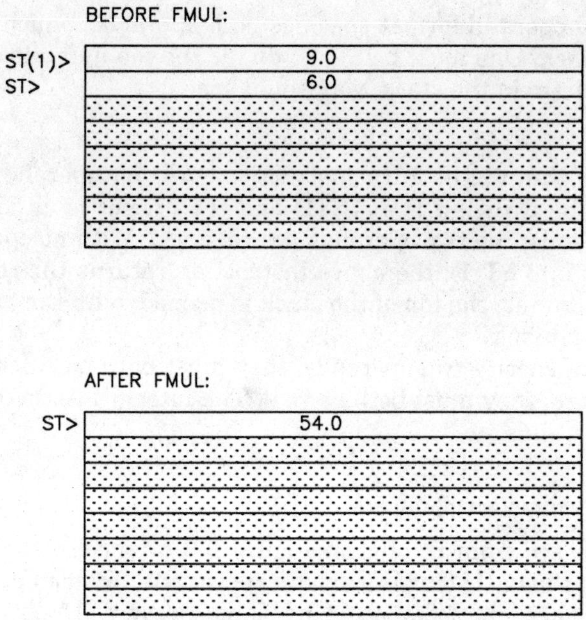

BEFORE FMUL:

ST(1)> [9.0   ]
ST>   [6.0   ]

AFTER FMUL:

ST>   [54.0   ]

Figure 6-7   Effect of Arithmetic Instruction with no Operands

following instruction adds the memory field named **month_end** to ST, returning the sum to ST:

```
fadd    month_end
```

The only memory types that can be addressed as arithmetic operands are single- and double-precision real values as well as word and short integers. BCD values, long integers, and extended-precision real values cannot be addressed this way; to use them as source values, you must load them into the register stack and use one of the other operand forms.

You must use the one-operand format with the integer instructions. The following instruction subtracts **loss**, which is defined as a short integer, from the top of the stack:

```
fisub   loss
```

Notice the use of **fisub**, since the source operand is an integer. The coprocessor will convert the value from **loss** to extended real format before subtracting it, although the source field is not changed in any way. It's crucial to match the opcode to the operand type correctly; if the above instruction used **fsub** instead of **fisub**, the source value would be converted incorrectly and the result would be garbage.

The third operand format specifies both operands, which must both be in the stack. One must be ST. To divide the top item in the stack by the second item in the stack, you would specify:

```
fdiv    st,st(1)
```

Compare this to the **fdiv** instruction with no operands. With no operands, the dividend is at ST(1) and the divisor is at ST; with the above operands, the two operands are reversed. With no operands, the result goes into ST(1); the above instruction returns the result to ST. With no operands, the top of the stack is popped; with the two-operand instruction, it isn't.

When you specify two operands, they must both be stack operands, and therefore, they must both be real. The integer instructions cannot use two operands.

The Basic Arithmetic Operations

As you can see from the list in Figure 6-6, a variety of instructions accomplish the basic four arithmetic operations. You can do real arithmetic, real arithmetic followed by a pop, reversed subtraction and division, and integer arithmetic.

Real Arithmetic. The "plain vanilla" real instructions are **fadd, fsub, fmul,** and **fdiv.** In each case, the operation performed is:

```
destination = destination op source
```

In the case of subtraction, the source is subtracted from the destination. In division, the destination is divided by the source. Any of the operand styles may be used with these instructions.

Real Arithmetic Followed by a Pop. You often need to delete the source operand at ST by an automatic pop as part of the operation. In such cases, you can use the pop arithmetic instructions: **faddp, fsubp, fsubrp, fmulp, fdivp,** and **fdivrp.** These instructions perform the operation, store the result in the destination operand, then pop the top of the stack. Generally, the source operand is at the top of the stack and the destination operand is somewhere else in the stack. Popping the top eliminates the source operand from the top of the stack after it is no longer needed.

Reversed Subtraction and Division. Addition and multiplication can be thought of as symmetrical operations in that the result is the same no matter which order the operands are in; the position of the operands is dictated by the one that should be replaced by the result, which becomes the destination operand. Subtraction and division do not have that same symmetrical nature. With **fsub**, for example, the destination operand must be the minuend. With **fdiv**, the destination operand must be the dividend. However, the reversed instructions provide symmetry by reversing the operands. The destination operand in **fsubr**, **fsubrp**, and **fisubr** is the subtrahend, not the minuend. The reversed subtraction operation is accomplished as follows:

```
destination = source - destination
```

Thus, to subtract ST from **total** and replace ST with the difference, you would code this instruction:

```
fsubr  total
```

To subtract ST(2) from ST, replace ST(2) with the total, and pop ST, you would code:

```
fsubrp st(2),st
```

In reversed division, the destination operand is the divisor instead of the dividend:

```
destination = source  destination
```

To divide ST by ST(1), return the result to ST(1), and pop ST, you would code this instruction:

```
fdivr
```

Integer Arithmetic. The integer instructions must use an integer stored in memory as the source operand. The destination is always ST. The basic integer instructions are **fiadd**, **fisub**, **fimul**, and **fidiv**. There are also reversed subtraction and division instructions: **fisubr** and **fidivr**.

Other Arithmetic Operations

Unlike the CPU instruction set, the coprocessor offers a number of other common arithmetic operations. The operands are assumed for all these operations.

Square Root. The square root instruction (**fsqrt**) replaces the top of the stack with its square root. To find the square root of **sum_total**, you would use this routine:

```
fld     sum_total
fsqrt
```

The square root is now at ST and can be saved to memory or used for further calculations. Compared to most microprocessors' square root algorithms, the **fsqrt** instruction is quite efficient, taking approximately 185 clock cycles on the '287 and 125 cycles on the '387. Thus, you need not avoid square roots in your numeric processing.

Scale. The scale instruction, **fscale**, takes no operands. It makes an integer out of the value in ST(1) by chopping it toward zero, then adds that integer to the exponent of the value in ST, effectively multiplying ST by $2^{ST(1)}$. This provides extremely rapid multiplication or division of ST by powers of 2.

Partial Remainders. Both of the partial remainder instructions, **fprem** and **fprem1**, divide ST by ST(1), producing an integer quotient. The functions don't save the quotient, only the remainder, which is returned to ST. The sign of the remainder is the sign of the original dividend from ST. The difference between **fprem** and **fprem1** is the way the integer quotient is determined, which of course influences the remainder. **Fprem** chops the quotient toward zero to produce an integer result, while **fprem1** rounds it to the nearest integer (taking the even integer if it's exactly halfway between two). **Fprem1** realizes the final IEEE standard.

The partial remainder instructions work by iterative subtraction and are quite time consuming, possibly preventing an interrupt from gaining control. Therefore, the instructions are limited in how much they can do in one operation. The value in ST can be reduced by 2^{64} at a time. If the final quotient and remainder have not yet been reached, the operation terminates with a 1 in condition code bit 2 of the status word. The value in ST at this point is a partial remainder. To continue to reduce it to a final remainder, you must repeat the operation on it until C2 is 0. At that point, C3, C1, and C0 are set to the three least significant bits of the quotient.

These partial remainder operations are useful in cases where you need to reduce arguments for transcendental functions, covered later in this chapter. For more information, see the Intel manual.

Round to Integer. The **frndint** instruction rounds the value in ST to an integer according to the current rounding control bits in the control word.

Extract Exponent and Significand. The **fxtract** instruction extracts the exponent and significand of the value in ST, storing the exponent in ST, then pushing the significand onto the stack. After the operation, the significand is addressable as ST, the exponent as ST(1). The significand is expressed as a real number with the sign of the original value, an exponent of biased 0, and the same significand as the original number. The bias is removed from the exponent, which is then expressed as a real number.

If the source value is zero, ST is set to signed zero and ST(1) is set to signed infinity.

Absolute Value. The **fabs** instruction returns the absolute value of ST by the simple expedient of changing its sign to positive.

Change Sign. The **fchs** instruction reverses the sign of the value in ST.

Arithmetic Example

Figure 6-8 shows a procedure that summarizes the arithmetic instructions and demonstrates how they fit into a regular assembler program. The procedure finds the total and mean average of a set of 1000 scores stored in the data segment.

The .287 directive on line 1 permits the coprocessor instructions to be assembled. Without it, this program would not assemble properly.

The relevant portions of the data segment are shown on lines 2 through 5. The constant 1000, which represents the total number of cases, is defined as an integer quadword on line 2. Why not just use an immediate value in the procedure? There isn't any way to push an immediate value onto the register stack. The only way to get this value onto the register stack is to place it in memory, then push it with **fild**.

The array of raw scores is defined on line 3 as 1000 uninitialized quadwords. Before the **mean_avg_proc** procedure is called, an input procedure loads the values into this array in real format. The two result variables are defined on lines 4 and 5.

The procedure itself is shown on lines 6 through 30. Notice that '287 instructions are interspersed with '286 instructions as if they were all

```
 1          .287
 2 n        dq     1000              ; number of entries
 3 raw_scores  dq 1000 dup (?)
 4 raw_total   dq ?
 5 mean     dq     ?
                ...
 6 mean_avg_proc  proc   near
 7          push   cx
 8          push   si
 9          mov    cx,n              ; loop counter
10          dec    cx
11 ; The loop counter is now set up for 999 loops.
12          mov    si,0
13          fld    raw_scores[si]
14 sum_loop:
15          inc    si
16          fadd   raw_scores[si]
17          loop   sum_loop
18 ; When control falls through to this point, the
19 ; running total has been completed and is at ST
20          fild   n
21          fdivr  st,st(1)
22          fstp   raw_total
23          fstp   mean
24 ; The register stack is now clear of all
25 ; operands placed there by this procedure.
26          pop    si
27          pop    cx
28          fwait
29          ret
30 mean_avg_proc  endp
```

Figure 6-8   Mean Average Program

part of the same instruction set, which, in a sense, they are. Lines 7 and 8 preserve the two CPU registers used by the procedure. Lines 9 and 10 initialize the counter for the loop that totals the raw scores. Since the first score is loaded into the register stack before the loop starts, the loop needs to be repeated only 999 times instead of 1000. That's why we decrement CX after loading 1000 into it.

Line 12 sets up the index register for the loop, and line 13 loads the first score into the register stack. This score will act as the base for the running total. The loop adds the next 999 scores to this one.

The summation loop is shown on lines 14 through 17. First, the index is incremented (line 15). Then the next score is added to the running total at ST (line 16). Then we loop back for the next score (line 17).

After the summation loop is completed, control falls through to line 20. The instructions that calculate the mean average are shown on lines 20 and 21. First, the number of scores is pushed onto the stack (line 20). It's important to use **fild** instead of **fld** to do this since the value is defined as an integer. (Why did we define it as an integer? So it can also be used to initialize CX on line 10.)

Now the division problem is set up. The total of all scores (the dividend) is at ST(1). The divisor (1000) is at ST. The dividend should not be replaced by the quotient because it is also a result of the procedure. Therefore, the reverse division instruction is used to replace the divisor with the answer. The **fdivr** instruction on line 21 divides ST(1) by ST, replacing ST with the quotient.

When line 22 is reached, the sum total is at ST and the mean is at ST(1). Lines 22 and 23 store these two results in the appropriate locations in memory. As noted in the procedure (lines 24 and 25), the procedure has now removed all its variables from the stack, leaving an empty stack for the next procedure. Then the two preserved registers can be restored (lines 26 and 27).

The **fwait** instruction on line 28 is discussed in detail later in this chapter. For now, let us just say that it is important to make sure the last **fstp** instruction (line 25) completes its operation before returning control to the calling procedure. Finally, lines 29 and 30 complete the procedure.

Comparisons

The comparison instructions shown in Figure 6-9 set the coprocessor condition codes (C3, C1, and C0 in the status word register). The comparison is done by hypothetically subtracting the source value

fcom	Compare real
fcomp	Compare real and pop
fcompp	Compare real and pop twice
ficom	Compare integer
ficomp	Compare integer and pop
fucom	Unordered compare real ('387 only)
fucomp	Unordered compare real and pop ('387 only)
fucompp	Unordered compare real and pop twice ('387 only)
ftst	Test against zero
fxam	Examine condition codes

Figure 6-9   The Comparison Instructions

from the destination. You can specify a memory or stack value for the source; ST is always the destination.

Figure 6-10 shows how the condition codes are set and what jumps are appropriate afterward. However, there are no coprocessor jump instructions. You must use the CPU instructions, which test the CPU status flags, not the coprocessor condition codes. Therefore, before you can jump, you must copy the coprocessor status word to the CPU (E)FLAGS register. You'll learn how to do that later in this chapter.

The Comparison Instructions

The **fcom** instruction compares two real items. ST is always the destination. If no operand is specified, ST(1) is the source. You can specify one source operand, which can be a stack register or a single-precision or double-precision real memory variable. The **fcomp** instruction is

condition	C3	C2	C0	jump
ST > source	0	0	0	jg
ST < source	0	0	1	jb, jc
ST = source	1	0	0	je, jz
unordered	1	1	1	jp

Figure 6-10   Condition Codes and Jumps

the same as **fcom** except it pops the top of the stack. The **fcompp** instruction pops both variables off the stack. You cannot specify an operand with **fcompp** since it assumes the source is at ST(1) and the destination is at ST.

The **ficom** instruction must specify a word or short integer variable as the source. It is converted to extended real format and compared to the stack top. The **ficomp** instruction is just like **ficom** but it pops the top of the stack. There is no **ficompp** instruction since the integer instructions must specify a memory variable as the source.

The unordered instructions (**fucom, fucomp,** and **fucompp**) are just like the ordinary real comparisons except that they don't trigger an exception if either one of the operands is a NaN. Instead, they yield a result of *unordered*, which can be tested for by the **jp** instruction. The unordered instructions are available only with the '387 and can have only stack operands. (You can specify a source operand, but it must be a stack register.) The ordinary real comparison instructions yield the same condition codes but trigger the invalid operation exception upon encountering a NaN operand. Always use **jp** before any other jumps following the unordered comparisons, because the 1's in all three condition codes could fool the other conditional jump instructions.

The **ftst** instruction compares ST to zero. The **fxam** instruction uses all four condition codes to identify the nature of the value at ST. The 16 possible results are shown in Figure 6-11. The values are arranged so

type	C3	C2	C1	C0
+Unnormal*	0	0	0	0
+NaN	0	0	0	1
-Unnormal*	0	0	1	0
-NaN	0	0	1	1
+Normal	0	1	0	0
+Infinity	0	1	0	1
-Normal	0	1	1	0
-Infinity	0	1	1	1
+0	1	0	0	0
Empty	1	0	0	1
-0	1	0	1	0
Empty	1	0	1	1
+Denormal	1	1	0	0
Empty	1	1	0	1
-Denormal	1	1	1	0
Empty	1	1	1	1

*Not supported on the '387

Figure 6-11   Results of Fxam

that C1 indicates whether the number is positive or negative. If C3 and C1 are both set, the register is empty.

The Transcendental Instructions

Figure 6-12 lists the transcendental instructions, which include the trigonometric, inverse trigonometric, hyperbolic, inverse hyperbolic, logarithmic, and exponential functions. These instructions take no operands. ST is always the implied destination; if a separate source operand is needed, ST(1) is the implied source. None of these functions can provide 100% accuracy, but they are programmed to minimize error.

Fsin, fcos, fsincos, and **fptan** all operate on the value at ST, which must be expressed in radians and have an absolute value less than 2^{63}. If the source value is too large or too small, C2 is set and ST is not replaced. The program must use **fprem** or **fprem1** to reduce the source value appropriately before executing one of these functions.

Fsin and **fcos** return the value SIN(ST) and COS(ST) respectively. **Fsincos** calculates both SIN(ST) and COS(ST). It returns the sine to ST, then pushes the cosine onto the stack. **Fptan** returns the TAN(ST) to ST. Then it pushes a 1 onto the stack. The stack is now set up to calculate other functions that are derivatives of the tangent. For example, the cotangent can be obtained by this instruction:

```
fdivr
```

This instruction divides 1 (in ST) by the tangent (in ST(1)), replaces the tangent with the result, and pops the 1.

fsin	Sine of ST
fcos	Cosine of ST
fsincos	Sine and Cosine of ST
fptan	Partial tangent of ST
fpatan	Partial arctangent of ST
f2xm1	$2^x - 1$
fyl2x	Y times $\log_2 X$
fyl2xp1	Y times $\log_2(X + 1)$

Figure 6-12   The Transcendental Instructions

Fpatan computes ARCTAN(ST/ST(1)), returns the answer to ST(1), and pops the top. For this instruction, the range of operands is not limited. Derivative functions such as arcsine and arccosine can be calculated from the arctangent.

The **f2xm1** instruction calculates $2^{ST}-1$ and replaces ST with the result. The value in ST must be in the range of −1 to +1. If the value is out of range, the results are undefined. The **fyl2x** instruction calculates Y times LOG_2X, where Y is at ST(1) and X is at ST. The result is returned to ST(1) and the top of the stack is popped so that the answer becomes the top of the stack. X must be positive and both X and Y must be finite. The **fyl2xp1** instruction calculates Y times $LOG_2(X+1)$, returning the answer to ST(1) and popping the top. X must be in the range −(1−SQRT(2)/2) to 1−SQRT(2)/2; Y is unlimited.

The Constant Instructions

Figure 6-13 shows the constant instructions. Each of these instructions loads the indicated constant into ST. With the '287, they are rounded to nearest. With the '387, they are rounded according to the rounding control bits.

The Control Instructions

A collection of instructions are used to control the actions of the coprocessor. Figure 6-14 lists these instructions. Most of them are used for system, rather than application, programming. However, you will need **fwait** in every coprocessor routine you write. You might also find use for **fstsw** and **fstsw ax**.

Synchronizing the Two Processors

The CPU and the coprocessor can both process instructions at the same time. When the main processor encounters a coprocessor instruc-

fldz	Load +0.0
fld1	Load +1.0
fldpi	Load pi
fldl2t	Load $log_2 10$
fldl2e	Load $log_2 e$
fldlg2	Load $log_{10} 2$
fldln2	Load $log_e 2$

Figure 6-13   The Constant Instructions

fwait	CPU wait
fstsw/fnstsw	Store status word
fstsw ax/	Store status word to AX
fnstsw ax	
fldcw	Load control word
fstcw/fnstcw	Store control word
fldenv	Load environment
fstenv/fnstenv	Store environment
fsave/fnsave	Save state
frstor	Restore state
fincstp	Increment stack pointer
fdecstp	Decrement stack pointer
finit/finnit	Initialize processor
fclex/fnclex	Clear exceptions
ffree	Free register
fnop	No operation

Figure 6-14   The Control Instructions

tion in the program, it checks the coprocessor's busy line to determine whether it is available. When the coprocessor is free, it transfers the instruction to the coprocessor for execution. Then, without waiting for the coprocessor to complete its task, it fetches the next instruction in the program. If that is a CPU instruction, it executes the instruction and fetches the next. Only when it encounters another coprocessor instruction is it forced to wait until the coprocessor is free. The '286 can execute a lot of instructions in the approximately 185 clock cycles it takes the '287 to calculate a square root.

For the most part, this system of parallel processing offers tremendous advantages. However, in two situations, it can cause problems. If a coprocessor instruction accesses a memory field, the processor must be careful not to change the value in that field until the coprocessor has finished with it. If a coprocessor instruction stores a value in memory, the main processor cannot access the stored item until it is sure the coprocessor has finished storing it. The **fwait** instruction forces the main processor to wait until the coprocessor busy signal clears—that is, until the coprocessor has finished the last instruction it received. You will also see the **wait** instruction in the main processor instruction set. This is another name for the same instruction. You can code it as **wait** or **fwait**.

Suppose you want to calculate the square root of **difference**, storing the answer in **square_root**, then move **square_root** to EAX for output. This routine will do it:

```
fild    difference

fsqrt

fist    square_root

fwait

mov     eax,square_root
```

The **fwait** instruction is crucial here. Without it, the main processor would execute the **mov** instruction long before the square root was stored in **square_root**. Suppose you want to load **difference** into the coprocessor register stack, then move 0 to **difference**. The following routine will do it:

```
fild    difference

fwait

mov     difference,0
```

Here again, the **fwait** instruction is crucial. Otherwise, the **mov** instruction might zero the value in **difference** before the coprocessor has a chance to load the original value. Intel strongly suggests that you document each **fwait** instruction thoroughly for fear that a naive maintenance programmer might remove it.

If the instruction that accesses data is followed by another coprocessor instruction, the synchronization is automatic and **fwait** is not needed. For example, suppose the above routine adds ST and ST(1) after loading **difference**. Now the routine can look like this:

```
fild    difference

fadd
```

```
mov     difference,0
```

Remember that the CPU automatically waits for the coprocessor to be free before it transfers the next instruction. In other words, each coprocessor instruction starts with an implied wait. Therefore, the **fadd** instruction forces the CPU to wait until the **fild** instruction is complete. The main processor will not get to the **mov** instruction until it has transferred the **fadd** instruction to the coprocessor after the **fild** instruction is finished. In this situation, the **fwait** instruction is unnecessary. However, if in doubt, wait.

You saw another example of the use of **fwait** in Figure 6-8. Line 23 issues a **fstp** instruction to store **mean**. It is safe to go on to pop the two registers on lines 26 and 27. But you should wait for the **fstp** instruction to complete its work before returning to the calling procedure, which might attempt to access **mean** immediately. Hence, the **fwait** instruction is coded on line 28. By coding the **pop** instructions before the **fwait** instruction, we let the CPU get as much work done as possible before waiting and give the coprocessor more time to get its work done before waiting for it.

There is also a hidden pitfall in unsynchronized programs. If any coprocessor instruction results in an unmasked exception, that exception will not be handled until the next coprocessor instruction is begun. By that time, the CPU environment at the time of the exception may be long gone, making recovery and debugging nearly impossible.

Back in the days of the 8086 and 8087, the main processor did not test the busy signal before shipping an instruction to the coprocessor. Therefore, every coprocessor instruction had to be preceded by **fwait** or **wait** to ensure synchronization of the coprocessor. You will see a lot more **(f)wait** instructions in 8086 programs. They won't do any harm when run on the '286 or '386; they just take up extra storage space. You can ignore them or remove the unnecessary ones, as you see fit.

Examining the Status Word

Many of the coprocessor instructions set bits in the status word to indicate various types of exceptions as well as the results of comparisons. To examine the status word after a coprocessor instruction, you must copy it to memory or AX, then test the relevant bits.

Suppose you want to find out whether the zero divide flag has been set after a **fdiv** operation. You might use this routine:

```
status_word dw      ?

        . . .

        fdiv
```

```
fstsw   status_word
fwait
test    status_word,0000000000000100b
jnz     divide_error
```

After the division, the status word is stored in a memory word called **status_word**. **Fwait** ensures that the word is stored before the **test** instruction accesses it. **Test** then checks the zero divide error flag, bit 2. If that bit is 0, the zero flag will be set, indicating no error. If that bit is 1, the zero flag will be cleared, indicating an error. The **jnz** instruction jumps to an error-processing routine if the zero flag is cleared, indicating an error. (The **test** instruction is explained in detail in Chapter 7.)

Most of the time, you will need to access condition code bits C0 (bit 8), C2 (bit 10), and C3 (bit 14). These are the bits set by the comparison instructions. If you copy the status word to AX with the **fstsw ax** instruction, then load the upper half into the flag register using the **sahf** instruction, the three condition code bits, load directly into the zero flag, parity flag, and carry flag, as shown in Figure 6-15. Suppose you want to find out whether the value in ST is zero. You could use the following routine:

```
ftst
fstsw ax
fwait
sahf
jz      zero_value
```

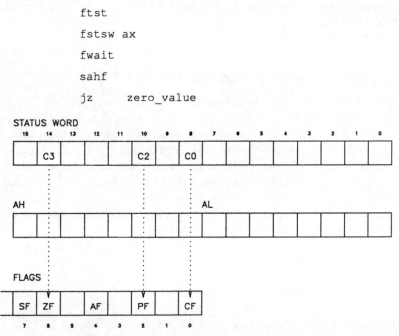

Figure 6-15   Moving the Condition Codes to the FLAGS Register

Ftst compares the value at ST to 0.0 and sets the condition code. C3 is set if the value equals zero and is cleared otherwise. That's the only bit of interest in this particular problem. The **fstsw ax** instruction stores the status word in AX. **Fwait** is important to force the instruction to complete before accessing AH. Then the **sahf** instruction loads selected bits from the upper half of the status word into FLAGS. Finally, the **jz** instruction jumps if the zero flag is set.

Initializing the Coprocessor

You might occasionally need to reset the coprocessor registers to their default values. For example, you might want to clear the condition codes or the exception flags, which are sticky. To reset all the registers, use **finit**. To reset just the exception flags, use **fclex**. You might want to issue **finit** at the beginning of your program just to clear any other program's data out of the coprocessor registers. And issue **finit** again at the end of your program to clear your values out of the register for the next program, especially if you reset any of the bits in the control word register.

Other Control Instructions

The remaining instructions in Figure 6-14 are normally not used in application programs. If you need to know more about them, check your Intel reference manual.

Differences among the Coprocessors

The numeric coprocessor has changed over the years, partly to keep up with the IEEE standard and partly to improve its functionality. Unfortunately, it has not been possible to maintain upward compatibility from the 8087 to the '287 to the '387. A program written for an earlier processor might function differently on a newer coprocessor. Most of the differences are slight, but even a slight difference can be crucial in some applications.

You have seen some of the differences in this chapter. The complete list of differences falls into these categories:

Initialization (**reset** and **finit**)

Data types (NaNs, pseudo-formats, unnormal format)

Exceptions (exceptions triggered by certain conditions; handling of exceptions)

Condition codes (**finit, fprem, fptan**)

Infinity control (affine vs. projective closure)

Status word (use of bit 6)

Tag word (use and interpretation of tags)

Instructions (range of values, special operands, condition codes, exceptions, rounding)

Several instructions have been dropped from the 8087 instruction set

If you are concerned about upward compatibility for your coprocessor routines, check your Intel coprocessor reference manual for detailed explanations of the differences.

Bit Manipulation

You've seen in previous chapters how to manipulate bytes, words, doublewords, quadwords, and tenbytes. One advantage of working with assembler language instead of a higher level language is the ability to access individual bits. This chapter completes our discussion of the assembler instruction set by showing you how to manipulate individual bits.

Logical Operations

The logical operation instructions, shown in Figure 7-1, turn bits on and off and test for bit combinations. The simplest operation is **not**, which complements every bit of the operand. Suppose you are maintaining the sign of a BCD value in **a_sign**, where 0FFh is negative and 0 is positive. To reverse the sign:

```
a_sign      db      0

            . . .

            not     a_sign
```

not	Complement bits
and	And source to destination
or	Or (inclusive) source to destination
xor	Or (exclusive) source to destination
test	Test destination bits
neg	Two's complement negation

Figure 7-1   The Logical Operation Instructions

The **and, or,** and **xor** operations each compare two fields and assign a value to the destination field accordingly. The comparison is done bit-by-bit. Figure 7-2 shows how the destination bit is assigned for each combination of input bits. Suppose **fielda** contains 10101110b and **fieldb** contains 00001111b. When you **and** them, the result is 00001110b. **Or** produces 10101111b. **Xor** produces 10100001b. This section explains how each of these operations is applied.

Turning Bits Off with And

The **and** operation sets the destination bit if both input bits are set (input A *and* input B) and clears it otherwise. **And** is generally used to turn bits off in the destination field because if you **and** a bit with 0, the bit is automatically cleared. If you **and** a bit with 1, the bit retains its original value.

Therefore, if you want to turn a bit off, **and** it with 0. If you want to leave it alone, **and** it with 1. To clear a field such as CX, you could code:

```
and    cx,0
```

This sets all the bits in CX to 0 and is as efficient as subtracting CX from itself.

It's rare that you **and** two unknown values together. Usually you **and** a source operand with an immediate value, called a *mask*. The mask specifies a pattern of 1's and 0's designed to affect certain bits in

	and	or	xor
source	0 0 1 1	0 0 1 1	0 0 1 1
dest	0 1 0 1	0 1 0 1	0 1 0 1
result	0 0 0 1	0 1 1 1	0 1 1 0

Figure 7-2   Results of Logical Operations

the destination field. Coding the mask in binary makes the effect of the **and** operation clear.

When you accept characters from the keyboard, they are in ASCII format. ASCII digits are coded as 30H through 39H. To convert an ASCII digit to an unpacked BCD format, all you need do is remove the 3 from the upper nibble. One way to do that is shown below:

```
in_digit    db      ?

            . . .

            and     in_digit,00001111b  ; clear upper nibble
```

The mask 00001111B turns off all the bits in the high-order nibble while leaving the low-order nibble intact.

Testing Bits

Test is similar to **and** except it doesn't change the destination bits, merely setting the flags *as if* the **and** operation had taken place. **And** and **test** both affect SF, PF, CF, OF, and ZF (CF and OF are automatically cleared and AF is undefined).

Test can be used to test one or more bits in the destination field and jump accordingly, without disturbing the destination field. Suppose you have created your own flag byte; each bit represents an on/off condition. Now you want to jump to **long_record** if bits 4 and 6 are off:

```
flag_byte   db      ?

            . . .

            test    flag_byte,01010000b

            jnz     long_record
```

The mask "turns off" every bit except 4 and 6. If the result is 0, then you know that bits 4 and 6 were also off. If the result is not 0, then you know that at least one of those bits was on.

Turning Bits On with Or

An **or** operation sets the destination bit if either input bit is set and clears it otherwise. The difference between the inclusive (**or**) and exclusive (**xor**) versions lies with the result when both input bits are on; **or** sets the result bit while **xor** clears it when both input bits are on.

Whereas **and** can be used to turn bits off, **or** can be used to turn them on. If you **or** any bit with 1, the destination bit is set. If you **or** a bit with 0, the bit retains its original value. Suppose you want to turn on all the bits in DX. You could do it this way:

```
        or      dx,1111111111111111b
```
This is the same as moving 0FFh to DX.

Suppose you need to convert an unpacked BCD digit to an ASCII character prior to displaying it on the monitor or printing it. All you have to do is set the upper nibble to 3 while leaving the lower nibble alone:

```
out_digit   db      ?

        . . .

        or      out_digit,00110000b
```

This **or** instruction forces bits 4 and 5 on while leaving the others alone. Assuming the destination was in correct unpacked BCD format to start with (i.e., the upper nibble was 0 and the lower nibble was 9 or less), this instruction creates a valid ASCII digit.

Reversing Bits with Xor

The **xor** instruction is used to complement (reverse) the value of some bits while leaving others alone. Anywhere a 1 bit appears in the mask, the corresponding destination bit is complemented. A zero mask bit leaves the corresponding destination bit unchanged.

Xor is frequently used to set the result sign in signed BCD multiplication and division. Suppose you are writing a routine to multiply two BCD values together. The signs are kept in **sign1** and **sign2**. All 1's indicates a negative number while all 0's indicates a positive number. The **xor** instruction will set the result sign (**sign3**) correctly.

```
sign1       db      ?
sign2       db      ?
sign3       db      ?

        . . .

        mov     al,sign1
        xor     al,sign2
        mov     sign3,al
```

Let's look at the four possible cases:

sign1	0000 (+)	0000 (+)	1111 (–)	1111 (–)
sign2	0000 (+)	1111 (–)	0000 (+)	1111 (–)
sign3	0000 (+)	1111 (–)	1111 (–)	0000 (+)

You can see that **xor** produces the correct result in all four cases. **Xor** is also frequently used to zero (clear) a field:

```
xor     ax,ax
```

This forces all the one bits off; the zero bits remain off.

Shifting Bits

The shift instructions move bits to the left or right within the destination field. The rightmost operand specifies the number of positions to shift the bits. A bit that is shifted out of the field goes into the carry flag, then disappears when the next bit is shifted into the carry flag. Bits shifted into the field depend on which instruction is used. Figure 7-3 lists the shift and rotate instructions and Figure 7-4 illustrates the function of the five shift instructions as well as the rotate instructions, which are discussed in the next section.

Suppose you want to shift the bits in DX four positions to the left, filling zeros in on the right. You could code this instruction:

```
sal     dx,4
```

To shift them to the right, filling zero bits in from the left, you could code:

```
shr     dx,4
```

sal/shl	Shift left
shr	Shift right (feed in 0)
sar	Shift right (duplicate MSB)
shld	Double precision shift to left ('386 only)
shrd	Double precision shift to right ('386 only)
rol	Rotate left
rcl	Rotate left through carry
ror	Rotate right
rcr	Rotate right through carry

Figure 7-3   The Shift and Rotate Instructions

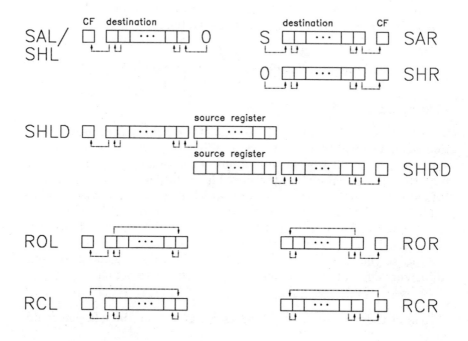

Figure 7-4   Function of Shift and Rotate Instructions

As you will see in the following discussion, the effect is to multiply or divide DX by 16.

Shifting to the Left

Sal and **shl** are identical; both shift the bits to the left, feeding 0's into the low-order bit on the right. The overall effect of this operation is to multiply the value by 2^n, where n is the number of shifts. The obvious advantage of shifting over ordinary multiplication with **mul** or **imul** is that you can shift the value where it lies; it need not be loaded into the accumulator, then stored again. The obvious disadvantage is that you have to multiply by powers of 2. But by combining shifts with addition, you can devise an algorithm for any multiplier you need. For example, to multiply ECX by 25:

1. Copy ECX to **temp.**
2. Multiply ECX by 16 (shift left 4 times).
3. Save this partial product in EDX.
4. Multiply ECX by 8 (shift left 3 times).

5. Add this product to the partial product in EDX, which now equals **temp** times 24.

6. Add **temp** to the partial product in EDX. EDX now equals **temp** times 25.

There are a few other advantages of shifting over **mul** and **imul**:

- Shifting can produce the final result more quickly, depending on how complex your algorithm is.

- In the '386, you can multiply doubleword values in EAX (as opposed to DX:AX) or any other doubleword field.

Shifting to produce arithmetic results has limitations, however.

- If a value has been stored in memory with the bytes reversed, **sal** will produce the wrong results. To shift such values, move them to a register to straighten out the bytes, then shift the register.

- If you shift more than once in one operation, you take the chance of shifting significant bits out of the destination field without being able to identify the loss. The carry flag tells you only what the last bit shifted out was. To avoid overflow, make sure the unshifted value has enough leading 0's (or 1's if it's negative) to accommodate the entire shift without overflowing. Otherwise, shift only one position at a time and test the carry flag after every shift.

- If the number is signed, you take the chance of reversing the sign without doing a proper two's complement negation. If you shift only once, the overflow flag will be set if the new sign bit doesn't match the original sign bit (now in the carry flag). If you shift more than once, the overflow flag becomes undefined and you lose this valuable piece of information. To avoid this problem, make sure the original value has enough leading sign bits to avoid both overflow and sign reversal, or shift only one position at a time and test the overflow flag after each shift.

- You can't multiply BCD values by shifting; the adjustments, which depend on the auxiliary flag, don't work properly after **sal/shl**.

Sal/shl is also useful in converting two unpacked decimal digits into one packed byte. If the digits are in BH and BL:

```
shl     bh,4
add     bh,bl
```

Shifting BH left four times puts the first digit in the upper nibble of BH. Adding BL to it puts the second digit in the lower nibble of BH. BH now contains the packed byte.

Shifting to the Right

Unlike **sal/shl**, **sar** and **shr** are not identical. They both shift bits to the right, but **shr** fills in the new high-order bit with 0 while **sar** duplicates the original sign bit. **Shr** is useful for unsigned binary values, while **sar** is designed for signed binary values.

Shifting binary values to the right has the effect of dividing by powers of two, but note these differences from **div** and **idiv**:

- **Shr** and **sar** do not automatically save the remainder. You have to code a routine specifically to catch the bits shifted out on the right and save them as the remainder.

- The divisor is always positive. If you want the divisor to be negative, negate the result using **neg**.

- **Idiv** truncates the quotient (which is the same effect as rounding every answer toward zero), but **sar** always rounds down towards negative infinity. This means that **idiv** and **sar** produce the same answer with positive quotients, but **sar**'s negative quotients will always be 1 less than **idiv**'s. For example, if you divide −9 by 4, **idiv** produces a −2 quotient and −1 remainder, but **sar** produces a −3 quotient, which would be the wrong answer in most applications. A simple increment is all that's needed to produce the same answer as **idiv**:

```
distance    dw      ?
rate        dw      ?
four        dw      4

            ...

            mov     ax,distance     ; dividend in AX
            cwd                     ; dividend in DX:AX
            idiv    four            ; quotient in AX
            mov     rate,ax         ; quotient to RATE
```

Compare this routine to the following, which accomplishes the same result using **sar**:

```
            mov     ax,distance     ; dividend in AX
```

```
              sar     ax,2                ; quotient in AX
              jns     store_rate          ; if quotient is neg...
              inc     ax                  ; ...round up
store_rate:
              mov     rate,ax             ; quotient to RATE
```

On the '386, the routine using **idiv** takes 37 machine cycles, while the routine using **sar** takes 16 or 21 machine cycles, depending on whether or not the jump is taken. Therefore, the extra step of identifying and incrementing negative quotients is well worth the trouble.

Shr is also useful for unpacking a packed BCD byte:

```
bcd_byte    db      ?                   ; packed
              ...
; The following two steps place the
; low-order nibble in BL
              mov     bl,bcd_byte
              and     bl,00001111b       ; delete upper digit
; The following three steps place the high_order
; nibble in BH
              mov     bh,bcd_byte
              and     bh,11110000b       ; delete lower digit
              shr     bh,4               ; position value in byte
```

At the end of this routine, BH:BL contains the two unpacked bytes.

Double Precision Shifts

Shld and **shrd** differ from **shl** and **shr** in the source of bits shifted into the destination field. Instead of zeros, input bits are taken from a source field, which must be a register and must be the same size as the destination. Therefore, three operands must be specified: destination, source, and count. To shift BH four bits to the left, filling in bits from BL, you could code:

```
              shld    bh,bl,4
```

For **shld**, imagine the source register located to the right of the destination field (as shown in Figure 7-2), with bits shifting from the high-order end of the source into the low-order end of the destination. The opposite takes place with **shrd**. The source is not shifted, but successive bits are taken from it as if it were.

Let's look at the actual results of some double-precision shifts:

```
before                    shift          after
AX: 1111 0000 0000 0000   shld ax,bx,4   AX: 0000 0000 0000 1001
BX: 1001 0000 0000 0110                  BX: (no change)

before                    shift          after
AX: 1111 0000 0000 0000   shrd ax,bx,4   AX: 0110 1111 0000 0000
BX: 1001 0000 0000 0110                  BX: (no change)
```

Let's look at a routine that multiplies the quadword in EDX:EAX by 4:

```
        shld    edx,eax,2

        shl     eax,2
```

The first step shifts EDX, bringing in the two high-order bits from EAX. However, this step does not affect EAX. The second step finishes the routine by shifting EAX.

Shld and **shrd** can be used to transfer a value from register to memory without swapping the bytes, which you might need to do when manipulating bit strings. You can overlay all or part of a memory field:

```
timer       dd      ?

            . . .

        shld    timer,ax,16
```

This **shld** instruction replaces the lowest 16 bits of **timer** with the contents of AX.

Rotates

A rotate differs from a shift by recirculating the bits around to the other end of the field. The **rol** instruction rotates bits to the left. Each bit that exits the field on the left becomes the low-order bit on the right. It is also copied to the carry flag. The **rcl** instruction rotates the bits to the left through the carry flag. That is, each bit that rotates out of the field on the left goes into the carry flag. The bit that rotates out of the carry flag goes into the low-order position in the field. Thus, **rcl** uses nine bits to rotate, while **rol** uses 8.

The **ror** and **rcr** instructions are just like **rol** and **rcl**, except the rotation is to the right instead of the left.

When the operation is finished, the carry flag always holds the last bit that was rotated. If you are concerned about not rotating any 1's out of the field, then rotate only 1 bit at a time and check the carry flag after each rotation. The overflow flag can indicate whether or not the sign of a signed value was changed by the rotation. If only one bit is rotated, the overflow flag is set if the value's sign was changed by the operation; it is cleared if the sign did not change. If you rotate more than one bit at once, then the overflow flag becomes undefined.

Suppose you want to reverse the bytes in AX. You could do it with this instruction:

```
        rol     ax,8
```

Ror would work as well.

Bit Tests

A bit test isolates a single bit in a field, copies it to the carry flag, and perhaps sets or clears the original bit. After the test, you can jump based on the value of the carry flag. Figure 7-5 lists the bit test instructions. These instructions are useful mostly in flag fields you have created yourself. For example, suppose you have created a file structure where the first word in each record contains 16 flags indicating status information about that record. They might indicate whether the record was changed since the last time the file was backed up, if it is currently accessed for update, if it has been marked for deletion, and so forth. To test a particular bit in this byte, you could use **bt**:

```
status_word dw      ?

            . . .

            bt      status_word,0
            jc      deleted
```

The **bt** instruction accesses the low-order bit of the word (bit 0), copying its value into the carry flag. The **jc** instruction then makes a decision based on the value of the carry flag. The following routine treats bit 3 of the status word as a semaphore, indicating whether another process is currently using the record:

```
get_record:
```

bt	Bit test
bts	Bit test and set
btr	Bit test and reset (clear)
btc	Bit test and complement

Figure 7-5   The Bit Test Instructions

```
bts    status_word,3

jc     get_record
```

Bts is used much like **xchg** is used for a semaphore field. It copies the current value of the semaphore bit into the carry flag, while at the same time setting the bit. If the bit was originally set, meaning that someone else has accessed the record, then the routine is repeated until the bit goes off, meaning someone else has released the record. Then you fall through the **jc** instruction into the routine that updates the record.

At the end of that routine, you could release the record with this instruction:

```
btr    status_word,3
```

In this case, you're using **btr** not as a test, but simply to clear the bit. Since you *know* its current value is 1, you could also clear it with this instruction:

```
btc    status_word,3
```

However, Murphy's Law suggests that **btr** is wiser than **btc**, just in case some other instruction cleared the bit after **bts** set it.

Any of the bit test functions can also be accomplished by **and, or, xor,** and **test,** but when dealing with only one bit, the bit test instructions are clearer and easier.

Bit Scans

Figure 7-6 shows the bit scan instructions. A bit scan starts at one end of a field and looks for the first 1 bit, setting the destination register to the position of the bit.

Suppose you want to find the position of the highest 1 bit in AX, storing the position in BX. You could code this instruction:

```
bsr    bx,ax
```

If AX contains 00000000 10110100b, the result in BX is 7, indicating that bit 7 of AX contains the highest order 1 bit.

Suppose you want to find the lowest order 1 bit in the value in the AX register. You need to start at the right end of the value and scan to

bsf	Bit scan forward (right to left) ('386 only)
bsr	Bit scan reverse (left to right) ('386 only)

Figure 7-6   The Bit Scan Instructions

the left, which is a backward scan. You could code the instruction shown below.

```
bsf     bx,ax
```

Given the same value for AX, the result in BX is 2.

If the source is zero, the result in the destination is undefined but the zero flag is set. You should always use **jz** or **jnz** after a bit scan to handle a zero value.

Let's look at a routine to *normalize* the value in AX; that is, we're going to rotate it to the left until the first 1 bit is in the high order position.

```
bsr     bx,ax
jz      short zero_value
mov     cx,15
sub     cx,bx              ; cx = lead zeros in ax
shl     ax,cx              ; shift lead zeros out
```

Even though **bsr** scans from the left, the number it places in the result field indicates the bit's position from the *right*, so you have to subtract it from 15 to figure out the number of leading zeros in the 16-bit field. You have to test for zero and bypass the next instructions, because if a zero value was found, the value in BX is undefined. If the zero flag was off, then we can subtract the result from CX, leaving the result in CX. CX now contains the number of leading zeros in AX and can be used as the count operand in the shift instruction. The value in CX should be saved with the normalized number so that the true value can be restored when necessary.

Like bit tests, bit scans treat memory bytes in the correct logical, not physical, order, so that a result of 2 means bit 2 in the value as if the bytes were stored in nonreversed order.

Setting and Clearing Flags

Figure 7-7 lists the instructions to set and clear flags. You have seen most of these instructions before. Notice that you can not only set and clear the carry flag, you can also complement it.

Normal applications don't need to manipulate flags other than carry and direction. If you do need to control another flag for some reason, push the flags register into the stack, use one of the bit manipulation instructions discussed in this chapter to set, clear, or complement the flag, then pop the flag register again.

stc	Set carry flag
clc	Clear carry flag
cmc	Complement carry flag
std	Set direction flag
cld	Clear direction flag

Figure 7-7   The Flag Manipulation Instructions

Defining and Using Data

You have now seen all the assembler instructions used for application programs. The next four chapters deal with assembler directives—source program statements that control not the processor but the assembler. They can vary from assembler to assembler since they aren't standardized by Intel (or any other organization), but the ones presented in this book tend to be available for most assemblers. They are all available for both MASM and the Phar Lap assemblers unless we specifically state otherwise. If you use a different assembler, you should check your assembler reference manual to see what is available to you.

You have already seen many assembler directives, as it is impossible to present program examples without segment declaration directives such as **.stack, .data**, and **segment**; data declaration directives such as **db** and **dd**; and procedure declaration directives such as **proc** and **endp**. Now you will learn the details of those directives and many others.

This chapter deals with data declarations. You'll learn how to create a symbol such as a variable name or a label, how to express a value for

a data declaration or an immediate operand, and how to define and
initialize variables with the data declaration directives.

Forming Symbols

A symbol is a name that stands for an address or a constant value,
such as **user_id** and **sum_loop**. A symbol can be any length, but the
assembler uses only the first 31 characters. You can usually create a
unique, meaningful name using far fewer characters, as in the many
examples you've already seen in this book.

Symbols can be formed from the following characters:

A through Z   a through z   0 through 9   _ ? $ @

Other characters, including the hyphen and space, are not permitted. The first character can be any character but a digit. All the
following are valid symbols:

```
record_flag

_text

$expenses

profit_loss?
```

The following are invalid for the reasons given:

```
profit/loss        The slash is illegal

287flag            Starts with a digit

password check     The space is illegal
```

Except for local names, which are discussed later in this chapter, the
first 31 characters of each name must be unique within the module.
The module consists of the source code file that you assemble as one
unit; it might be combined with other modules at link editing time. If
you create a global symbol (one that can be accessed by other modules
in the program), then it must be unique within the entire program.
You'll see how to create and use global symbols later in this chapter.

By default, the assembler ignores case. You can define a symbol as
work_space, then refer to it later as **Work_Space**, **WORK_SPACE**,
or any other combination of upper- and lowercase letters. If you wish,
you can make the assembler and link editor case-sensitive, so that the
above are three different symbols, by setting special switches when
you assemble and link edit the program. You'll see how to do that later
in this book.

Many names are reserved for system use and cannot be specified as user-defined symbols. These include the register names (such as AX and ESP), the instruction and directive mnemonics (such as **mov** and **fld**), the expression operators (such as **dup** and **offset**), and words which have predefined meanings for particular instructions and directives (such as **public** and **far**). Since different assemblers have different directives, which contribute many words to the reserved word list, you'll have to look in your assembler reference manual to see the complete list of reserved words for your system. You can use variations on reserved words with no problems. For example, you can't define a variable named **far**, but you can define ones named **far1, afar, @far, _far,** and **far?.** Case sensitivity does not apply to the reserved words. That is, even when the assembler and link editor have been instructed to recognize the difference between upper- and lowercase letters, you still cannot define **mov, Mov,** or **MOV** as a symbol.

Values

Many directives and instructions allow values to be included in them. For example, when you define a data field, you can give it an initial value, as in this definition:

```
return_code dw      0
```

You might also include a value in an instruction as an immediate operand, as in this instruction:

```
mov     cx,5
```

Values can be coded as constants or expressions. A constant states the desired value directly, as in the preceding two examples. An expression lets the assembler determine the value. Some expressions you have seen in previous chapters are italicized in these examples:

```
msg_len     dw      $ - msg
            push    offset add_proc
            push    length what_msg
```

Constants

The way you express a constant depends on the data type: integer, real, BCD, or ASCII string. Each type is discussed in the following sections.

Integers. An integer is expressed as a string of digits with an optional sign and an optional radix specifier. The radix specifiers are B for binary, D for decimal, O or Q for octal, and H for hexadecimal. Usually the default radix is decimal, so you don't need the D. The following directives define integers:

```
return_code dw      0

x_factor    dq      -7

mask        db      11111110b

table_length dd     75000

jump_code   dw      0A48h

strength    dd      -45ABh
```

The following instructions use integer immediate values:

```
            mov     ah,4Ch

            add     esi,2

            and     ax,0000011000000110b

            mul     ax,-8
```

Hexadecimal constants must start with a digit to differentiate them from names. If a hexadecimal value starts with a letter, insert a leading zero.

Changing the Default Radix. You can change the default radix with the **.radix** directive, which has this format:

```
.radix value
```

The value must be a number between 2 and 16 indicating the base of the number system to be used as default. Thus, if you want constants without radix specifiers to be interpreted as hexadecimal rather than decimal, code this directive:

```
.radix 16
```

The value of the radix directive is always interpreted as a decimal number, no matter what the current default radix is. If you change the radix to any system other than decimal, then you must use the D specifier to define decimal numbers. The following routine changes the radix to hexadecimal, then defines both a hexadecimal and a decimal value:

```
.radix 16

decimal_num dw      300d
```

```
hex_num     dw      0FFFF
```

The radix specifier is required for **decimal_num** because the default is now hexadecimal. No radix specifier is required for **hex_num** for the same reason. However, if **hex_num**'s value ended in D, then you would need to add the H specifier so the D wouldn't look like a decimal radix specifier.

Notice that the **.radix** directive lets you create values in number systems other than the standard four. Suppose you needed to create some duodecimal values. There is no radix specifier for duodecimal, but you could make it the default temporarily with this set of directives:

```
            .radix 12
ddnum1      dd      0325A0
ddnum2      dd      1000
ddnum3      dd      100B
            .radix 10
```

The three duodecimal numbers would be translated into their correct binary equivalents by the assembler. You would see the hexadecimal equivalent on the assembler listing. The **.radix 10** directive at the end restores the normal decimal default so that subsequent integers and immediate values will be interpreted correctly.

The default radix affects integers and immediate values. It does not affect the definition of real values, which are assumed to be decimal, or tenbytes, which are assumed to be packed BCD when an integer without a radix specifier is coded.

Real Numbers. Real numbers are expressed in decimal or hexadecimal. The most common method is decimal, which takes this form:

[±]digits.[digits][E[±]digits]

That is, there must be at least one digit and a decimal point, as in these examples:

```
p1          dd      1.
nonentity   dq      0.
transfer    dd      345.
```

You can include a sign and fractional digits if appropriate, as in these examples:

```
tax_rate    dd    0.075

minrate     dq    -225.0003
```

You can also include an exponent to indicate the desired position of the decimal point. The exponent may be signed if appropriate:

```
fudge_factor  dd  0.475E-3

maxrate     dq    4.222E5
```

For the most part, the above system will let you code real values in the easiest and clearest possible manner. However, if you want to specify a real value that can't be expressed in decimal form, then you can code the exact pattern of bits in *encoded real* format, which involves a hexadecimal value followed by an R specifier. You must specify every bit in the value when using encoded real constants. Therefore, doublewords must be expressed in exactly 8 hexadecimal digits, quadwords in exactly 16 hexadecimal digits, and tenbytes in exactly 20 hexadecimal digits. If the leading digit is a letter, then you must prefix a 0, giving a total of 9, 17, or 21 digits.

The bit pattern expressed in hexadecimal will be loaded directly into memory without any conversion or interpretation, so you have to figure out the correct sign bit, biased exponent, and significand for the value you want. For example, to define a quadword with the initial value of negative infinity, you could use this directive:

```
neg_infinity        dq          0FFF0000000000000r
```

This value sets the sign bit to 1, the 11 exponent bits to 1s, and the 52 significand bits to 0. You can create any of the coprocessor special values this way.

Binary Coded Decimal. To code a packed BCD value for a tenbyte, all you have to do is specify an integer with no radix specifier. BCD is the default data type for tenbytes, regardless of the current default radix. The maximum number of digits is 18. The following instruction creates a packed BCD tenbyte containing 1,234,567,890:

```
audience    dt    1234567890
```

To code a BCD value for any other size field, you must code it in hexadecimal because there is no radix specifier for BCD. The following instruction stores the maximum packed BCD value in a doubleword:

```
audience    dd    99999999h
```

When you define an unpacked BCD number, you must specify a 0 as the upper nibble of each byte. The following instruction stores the maximum unpacked BCD value in a doubleword:

```
max-val      dd    09090909h
```

ASCII Strings. You can specify any printable ASCII character by placing the value in single or double quotes. The assembler will provide the correct numeric code. These instructions all create fields initialized with ASCII values:

```
low_letter  db    "a"

high_letter db    'z'

radix_point db    "."
```

You cannot mix the two types of quotes in one string; the closing quote must match the opening quote. Any characters inside quotes are case sensitive; "A" yields a different code than "a." Nonprintable characters can be specified by any integer that yields the correct numeric code. Hexadecimal is the most common, as in these examples:

```
cr          db    0Dh              ; carriage return

lf          db    0Ah              ; line feed
```

You can string values together in one definition by connecting them with commas, as in these examples:

```
new_line    db    0Dh,0Ah

message_end db    ".",0Dh,0Ah,"$"
```

Be sure to use the commas to indicate that you are defining separate string bytes. The following definition would cause an assembler error because it defines a two-byte value for a one-byte field:

```
new_line    db    0D0Ah
```

Printable strings do not need to be separated by commas. In fact, you can place them inside one pair of quotes:

```
id_msg      db    "User ID: "
```

If you need to include a quotation mark in the string, use the other type of quotes to enclose it:

```
help_msg    db    "Help! I'm being held prisoner"

yn_message  db    'Please enter "Y" or "N"'
```

Alternatively, you can use the same type of quote in both places but double the internal quote:

```
help_msg    db      'Help! I''m being held prisoner'
yn_msg      db      "Please enter ""Y"" or ""N"""
```

You can combine quoted strings with separate ASCII characters in one operand, using commas to connect the parts:

```
hello_msg   db      'Hello',0Dh,0Ah,'$'
```

Some people confuse ASCII numbers with binary integers. The value '1' has a different internal representation than the value 1. ASCII numbers are stored internally as 30h through 39h. Thus, '1' is stored internally as 31h. This is a character that can be displayed on a monitor and printed. The value 1 is stored internally as 01h, which can neither be displayed nor printed. Therefore, in defining ASCII numbers, be sure to use quotes. The following directive defines a 5-byte field containing the ASCII number 12345:

```
code        db      '12345'
```

Comparing the Data Types. Let's look at directives to store the value 555 in each of the data types. We'll use doublewords except for the ASCII value and the BCD tenbyte.

```
int_value   dd      555         ; doubleword integer
real_value  dd      555.        ; real doubleword
BCD_value   dd      050505      ; unpacked BCD dword
packed_value dt     555         ; packed BCD tenbyte
ASCII_value db      "555"       ; ASCII string
```

Expressions

An expression combines one or more operands with expression operators. In this context, an "operand" is an entity that is operated on to find the value of the expression, as differentiated from an operand of an instruction or directive. The following directive has an expression for an operand; the expression has $ and **what_msg** as its operands and a minus sign as the operator:

```
what_msg_len dw     $ - what_msg
```

Types of Expression Operands. An expression operand can be a constant, the name of a data field or label, or one of several reserved words. The expression in the following directive has a data name and a constant as operands:

```
new_loc    dw    old_loc + 2
```

Symbolic names such as **old_loc** have address offset values. There-fore, the value placed in **new_loc** is the address offset of **old_loc** plus two bytes.

Expression Operators. Figure 8-1 lists all the various expression oper-ators, which fall into four major classes: arithmetic, bitwise, relational, and special.

The arithmetic operators perform an arithmetic operation on one or two operands. Unary + basically has no effect. Unary − reverses the operand's sign. The four standard arithmetic signs have standard

Operator	Format	Meaning
arithmetic operators		
unary +	+*op*	Plus sign
unary -	-*op*	Minus sign
+	*op* + *op*	Adds two operands
-	*op* - *op*	Subtracts two operands
*	*op* * *op*	Multiplies two operands
/	*op* / *op*	Divides two operands
mod	*op* mod *op*	Divides two operands and returns remainder
bitwise operators		
not	not *op*	Complements each bit
and	*op* and *op*	Ands two operands
or	*op* or *op*	Ors two operands
xor	*op* xor *op*	Xors two operands
shl	*op* shl *count*	Shifts operand left *count* times
shr	*op* shr *count*	Shifts operand right *count* times
low	low *exp*	Returns low-order byte from value of *expression*
high	high *exp*	Returns high-order byte from value of *expression*
loww	loww *exp*	Returns low-order word from value of *expression*
highw	highw *exp*	Returns high-order word from value of *expression*
relational operators		
eq	*exp* eq *exp*	Returns true if expressions are equal
ne	*exp* ne *exp*	Returns true if expressions are not equal
lt	*exp* lt *exp*	Returns true if first < second
le	*exp* le *exp*	Returns true if first < or = second
gt	*exp* gt *exp*	Returns true if first > second
ge	*exp* ge *exp*	Return true if first > or = second

Figure 8-1   Expression Operators (part 1 of 2)

special operators

length	length *var*	Returns the number of elements in variable
size	size *var*	Returns the size in bytes of the variable
width	width *recname*	Returns the number of bits in the record definition or the record field
mask	mask *recname*	Returns a mask for the defined bits in the record or the field
type	type *symbol*	Returns the data type of the symbol
seg	seg *symbol*	Returns the segment selector of the symbol
offset	offset *symbol*	Returns the offset of the symbol
this	this *type*	Returns the current instruction's offset
ptr	*type* ptr *exp*	Assigns the type to the expression
short	short *label*	Tells the assembler to use a short jump
.type	.type *exp*	Returns a value indicating the characteristics of the expression
:	*seg:offset*	Directly specifies the segment selector for the operand
[]	[*register*]	Indicates register should be used as indirect address (also used to indicate an element to be added to form the effective address)
.	*name.name*	Concatenates structure name with field name

Figure 8-1   Expression Operators (part 2 of 2)

meanings. **Mod** finds the remainder of a division problem. The expression **20 mod 6** evaluates to 2.

The bitwise operators perform bit manipulation on the operand(s), just like the bit manipulation instructions. **Not** complements each bit in the operand. **Not 00001111b** evaluates to 11110000b. **And, or,** and **xor,** performs the indicated operation on the two operands to derive the desired value. **Shl** and **shr** shift the first operand left or right by the number of bits specified by the second operand. **Low** and **high** extract byte 0 and byte 1, respectively, from the operand. If the field being defined is larger than a byte, the value is filled in with leading zeros. **Loww** and **highw** extract word 0 and word 1 of the operand. If the field being defined is larger than a word, the value is filled in with leading zeros.

The relational operators compare two operands and yield a result of true (all 0's) or false (all 1's). The expression **2 gt 3** applied to a word would evaluate to 0FFFFh.

The **length** operator returns the number of elements defined for a variable, which is not necessarily the number of bytes in the field. For example:

```
scores        dw      100 dup (?)
```

```
array_size dw      length scores
```

The value of **array_size** evaluates to 100, since there are 100 words in **scores**.

The **size**, **width**, and **mask** operators pertain to structures and records, which are covered later in this chapter.

The **type** operator returns a number indicating the data type of the operand, which must be a symbolic name. The value returned represents the size in bytes of the operand. You might use this function in macros or procedures where you are not sure what type of parameter was passed from the calling routine. Suppose you wanted **array_size** in the above example to reflect the number of bytes in **scores**. You could use this directive:

```
array_size dw      length scores * type scores
```

This compound expression means to multiply the length of **scores** by the type of **scores**. The length is 100, because there are 100 elements in **scores**. The type is 2 because **scores** is defined with the **dw** directive. Therefore, the expression evaluates to 200, which is the correct number of bytes in **scores**.

The **seg** operator returns the 16-bit segment selector value of the operand, and the **offset** operator returns the address offset value, which is either 16 bits or 32 bits, depending on the processor and the mode. In both cases, the operand must be a data name or a label. For real mode, the segment selector value is the beginning address of the segment rotated four bits to the right (real-mode segments always begin on paragraph boundaries, so the right four bits are always 0). To find the true segment address, rotate the segment selector four bits to the left, producing a 20-bit address. That is, if the segment selector is 4545h, the segment begins at address 45450.

The **this** operator makes the current address offset into an operand of the type specified. The following instruction moves its own offset into EAX:

```
        mov    eax,this dword
```

The **ptr** operator assigns a data type to an expression. Use **byte**, **word**, **dword**, **pword** (six bytes), **qword**, **tbyte**, **near**, **far**, or **proc**. The following expression can be used to tell the assembler the correct size of a forward reference:

```
        jmp    far ptr sum_proc
```

It can also be used to override the defined data type of an operand, as in this example:

```
good_string db     "Good"
```

```
    . . .
    mov    eax,dword ptr good_string
```

Without the **ptr** operator, the assembler would treat **good_string** as a byte-sized operand, and the **mov** instruction would fail because you can't move a byte to a doubleword. It should be noted, however, that treating **good_string** as a doubleword means that the processor will reverse its bytes when loading it into EAX, producing the value "dooG."

You can also use the **ptr** operator to define the size of an operation when the operands don't make it clear. For example, the number of bytes to be pushed in the following instruction is unclear:

```
    push   [ax]
```

[Ax] identifies the memory address of the value to be pushed, but not its size. The instruction should read:

```
    push word ptr [ax]
```

or

```
    push dword ptr [ax]
```

The **short** operator compensates for the fact that there is no short data type for the **ptr** operator. Therefore, there is no way to warn the assembler of a short jump using **ptr**. The **short** operator fills in the gap. To warn the assembler of a short jump, use an expression like this:

```
    jmp    short no_records
```

The assembler assumes near jumps for forward references on the first pass. If a jump turns out to be short, the assembler must fill in the extra byte of the **jmp** instruction with a **nop** instruction. To save space, inform the assembler of short forward jumps (within 127 bytes) with the **short** operator.

The **.type** operator tells you whether the operand is a label or a variable name, and whether it contains any undefined or external operands. To do this, **.type** returns a value in which only the following bits are important:

- Bit 0 is set only if the operand is a label.

- Bit 1 is set only if the operand is a variable.

- Bit 5 is set if the expression contains no undefined symbols. If it contains one or more undefined symbols, then all the bits in the value are set to 0.

- Bit 7 is set if the expression contains an external symbol.

All other bits in the value are undefined.

The expression operators also include three punctuation marks. You already know how to use the segment override operator (:) to override the segment of an operand, as in **ax:dx**. And you know how to use the indirection operator ([ ]) to specify a register as an indirect address or to cause two address elements to be added together, as in **[bp][si]**. The structure field operator (.) pertains to structures and is discussed later in this chapter.

Equates

An equate is a symbol for a value. You can define equates for five different types of values: integer constants, aliases for reserved words, character strings, labels, and variables. You've already seen many examples of symbols equated to integer constants, as in these directives:

```
return_code equ    0
std_handle  equ    1
```

Symbols for integer constants simply help make the program easier to read and understand. They can be used anywhere in the program that an integer is appropriate. The assembler substitutes the integer for the symbol when assembling the statement.

An alias for a reserved word lets you assign a more meaningful name in the context of a program or a procedure. For example, the following routine assigns the name **loop_counter** to CX, then uses the alias to make the purpose of the routine clearer:

```
loop_counter equ   CX

             mov    loop_counter,10
```

The symbol **loop_counter** can be used anywhere in the module that CX is appropriate.

You can also establish a symbol to represent any string of characters, as in this example:

```
clearax      equ    sub ax,ax
             ...
```

```
clearax
```

This routine establishes the symbol **clearax** as meaning "sub ax,ax." When the assembler encounters the second instruction, it substitutes **sub ax,ax** for **clearax**. Thus, **clearax** has become a macro that sets AX to zero. Only very simple macros can be created this way, because the character string is limited to one line.

You can also equate symbols to address offsets. If the symbol has a data type associated with it, then it is a variable symbol. If it has a type of **near** or **far**, then it is a label symbol. For example, suppose you need to address separately the first word of a doubleword. These instructions will accomplish it:

```
incidence    dd      ?
remains      equ     word ptr incidence+2
             . . .
             mov     ax,remains
```

Incidence is defined as a doubleword, and **remains** is defined as a single word starting at the third byte of **incidence**. **Remains** has no storage space itself; it is simply a symbol with an address value and a word size. Since the bytes in **incidence** would be stored in reversed order, the first word of its value is stored at **incidence+2** and **incidence+3**. That's why we define **remains** to start at **incidence+2** to access the first word of the value. The reference to **remains**, therefore, accesses one word—the first word of **incidence**.

The Difference between Equ and =

Both **equ** and **=** equate a symbol to a value, as described in the preceding paragraphs. For example, you could define **return_code** and **std_handle** this way:

```
return_code =      0
std_handle  =      1
```

However, **=** cannot be used to create aliases or character strings. The symbol defined by **equ** must be unique within the program. Once defined, it cannot be redefined. The symbol defined by **=**, on the other hand, can be redefined as often as necessary within the program. You might, for example, want to equate **back_step** with **ending – 2** for one procedure, with **[esp] + 4** for another procedure, and with **this – 16** for a third procedure. The current definition of a symbol defined by **=** pertains to all lines that follow it in the source file until it is redefined by another **=** directive.

Variables

A variable is a user-defined symbol that has an address and a data type. Data values may be stored at the address. The directive that creates the variable may assign an initial value to the address. Later instructions may overlay that value with other values.

Defining Variables

Variables are defined with data declarations, which are listed in Figure 8-2. You have already seen most of the data declarations: **db, dw, dd, dq,** and **dt.** The **df** declaration creates a 48-bit field, the correct size to hold a full pointer when 32-bit addressing is in use. **Dp** is a synonym for **df.**

The general format for a data declaration is:

[*name*]   opcode *value,...*

The *name* is optional; if present, it becomes the variable symbol. The value stored at that address can be referenced by *name*, which must be unique within the module.

At least one *value* must be coded. A question mark (?) for *value* leaves the value undefined. If more than one value is coded, a storage element is created for each specified value. You have already seen how this works for ASCII strings:

```
command_prompt      db              0Dh, 0Ah, ' - '
```

This creates three bytes; the first is initialized with 0Dh, the second is initialized with 0Ah, and the third is initialized with '–'. The symbol **command_prompt** has the address of the first byte and the type of byte. Its length is 3, and its size is 3. You can also create multiple elements of other types using the same format. The following directive creates four words:

db	Define byte
dw	Define word
dd	Define doubleword
df	Define full pointer
dp	Define full pointer
dq	Define quadword
dt	Define tenbyte

Figure 8-2   Data Declaration Directives

```
constants   dw      0,1,2,3
```

The first word is initialized with 0, the second with 1, and so forth. The symbol **constants** has the address of the first byte of the first word. Its length is 4, and its size is 8.

When words, doublewords, and quadwords are created in memory, the bytes in their values are reversed. But the bytes are not reversed among neighboring elements. The **constants** definition above creates four elements. The bytes are reversed within each element, but not from element to element. That is, the second element is stored as 1000h, the third element as 2000h, and the fourth as 3000h. If you move **constants+2** to AX, the value in AX would be 1.

The Dup Operator

Another way to specify multiple elements for a field, when all the elements have the same initial value, is to use the **dup** operator. **Dup** must be followed by parentheses containing at least one value. If more than one value is specified, the entire series of values is repeated the indicated number of times. The following directive creates 20 bytes; the first, third, fifth, etc. bytes contain 0.0, and the second, fourth, sixth, etc. bytes contain 1.0:

```
initial_array       dd              10 dup (0.0,1.0)
```

You can nest **dup** operators inside the parentheses, up to 17 levels. Thus, you could define a three-dimensional table this way:

```
week-table  dw      7 dup (5 dup (10 dup (?)))
```

The total number of elements defined in this example is 350 words. (Usually, the data declaration operand spacing is optional.)

Data Structures

Both the MASM and the Phar Lap assemblers let you create and use *structures* in your source program. A structure is a set of data declarations that is used several times in the program. For example, suppose you are writing an electronic mail system. The data for one user looks like this:

```
user_id     db      5 dup (?)
user_name   db      30 dup (?)
terminal    db      3 dup (?)
```

Throughout the program, you must use this data structure several times: the sender and receiver of a letter, the master user, a table of all users currently logged on, and a table of all the users registered with the system. Do you really need to code the three data declarations over and over again in the data segment, devising unique data names every time? The answer is no. You can define it once and refer back to that one definition every time you need another occurrence of the data structure in memory.

The original definition, called a *structure definition*, looks like this:

```
user        struc
id          db      5 dup (?)
name        db      30 dup (?)
terminal    db      3 dup (?)
            ends
```

Each time you want to use the structure in memory, you code a *structure declaration* instead of a data declaration. The structure declarations for the transaction sender and receiver might look like this:

```
sender      user    <>
receiver    user    <>
```

When the assembler sees **user** as a pseudo-op, it copies the **user** structure definition. (The angle brackets are discussed shortly.) You can refer to the individual fields in the **sender** structure as **sender.id**, **sender.name**, and **sender.terminal**. The **receiver** field names are **receiver.id**, **receiver.name**, and **receiver.terminal**.

Structure Definitions

You define a structure with **struc** and **ends** directives. All the data declarations contained between the two lay out the format of the structure. Suppose you are writing a program to handle cells in a data base. Each cell entry contains a row, a column, a value, a formula, a format, and a notation. The default row is 1 and the default column is A. The default value is 0. There is no default formula, format, or notation. The structure can be defined this way:

```
cell        struc
row         db      1
column      db      "A"
value       dd      0
formula     db      100 dup (?)
format      db      20 dup (?)
```

```
notation    db      500 dup (?)
cell        ends
```

This definition does not allocate or initialize any storage. It simply sets up the layout of the structure. It must precede any declarations of the structure.

Structure Declarations

To create an instance of a structure in memory, you use the structure name as if it were an opcode of a data declaration. The format of the structure declaration is:

> [name] structure-name <[value,...]>

The *name*, if specified, becomes the name of this instance of the structure. The angle brackets (<>) must be coded even if they are empty. If you place values inside the brackets, they supply values for the fields in the structure, overlaying the default values if appropriate. The first *value* specified pertains to the first field in the structure, the second *value* to the second field, and so on. To skip a field, code its comma without a value and the default value will be used.

The following declaration allocates storage for one instance of the **cell** structure defined above:

```
first       cell    <>
```

In this case, all the default values are accepted. The following declaration creates another instance of the cell structure:

```
last        cell    <,"Z",-1>
```

This declaration overrides the default values for **column** and **value**. The initial comma in the operand indicates that the value for **row** should not be overridden.

You cannot include string values in a structure declaration. The values for **row, column,** and **value** can be overridden because they are not strings, but the values for **formula, format,** and **notation** can't be supplied in the **cell** declaration. To assign values to those string fields, you must move values to **last.formula, last.format,** and **last.notation** via the procedure that works with the cell.

Declaring Multiple Structure Occurrences

You can use the **dup** operator to declare multiple instances of a structure, as in this declaration:

```
row1        cell    500 dup
```

This creates 500 instances of the **cell** structure, each with the default values.

Referencing Fields in Structures

Once you have declared instances of a structure, you can reference the fields just like any data fields in memory. For names, concatenate the name of the instance, which appears on the declaration, with the name of the field as defined in the structure. Use the structure field operator (.) to concatenate the names. For example, to refer to **row** in the **first** structure, you would use the name **first.row**. To refer to **notation** in the **last** structure, use the name **last.notation**. The name of the instance itself, such as **first, last,** or **row1**, has an address offset value but has no data type. Therefore, you cannot use it as an operand without using the **ptr** operator to give it a type.

The **size** operator can apply to a structure name to return the size, in bytes, of the structure.

Records

A record is a byte, word, or doubleword ('386 only) that is broken into subfields. Like structures, records are defined first without allocating any storage, then specific occurrences of the record are declared. You can access fields in a record with the bit manipulation instructions you learned in Chapter 7.

Defining Records

You define a record with the **record** directive, which has this format:

name record *fname:width*[*=value*],...

The name of the record becomes the name you use to declare specific instances of it. *Fname* is the name of a field, *width* is its size in bits, and *value* is its default value, if any. Suppose you want to define a record for a date value containing the year (7 bits), the month (4 bits), and the day (5 bits). Figure 8-3 diagrams this field. The definition would be:

```
date        record year:7,month:4,day:5
```

When the assembler processes the definition, it decides what size field to assign to the record according to the total number of bits

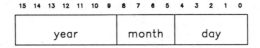

Figure 8-3   The Date Record

involved. In the **date** example above, a word would be selected because the total number of bits is 16. If the record is not a perfect fit, the assembler selects the next largest size. The record is rotated to the right in the field to take up the least significant bits, and it is padded with leading zeros. The following definition creates a 5-bit record:

```
file_flags     record  busy:1=0,rectype:2=2,deleted:1=0,archive:1=0
```

The assembler will place this record in a byte. The **archive** field will appear in bit 0, the **deleted** field in bit 1, and so forth. Bits 5–7 will always be 0.

The **file_flags** definition shows the use of default values. Each instance of the record will be initialized with these values unless they are overridden. Each value can be an expression that evaluates to a value of the correct size. Since you're dealing with bits, you might think that the values are automatically expressed in binary, but that is not the case. The default radix applies to these values. If you want to declare the values in binary, be sure to use the binary radix specifier unless binary is the default radix. The following definition would cause an assembler error:

```
file_flags     record  busy:1=0,rectype:2=10,deleted:1=0,archive:1=0
```

The error results from the value specified for **rectype**. Two bits cannot hold the decimal value 10. Since 10b was intended, the definition can be fixed two ways:

```
file_flags     record  busy:1=0,rectype:2=10b,deleted:1=0,archive:1=0
```

or

```
file_flags     record  busy:1=0,rectype:2=2,deleted:1=0,archive:1=0
```

Record Declarations

A record declaration creates a specific instance of a record, allocating memory space and initializing the fields if appropriate. The format of a record declaration is:

[name] record-name <[value,...]>

This format is almost identical to a structure declaration except that it references a record name. To define an instance of a **date** record, you could use this declaration:

```
today        date    <>
```

This creates a word in memory addressable as **today**, in which the **date** subfields can be accessed. The word has no initial value because neither the original definition nor this declaration assign any. To define an instance of the **file_flags** record, you could use this definition:

```
next_rec    file_flags   <>
```

This creates a byte in memory that you can access under the name **next_rec**. It will be initialized with the default values of the **file_flags** record. The following declaration overrides some of the default values:

```
update_rec  file_flags   <1,,,1>
```

The values in this declaration override the default values for the **busy** and **archive** fields.

Addressing Records and Fields

You can access any record instance by its name. To move **update_rec** into the accumulator, you would code:

```
        mov     al,update_rec
```

We chose AL because we know that **update_rec** is one byte long.

With MASM, you can also use a record declaration as an operand. The operand takes on the size of the defined record and its default values unless you override them. The following instruction moves a byte into AL with the value 00001000b, obtained from the definition of **file_flags**:

```
        mov     al,file_flags
```

The following instruction moves a byte with the value 00011111b into AL:

```
        mov     al,file_flags <1,3,1,1>
```

The individual field names cannot be used as the operands of instructions such as **mov**, **add**, and **push**. However, you can access the fields with the bit manipulation instructions. Suppose you need to set the **deleted** bit in **update_rec**. You could do it this way:

```
        or      update_rec,00000010b
```

The Mask Operator

What good does it do to create a record and assign names to subfields if you can't access the subfields in instructions? The answer lies in the **mask** operator, which creates a bit mask for a subfield. The bit mask has 0 bits for every field except the referenced subfield, which has all 1 bits. **Not mask** reverses the operation. Here are some examples of expressions and their results:

```
expression         result

mask year          1111111000000000b

mask month         0000000111100000b

not mask day       1111111111100000b

mask busy          00010000b

mask rectype       00001100b

not mask rectype   11110011b

mask deleted       00000010b

not mask archive   11111110b
```

You can use these expressions in bit instructions to turn bits on and off as needed. An alternative instruction to set the **deleted** bit would be:

```
or      update_rec,mask deleted
```

To clear the **rectype** field, you could use this instruction:

```
and     update_rec,not mask rectype
```

Suppose you don't want to completely set or clear a field, but to assign it a particular value. For example, suppose you want to set **month** in **today** to 8. You could either set each bit individually or clear all the bits and **or** the word with a mask that sets the desired value. Here is a routine that executes the second procedure:

```
and     today,not mask month          ; clears month

or      today,0000000100000000b       ; month = 12
```

The Width Operator

The **width** operator returns a width in bits of a record or field. For example, **width year** returns the value 7, **width file_flags** returns the value 8. **Width month** returns the value 4, while **width deleted** returns the value 1.

Labels

A label is a symbol with an address value and a data type of **near** or **far**. You've already seen how to define **near** labels with the colon (:) operator and both types of labels with the **label** directive.

Global Symbols

When a program has multiple modules, the symbols are available only to the modules where they are defined unless they are made global. To make a symbol global, include it in a **public** directive where it is defined. To access a global symbol from another segment, include it in an **extrn** directive.

Making Symbols Public

The **public** directive lists symbols in a module that should be made available to other modules in the same program. The following directive makes five symbols public:

```
public uid,pword,monitor,p_driver,handle
```

This directive appears only in the module that defines the symbol. Other modules declare the symbol in an **extrn** directive (explained in the next section), then use the symbol as if it were local. (If more than one module declares the symbol public, the link editor will consider it an error.)

A public symbol must be unique throughout the whole program, not just the module it appears in. In other words, no other module in the program could define **uid** or any of the other symbols listed in the above statement.

Using Global Symbols

The **extrn** directive tells the assembler that the module references symbols defined in other modules. The assembler bypasses references to those symbols, letting the link editor resolve them when it brings all the modules together into one program.

In the **extrn** directive, list each global symbol the module references. You have to indicate the type for each one so the assembler knows how much room to leave when the symbol is referenced as an operand. You've already seen how to declare **far** externals for the OS/2 API modules. You can also have **near** symbols (when linking a segment together from different modules), and various data types. For

example, the symbols declared public above might be referenced this
way:

```
extrn  uid:byte,pword:word,monitor:byte

extrn  p_driver:byte,handle:byte
```

You can also use structure names and record names as types.

To make large programs a little easier to code with the 386 | ASM
system, you can develop one **extrn** statement that applies to all the
modules in the program and copy that definition to each module in the
program. This means that, in some modules, a symbol will be declared
as both external and public. That's okay, as long as the **extrn** statement comes first, the **public** statement next, and then the definition
and references to the symbol. Any other order will cause an assembler
error.

If you code an **extrn** directive inside a segment, the assembler
assumes that the definitions for all the symbols in the directive will
appear inside that segment when the program is linked. Segment
prefixes and overrides for operands are generated accordingly. If the
extrn directive appears outside any segment, say as the first line of
the program, then the assembler assumes no segments, which might
mean you have to code more overrides yourself. You'll have to decide
for yourself, based on the needs of the program you're working on,
which approach is best. You can specify more than one **extrn** statement per module, so you can reference symbols only in the segments
they are used in, if you prefer.

Local Symbols

A local symbol is a symbol that pertains to the current procedure only.
It needs to be unique only within the procedure (as delimited by the
proc and **endp** directives). A local symbol name begins with #, as in
the following example:

```
edit_proc   proc    near

            cmp     quan,#low_value

            jna     short #too_low

            cmp     quan,#high_value

            jnb     short #too_high

            mov     quan_flag,0

            ret
```

```
#too_low:
            mov     quan_flag,1
            ret
#too_high:
            mov     quan_flag,2
            ret
#low_value dd       -1.5
#high_value dd      +9.9E7
edit_proc   endp
```

This short procedure makes sure that the value in **quan** (which is not local) is between –1.5 and 9.9E7. It sets **quan_flag** (also not local) to 0, 1, or 2 to indicate the result. The labels **#too_low** and **#too_high** are local labels. They can be referenced only from within the procedure and need to be unique only to this procedure. The same is true for the two variables: **#low_value** and **#high_value**.

You should use local symbols wherever possible in a procedure, especially if you are working on a programming team or using **include** to insert previously written procedures into your module. By using local symbols, you need not worry if your symbols are unique within the module.

Macros

If you have a set of definitions or a routine that you use several times in a module, you can make it into a macro. You code the macro once to define it, then you call it from other points in the program. The assembler replaces each macro call with the lines from the macro definition.

Suppose there are several points in your program where you zero all the general registers except SP. You could define a macro named **zregs** like this:

```
zregs     macro

          xor     ax,ax

          xor     bx,bx

          xor     cx,cx

          xor     dx,dx

          xor     si,si

          xor     di,di

          xor     bp,bp
```

```
                   endm
```

Every time you want to zero the registers, all you have to do is use **zregs** as a pseudo-op, like this:

```
                   zregs
```

The assembler replaces the pseudo-op with the seven **xor** instructions that comprise the **zregs** macro definition.

Defining a Macro

A macro definition is enclosed in **macro** and **endm** directives. All the statements between **macro** and **endm** are part of the macro. The following set of statements defines a macro to exchange two memory words:

```
xmem         macro

             push    mem1

             push    mem2

             pop     mem1

             pop     mem2

             endm
```

The **macro** directive identifies the beginning of the macro and gives it a name. In this case, the macro is named **xmem**. Once it is defined, a macro name can be used as an opcode in the remainder of the module. Anywhere you use **xmem** as an opcode, the assembler substitutes the four instructions that comprise the macro. You might use the same macro several times within the module.

A macro definition does not in itself generate any object code. It simply prepares the assembler for subsequent references to the macro. The macro definition is saved in memory for the remainder of the assembly job unless you specifically replace or purge it.

A macro name should be unique unless you are intentionally redefining a previously defined macro. Don't use any reserved words as macro names. Put the macro definition near the beginning of the program, before the first reference to it.

Using Macros

To use a macro, simply code the macro name as an opcode. For example, suppose you want to copy EAX to mem1, EDX to mem2, call a procedure to process them, then exchange them. You could code this routine:

```
mov    mem1,eax
mov    mem2,edx
call   mem_proc
xmem
```

The assembler expands this to:

```
mov    mem1,eax
mov    mem2,edx
call   mem_proc
push   mem1
push   mem2
pop    mem1
pop    mem2
```

Comments in Macros

You can include regular comments in a macro just as in other parts of the program. They are included in each expansion of the macro. If you want to include comments only in the definition that are not copied to the expansions, use two semicolons (;;) to start the comment.

You could document **xmem** this way:

```
xmem      macro  mem1,mem2
;; use to exchange two memory items
;; mem1 and mem2 can be words or doublewords
          push   mem1
          push   mem2
          pop    mem1           ;  mem2 value in mem1
          pop    mem2           ;  mem1 value in mem2
```

The assembler expands this as:

```
          push   mem1
          push   mem2
          pop    mem1           ;  mem2 value in mem1
          pop    mem2           ;  mem1 value in mem2
```

Using Parameters in Macros

The **xmem** example above has limited application because it always exchanges the same two memory fields: **mem1** and **mem2**. It can be made much more useful if the operands can be filled in by the assembler when the macro is expanded, letting it reference different operands each time. You can do this by specifying a list of macro parameters in the **macro** statement, using those parameters instead of actual operand references within the macro definition, then supplying the real arguments each time the macro is expanded. For example, to replace **mem1** and **mem2** with macro parameters, you could code the macro like this:

```
xmem        macro m1,m2

            push    m1

            push    m2

            pop     m1

            pop     m2

            endm
```

The operands on the **macro** statement inform the assembler that **m1** and **m2** are macro parameters. They are used just like actual operands within the macro definition, but whenever the macro is expanded, the assembler will replace them with the arguments supplied in the macro call.

Xmem can be referenced from a routine like this:

```
xmem    apples,oranges
```

The assembler substitutes **apples** for **m1** and **oranges** for **m2** when it expands the macro. The result looks like this:

```
push    apples

push    oranges

pop     apples

pop     oranges
```

At another point in the module, the following statement could appear:

```
xmem    blue,green
```

The expansion looks like this:

```
push    blue

push    green
```

```
pop    blue

pop    green
```

If a macro reference does not contain an argument for a macro parameter, the macro parameter is left blank. For example, suppose the module contained this statement:

```
xmem    gradeA
```

The expansion would look like this:

```
push    gradeA

push

pop    gradeA

pop
```

The **push** and **pop** instructions with missing parameters would cause an assembler error.

You can specify as many parameters as needed for a macro, with the restriction that they must all fit on one line, and their arguments must all fit on one line when you reference the macro.

A parameter doesn't need to be an operand. It can be an opcode, a label, even a comment. As you'll see in the next section, it can even be part of a word.

The Macro Operators

Four special operators can be used in conjunction with macro parameters, as listed in Figure 9-1.

Concatenation. The concatenation operator (&) lets you concatenate a macro parameter with other text. In the expansion, the & is removed, leaving the argument and the other text to form one word. For example, suppose you want to create a division macro to use either

```
operator    meaning
&           concatenation
!           literal character
<>          literal text
%           expression
```

Figure 9-1   The Macro Operators

DX:AX or EDX:EAX, whichever is more appropriate. You could define the macro this way:

```
divmem       macro  m1,m2,z
;; divides m1 by m2
;; places quotient in m1 and remainder in m2
;; m1 and m2 must be unsigned
        mov    z&ax,m1
        xor    z&dx,z&dx        ; clears z&dx
        div    m2
        mov    m1,z&ax
        mov    m2,z&dx
        endm
```

To use the macro with doubleword operands, you could code:

```
divmem tot,num,e
```

The assembler substitutes each occurrence of **z&** with **e**, producing this result:

```
        mov    eax,tot
        xor    edx,edx
        div    num
        mov    tot,eax
        mov    num,edx
```

If you want to use word operands, just leave out the third argument, which means that the parameter will be blanked out. The following statement would cause DX:AX to be used:

```
divmem tot,num
```

This would be expanded to:

```
        mov    ax,tot
        xor    dx,dx
        div    num
        mov    tot,ax
        mov    num,dx
```

If you tried to concatenate without using the & operator, the assembler would not find the macro parameter in the word. For example, if you defined **divmem** this way:

```
divmem      macro  m1,m2,z
            mov    zax,tot
            ...
```

The assembler would try to read **zax** as a variable name, causing an assembler error when the macro is expanded. It is the concatenation operator that makes it possible to substitute part of a word in a macro expansion.

The concatenation operator also makes it possible for the assembler to recognize a macro parameter inside a text string. Ordinarily, anything inside quotes is seen as ASCII text by the assembler and is not processed. Therefore, you must use the concatenation operator both before and after a parameter name to get the assembler to recognize a parameter inside quotes. Suppose you want to define this message as part of a macro:

```
Error nnnn: text
```

The *nnnn* and *text* should be replaced by a specific error number and message each time the macro is expanded. Here's the macro:

```
def_err      macro  num,tex
err_msg      db     'Error &num&: &tex&'
err_msg_len dw     $ - err_msg
             endm
```

To use the macro, you would specify both the error number and the text:

```
            def_err   0001,Diskerror
```

This would expand the macro to read as follows:

```
err_msg      db     'Error 0001: Diskerror'
err_msg_len dw     $ - err_msg
```

(The variable names in this macro would cause problems if the macro is expanded more than once in a module. We'll deal with that problem shortly.)

If you are concatenating two macro parameters, you need to use two operators, one for each parameter. For example, to concatenate **m1** and **m2**, you would code **m1&&m2**.

Literals. The literal character operator (!) makes it possible to use special characters as ordinary text in a macro without their being interpreted as macro operators or parameter separators. For example, the list of parameters on the macro line can be separated by commas, spaces, or tabs. Suppose you want to use the **def_err** macro defined above, but the message you want to display is "File not found." If you code this statement:

```
def_err   0002,File not found
```

The assembler will see four parameters: **0002, file, not,** and **found.** To force the assembler to treat the spaces as part of the text and not as separators, you must code:

```
def_err   0002,File! not! found
```

The literal text operator (<>) causes all the text within the angle brackets to be treated as literal text, so another way to solve the above problem would be to code the statement this way:

```
def_err   0002<File not found>
```

The left angle bracket (<) also acts as a parameter separator. That's why the comma was removed after 0002. Otherwise, the assembler would see two separators after 0002 and assume that the second argument was missing.

The literal text operator does not override !, %, or nested angle brackets. Thus you can continue to use ! even inside the angle brackets to force the assembler to treat % and nested angle brackets as text. (Nested angle brackets are handy when defining nested macros, which are discussed later in this chapter.) Suppose you want to define this message:

```
0003: An unmatched < was found
```

Here is the statement you could use:

```
def_err   0003<An unmatched !< was found>
```

Expressions. The expression operator (%) causes an expression to be evaluated and the result becomes the parameter. The result must be an integer constant.

Local Symbols

Symbol definitions can be a problem in macros if the same symbols get defined every time the macro is expanded. You've already seen an example of this in the **def_err** macro above. The first time **def_err** is expanded in a module, the symbols **err_msg** and **err_msg_len** will be defined. The next time the macro is expanded in the same module, those two symbols will be defined again, causing assembler errors. To circumvent such problems, you must use only local symbols in macros.

The macro local symbol definition is different from that of a procedure. In a macro, you declare the local symbols with the **local** directive. If we add the **local** directive to the **def_err** macro, it will look like this:

```
def_err     macro   num,tex
            local   err_msg,err_msg_len
err_msg     db      'Error &num&: &tex&'
err_msg_len dw      $ - err_msg
def_err     endm
```

When the assembler expands a macro, it replaces each occurrence of a local symbol with the generated name ??*nnnn*, where *nnnn* is a four-digit hexadecimal number. The first generated name is ??0000, the second is ??0001, and so forth up through ??FFFF. Thus, the first time the revised **def_err** macro is expanded, presuming it is the first macro expansion in the module containing local symbols, it would look like this:

```
??0000      db      'Error 0000: Diskerror'
??0001      dw      $ - ??0000
```

The next time it is expanded, presuming no other macros are expanded in the meantime containing local symbols, it would look like this:

```
??0002      db      'Error 0001: File not found'
??0003      dw      $ - ??0002
```

This method of generating names guarantees that all names defined within macros as local symbols will have unique names. It is essential that all variable names and labels defined within a macro be listed as local symbols unless you know for a fact that you are only going to expand the macro once in the entire module.

Repeat Blocks

A repeat block is a special form of macro that causes a set of statements to be repeated a specified number of times in a row. You define it with **rept** and **endm** directives instead of **macro** and **endm**. For example, suppose you need to define 100 pairs of fields, the first a doubleword and the second a word. This definition would be the easiest way to do it:

```
rept    100

dd      ?

dw      ?

endm
```

The **rept** directive tells the assembler to repeat the macro 100 times in a row. The **endm** directive marks the end of the macro. Everything in between is repeated the specified number of times. The operand of the **rept** directive can be an expression that returns an integer value. You can't use local names in a repeat block.

You also can't use macro parameters with the **rept** directive, but you can use them with a variation called **irp**. In **irp**, you specify a parameter name that is used within the repeat block, then specify a list of values for the parameter. The block is repeated once for each value in the list. For example, to create an array of ten words in memory containing the values 0, 1...9, you could code this definition:

```
irp     v,<0,1,2,3,4,5,6,7,8,9>

dw      v

endm
```

Notice that the values are enclosed in angle brackets and separated by commas. Also, a comma separates the parameter name from the values. A variation of **irp**, called **irpc**, uses each character in a string as the substitution value. This format is easier to code, but the values are limited to single characters:

```
irpc    v,0123456789

dw      v

endm    .
```

The two repeat blocks above have exactly the same effect. However, the following macro could be done only with **irp**:

```
irp     v,<'John','Judi','Joan','Angel','Sam'>

db      v

endm
```

This is expanded to:

```
db      'John'

db      'Judi'

db      'Joan'

db      'Angel'
```

```
db      'Sam'
```

The **zregs** macro at the beginning of this chapter could be coded this way:

```
zregs       macro
            irp     reg,<ax,bx,cx,dx,si,di,bp>
            xor     reg,reg
            endm
            endm
```

This defines a macro within a macro, which is perfectly acceptable. You'll see more about nested macros shortly. The **irp** block in this example generates seven **xor** instructions, one for each register in the parameter list.

You can use either regular comments or macro comments inside a repeat block.

Macro Libraries

Many macros are useful not just in one program but in a variety of contexts. The **xmem** macro defined earlier in this chapter, for example, might come in handy in many different programs. However, there is no way to make a macro definition global. It must be defined in every module that uses it. Macro libraries, used in conjunction with the **include** and **purge** directives, let you pull in macro definitions where you need them.

You can create a macro library with any text editor. Simply store one or more macro definitions in a file on disk. If you include more than one in the file, try to group related macros together. When you reference a macro library, all the macro definitions in that library are copied into your module; you don't want to fill your module with macro definitions you don't need.

The Include Directive

Suppose you have created four macros that you use frequently: **xmem** (to exchange two memory items), **mmem** (to move an item from one memory location to another, deleting it from the source field), **cmem** (to copy an item from one memory location to another), and **dmem** (to display a memory item on the monitor). You could use your favorite text editor to store all four definitions in one file called **mem.mac**, which you store on disk in your assembler program directory. To include the file in a module, use this directive:

```
include    mem.mac
```

This directive copies the file named **mem.mac** into the source program at the point of the **include** directive. Since **mem.mac** contains the four macro definitions, they are now copied into the module and can be referenced in subsequent directives.

The **include** directive can be used to include any text file in your source program; it doesn't have to be a macro file. For example, suppose you have a complicated data structure definition that you use in many programs. You could store it in a file called **empdata.ds** and copy it into new programs with this directive:

```
include    empdata.ds
```

You could copy blocks of definitions, code, or even comments this way.

The **include** directive assumes the default directory and path. If your library file is in another directory, specify the path with the name, as in:

```
include    d:\macros\empdata.ds
```

With some systems, you can also set up a default path for include libraries so that the assembler will search for them.

The Purge Directive

Every macro you define in a module, whether the definition is new with the module or included by the **include** directive, takes up space in memory. You can free up memory for other use by the assembler, possibly speeding up the assembly job, by purging unneeded macros from memory with the **purge** directive. For example, to purge the **def_err** macro after the last time you call it in the module, you could code:

```
purge  def_err
```

To include the **mem.mac** file but eliminate two macros that this module doesn't use, you could code:

```
include  mem.mac

purge  cmem,mmem
```

Nested Macros

A macro definition can call other macros. For example, suppose you have a macro to copy a string, defined like this:

```
cstring    macro m1,m2,l
```

```
;; m1 is the beginning address of the destination string
;; m2 is the beginning address of the source string
;; l is the length of each string
        push    cx
        push    si
        push    di
        lea     di,m1
        lea     si,m2
        mov     cx,l
        rep movs    m2,m1
        pop     di
        pop     si
        pop     cx
        endm
```

Now you want to write a macro to move the string; that is, after the string is copied, the source string is deleted by filling it with nulls (zeros). You could define the new macro this way:

```
mstring     macro   s1,s2,len
;; s1 is the beginning address of the destination string
;; s2 is the beginning address of the source string
;; len is the length of each string
        cstring  s1,s2,len       ;; calls cstring macro
        push    ax
        push    di
        push    cx
        xor     ax,ax           ; zero ax
        mov     di,s1
        mov     cx,len
        rep stos    s2
        pop     cx
        pop     di
        pop     ax
        endm
```

You can see the **mstring** macro calls **cstring**. **Cstring** requires three parameters, which it calls **m1, m2,** and **l**. The macro call to **cstring** provides values for those three parameters by passing on its own three parameters—**s1, s2,** and **len**.

Suppose you call **mstring** this way:

```
mstring    new_pword,old_pword,5
```

The instructions inserted into the program are as follows:

```
push   cx

push   si

push   di

lea    di,new_pword

lea    si,old_pword

mov    cx,5

rep movs    new_pword,old_pword

pop    di

pop    si

pop    cx

push   ax

push   di

push   cx

xor    ax,ax              ; zero ax

mov    di,new_pword

mov    cx,5

rep stos    old_pword

pop    cx

pop    di

pop    ax
```

Advantages and Disadvantages of Macros

As you have seen in this chapter, macros can save you from coding the same routine over and over again. But the macro expansion of mstring points out that macros can be inefficient compared to coding from scratch. The expansion of **mstring** includes more **push** and **pop** instructions than you would code for that same routine. They appear because both the outer macro and the inner macro must preserve and restore the registers they use. But if you were coding that same routine from scratch, you would not pop DI and CX in the middle of the routine, then push them again. So, you gain programmer time by using the macro, but you can lose program efficiency.

Macros and procedures accomplish much the same thing—they each let you repeat a block of code several times, altering it somewhat to suit the current situation. A macro is generally easier to code because it doesn't get involved with passing data via the stack. Also, a macro takes less overhead time to execute since it is expanded directly in the routine and doesn't involve **call** and **return** processing. On the other hand, a macro is copied into the program each time it is used, whereas a procedure appears only once and can be executed many times without taking up any extra space in the program. If a block is large and repeated many times, a procedure is the better choice. If it's small and repeated only a few times, then a macro would be better. If it's somewhere between those two extremes, then you'll have to decide which is the better choice.

Conditional Assembly and Errors

Most assemblers provide **if...else...endif** directives to decide whether a block of source code will be assembled. This facility is used almost exclusively within macro definitions to tailor the macros at the time they are expanded. For example, you could code an arithmetic macro to use either the CPU or the numeric coprocessor depending on which argument is passed to it when it is called. You will see an example of such a macro in this chapter.

You frequently want to terminate a macro, display an error message, and suppress the object module if a macro cannot be expanded properly because of invalid arguments. You will also learn how to do that in this chapter.

Conditional Assembly

The most basic form of conditional assembly involves a block of code that is assembled if a condition is true; otherwise, it is not assembled. The condition, of course, must be evaluated at assembly time, not run time.

For example, suppose you are creating a generalizable macro to add two memory operands. Three parameters are supplied. The first two identify the operands to be added. The third indicates whether or not the original value of AX should be preserved. If the parameter is a 1, AX should be preserved. If it is any other value, AX need not be preserved.

```
amem        macro  dest,source,pax
if pax eq 1
            push ax
endif
            mov    ax,source
            add    dest,ax
if pax eq 1
            pop ax
endif
            endm
```

The **if** statement determines whether or not the third parameter is 1. If so, then the **push ax** instruction is assembled. Otherwise, it is not assembled. In all cases, the **mov** and **add** instructions are assembled. Then the second **if** directive determines whether or not to pop AX again.

Suppose you write a program that calls this macro twice. The first time, you don't care to preserve AX. The second time, you do. You would code the macros like this:

```
            . . .
amem     profit,loss,0
            . .
amem     credit,return,1
            . . .
```

The assembler would expand the two macros like this:

```
            . . .
mov      ax,loss
add      profit,ax
            . . .
push     ax
```

```
        mov     ax,return
        add     credit,ax
        pop     ax
        ...
```

The first time, the assembler did not include the **push** and **pop** instructions in the expansion because the third argument did not equal 1. The second time, the third argument was 1 and the instructions were assembled.

Sometimes, you want to choose between two alternate routines depending on a condition. In that case, you code an **if...else...endif** structure. For example, suppose you are recoding the above macro to use either main processor arithmetic if the third argument is 0 or the numeric coprocessor if the third argument is 1. You could code the macro like this:

```
amem        macro   dest,source,p
if p eq 1
            fild    source
            fiadd   dest
            fistp   dest
            fwait
else
            mov     ax,source
            add     dest,ax
endif
            endm
```

Now let's look at two expansions of this macro. In the first one, this statement is coded:

```
        amem    profit,loss,0
```

Because the third argument is 0, the macro will be expanded like this:

```
        mov     ax,loss
        add     profit,ax
```

The second reference to **amem** looks like this:

```
        amem    credit,return,1
```

This will be expanded as follows:

```
fild    return
fiadd   credit
fistp   credit
fwait
```

Thus, the **if...else...endif** pattern sets up an alternate branch structure.

There are eight types of **if** directives, depending on what type of condition you need. Figure 10-1 shows all the types of **if** statements, along with **else** and **endif**.

Conditions Based on Expressions

Two **if** directives test the value of expressions: **if** and **ife**. The **if** condition is true if the expression evaluates to any value but 0, whereas **ife** is true if the expression evaluates to 0.

Format	Assemble the true block if:
if *expression*	Expression evaluates to anything but 0
ife *expression*	Expression evaluates to 0
ifdef *name*	Name is defined
ifndef *name*	Name is not defined
ifb <*string*>	String is blank
ifnb <*string*>	String is not blank
ifidn <*string*>,<*string*>	Two strings are identical
ifdif <*string*>,<*string*>	Two strings are different

Format	Function
else	Marks the end of true block and beginning of false block
endif	Marks the end of conditional block

Figure 10-1   Conditional Assembly Directives

```
Arithmetic operators      - +  * / mod
    All the arithmetic operators perform the indicated operation
    on two expressions to produce a numeric value

Bitwise operators       not and or xor shl shr low high loww highw
    All the bitwise operators perform a logical operation on one or
    two expressions to produce a numeric value

Relational operators        eq ne lt gt le ge
    All the relational operators yield a result of true or false.
    True evaluates to -1 and false evaluates to 0.

Length, size, width
    These operators all return a number indicating the number of
    bytes or bits in the variable

Type
    Type returns a number indicating the number of bytes in the
    variable. Thus, a byte type evaluates to 1 while a tbyte type
    evaluates to 10. Near evaluates to -1 and far evaluates to -2.

Seg and Offset
    These operators return address values.
```

Figure 10-2   Expression Operators

Some of the expression operators come in handy in creating conditions to test. Figure 10-2 lists the ones that are useful and shows how they produce numeric results that might or might not be 0.

Notice how the relational operators evaluate to 0 or −1. Let's look at how this condition evaluates:

```
if p eq 1
```

If **p** does equal 1, the expression is true and the result is −1. The **if** directive assembles the true branch if the expression evaluates to nonzero. Since −1 is not zero, the condition is true when the expression is true. When the expression is false, its value is 0 and the condition becomes false also.

The sample **amem** macro shown earlier that selects the main processor or the numeric coprocessor doesn't really need to code a relational condition. According to the design of the macro, the third argument is 0 for the numeric coprocessor or 1 for the main processor. All you need to code is:

```
amem      macro  dest,source,p

if p                            ; if p is not 0

          mov    ax,source
```

```
          add     dest,ax
else                                  ; if p is 0
          fild    source
          fiadd   dest
          fistp   dest
          fwait
endif
          endm
```

When the third argument is 1 (for the main processor), the condition is true and the main processor instructions are assembled. When the third argument is 0, the condition is false and the coprocessor instructions are assembled.

Conditions Based on Definitions

Two of the **if** directives shown in Figure 10-1 test whether or not a symbol has been defined. **Ifdef** assembles the true block if the symbol has been defined, while **ifndef** assembles the true block if it hasn't. These two definitions are used in conjunction with a switch on the assembler command line and are discussed in more detail in Chapter 12.

Conditions Based on Strings

Two **if** directives test whether or not a string is blank: **ifb** and **ifnb**. These two directives come in very handy for determining whether or not an argument has been supplied for a particular macro parameter.

Let's look at how you might use these directives. Suppose you are developing a macro to reverse from two to four fields in memory. When you expand the macro, you might supply two, three, or four arguments. Here's what the macro definition might look like:

```
rmem        macro m1,m2,m3,m4
;; You can supply 2 - 4 memory fields
;; They can be any size, but all must be the same size
            push    m1
            push    m2
ifnb <m3>   ; if m3 is not blank
            push    m3
```

```
        endif
        ifnb  <m4>    ; if m4 is not blank
                push m4
        endif
                pop     m1
                pop     m2
        ifnb  <m3>    ; if m3 is not blank
                pop     m3
        endif
        ifnb  <m4>    ; if m4 is not blank
                pop     m4
        endif
                endm
```

Let's look at the first **ifnb** directive. If no argument has been supplied for **m3**, recall that the assembler blanks out the parameter. Thus, the assembler sees this directive:

```
ifnb  <>
```

The string is blank, making the condition false, and so the true block is not assembled. The same holds true for the other **ifnb** directives in the macro. If the macro is invoked by this directive:

```
        rmem    mon,tues,wed
```

The resulting macro looks like this:

```
                push    mon
                push    tues
                push    wed
                pop     mon
                pop     tues
                pop     wed
```

You could recode the macro that adds two memory fields so that any third parameter causes the coprocessor to be used; if no third parameter is supplied, the main processor is used. Here's what the macro might look like:

```
amem            macro  source,dest,p
;; If you code anything at all as the third parameter
```

```
;; the numeric coprocessor will be used. If you leave
;; the third parameter blank, the main processor will
;; be used.
ifb <p>                          ;; If 3rd is blank
        mov     ax,source
        add     dest,ax
else
        fild    source
        fiadd   dest
        fistp   dest
        fwait
endif
        endm
```

Conditions Based on String Comparisons

The **ifidn** and **ifdif** directives make a decision based on whether or not two strings are identical. These directives are good for determining whether or not a macro argument has a particular value.

Both strings must be supplied, each must be enclosed in angle brackets, and they must be separated by commas. Let's revise the **amem** macro so that you enter either 'C' (for CPU) or 'N' (for numeric coprocessor) to select the arithmetic processor.

```
amem        macro dest,source,p
;; For the third operand, enter 'C' for the CPU
;; or 'N' for the numeric coprocessor.
ifidn <m3>,<C>
        mov     ax,source
        add     dest,ax
else
        fild    source
        fiadd   dest
        fistp   dest
        fwait
endif
```

```
        endm
```

Now let's look at what happens when you enter a 'C' as the third operand. The assembler sees this directive:

```
ifidn <C>,<C>
```

The two strings are identical, the condition is true, and the true block is assembled. Any other value would cause the condition to be false, and the false block would be assembled. Case counts in this context. If you enter a 'c' instead of a 'C,' the assembler sees **ifidn <C>,<c>**. The two values are not identical and the false block is assembled.

Exiting the Macro Early

Sometimes it is handy to be able to exit a macro before it finishes assembling. The **exitm** macro has been designed for that purpose. It has no operands. It simply terminates expansion of the macro. Suppose you want to make sure that at least two arguments have been supplied for the **rmem** macro defined above. You might use this definition:

```
rmem        macro  m1,m2,m3,m4
;; You can supply 2 - 4 memory fields
;; They can be any size, but all must be the same size
ifb <m1>
            ; WARNING! RMEM macro has not been expanded
            ; because no arguments were supplied.
            exitm
endif
ifb <m2>
            ; WARNING! RMEM macro has not been expanded
            ; because one argument is missing.
            exitm
endif
            push   m1
            push   m2
ifnb <3>    ; if m3 is not blank
            push   m3
```

```
        endif
        ifnb <4>    ; if m4 is not blank
                    push m4
        endif
                    pop     m1
                    pop     m2
        ifnb <3>    ; if m3 is not blank
                    pop     m3
        endif
        ifnb <4>    ; if m4 is not blank
                    pop     m4
        endif
                    endm
```

The new parts of the macro are the two **ifb** blocks following the initial comment. The comments they contain are regular comments, not macro comments. However, they will be carried over to the expansion only if their true blocks are being assembled. Thus, if no arguments are supplied, the entire macro expansion will look like this:

```
        ; WARNING! RMEM macro has not been expanded
        ; because no arguments were supplied.
```

If only one argument is supplied, the macro expands like this:

```
        ; WARNING! RMEM macro has not been expanded
        ; because one argument is missing.
```

If two or more arguments are supplied, the macro expands normally. (Are you curious about what happens if five or more arguments are supplied? The assembler ignores excess arguments.)

Forcing Assembly Errors

The preceding definition of **rmem** shows one way of handling possible error situations, but it would not prevent the remainder of the module from assembling. In a case where a macro could not be expanded, the validity of the entire program is threatened and an object module should not be produced. A set of error directives lets you force an assembler error, causing the assembler to delete the object module, and display a "forced error" message. Figure 10-3 shows all the error directives, including **.err**.

Forcing an Unconditional Error

The **.err** directive forces an error unconditionally. You'll usually enclose this in the true or false block of an **if** directive. You can also enclose an explanatory message with it and terminate macro expansion, if a macro is involved. For example, you might want to revise the two **ifb** blocks in the definition of **rmem** above to force an error. (We'll just show the **ifb** blocks; you've already seen the rest of the macro several times.)

```
ifb <m1>
            ; FATAL ERROR! RMEM macro has not been expanded
            ; because no arguments were supplied.
            .err
            exitm
endif
ifb <m2>
            ; WARNING! RMEM macro has not been expanded
            ; because one argument is missing.
            .err
            exitm
endif
```

Conditional Errors

A complete set of conditional error directives also exists, as you can see in Figure 10-3. The conditions here are the same as the ones for the **if** directives, so you shouldn't have any trouble figuring out how to use them.

Nested Conditions

You can nest conditional assembly directives. For example, recall the **amem** macro defined previously. You might want to make the **fwait** instruction optional in this macro. You can indicate whether **fwait** should be included each time you call the macro for expansion in your source program. If you want to suppress the **fwait** instruction, code a fourth argument (*any* fourth argument will do). If you want to include

.err	Force error unconditionally
.erre *expression*	Force error if *expression* evaluates to zero.
.errnz *expression*	Force error if *expression* evaluates to anything but zero.
.errdef *name*	Force error if *name* is defined.
.errndef *name*	Force error if *name* is not defined.
.errb *<string>*	Force error is *string* is blank.
.errnb *<string>*	Force error if *string* is not blank.
.erridn *<string1>,<string2>*	Force error if *string1* equals *string2*
.errdif *<string1>,<string2>*	Force error if *string1* differs from *string2*

Figure 10-3   Error Directives

fwait, omit the fourth argument. Here's how the revised macro might look:

```
amem          macro  dest,source,p,q
;; For the third operand, enter 'C' for the main processor
;; or 'N' for the numeric coprocessor.
;; Enter any fourth operand to suppress fwait.
ifidn <p>,<C>
              mov    ax,source
              add    dest,ax
else
              fild   source
              fiadd  dest
              fistp  dest
ifb <q>
              fwait
endif
endif
```

if1	Assemble block on pass 1 only
if2	Assemble block on pass 2 only

Figure 10-4   Pass Conditional Directives (MASM only)

```
endm
```

The **ifb** block is nested inside the false block of the **ifidn** routine. Therefore, it will be examined only if the false block is assembled. You can nest up to 255 levels of conditional directives. Be sure to provide an **endif** directive for each **if** directive. Each **endif** is paired with the most recent **if**.

MASM's Pass Conditionals

The MASM assembler provides pass-specific conditionals, as shown in Figure 10-4. You can use these conditionals to specify the assembler pass on which the condition should be examined. If you find that a statement is being assembled twice (as happens with some directives) or an error is being generated twice, then try using one of these conditionals. In the next chapter, you will see how to use these conditionals to display a message on the monitor during either pass 1 or pass 2.

Assembler Control Directives

Most assemblers include groups of directives that let you select from a variety of assembler features. You can indicate which CPU and co-processor, if any, to assemble the program for. You can control the contents and format of the assembler listing. You can adjust the location counter that keeps track of the current address offset. You can display your own messages on the monitor. And, most significantly, you can define the program and segment structure. This chapter shows you how to use assembler directives for all these functions.

Instruction Sets

Each assembler has a default instruction set. The MASM assembler uses the 8086 instruction set if no other set is specified. This means that instructions not in the 8086 set, such as numeric coprocessor instructions, most of the bit manipulation instructions, all the string instructions suffixed by **b**, **w**, and **d**, and many other instructions will be rejected by the assembler. The 386|ASM assembler uses the '386 instruction set. All instructions are available except the protected instructions.

If you are assembling a program for a processor other than the default, it is important to specify the correct instruction set. If the target processor is more sophisticated than the default processor, as is often the case with MASM, the instruction set directive enables the use of the more sophisticated instructions. If the target processor is less sophisticated than the default processor, as would often happen with 386|ASM, then you need to disable the advanced instructions, just in case you coded some in the program. (For 386|ASM, specifying an earlier processor also disables the default 32-bit addressing.)

Figure 11-1 shows the instruction set directives. Each CPU instruction set includes all the instructions in the previous sets, so you need specify only one directive to identify the CPU. If you want to include privileged instructions in your program, include either the **p** suffix on the processor directive or add a **.priv** (MASM) or **.prot** (386|ASM) directive after the CPU directive. (Don't put it first or the CPU direc-

.8086	Limits assembler to the 8086 instruction set.
.186	Enables 80186/80188 instruction set.
.286	Enables 80286 instruction set excluding privileged instructions.
.286c	Synonymous with .286.
.286p	Enables 80286 instruction set including privileged instructions.
.386	Enables 80386 instruction set excluding privileged instructions.
.386c	Synonymous with .386.
.386p	Enables 80386 instruction set including privileged instructions.
.priv or **.prot**	Enables privileged instructions for current instruction set. .Priv is used with MASM; .prot is used with 386|ASM.
.8087	Enables 8087 instruction set. (Fwait automatically generated.)
.287	Enables 80287 instruction set.
.387	Enables 80387 instruction set.

Figure 11-1   Instruction Set Directives

tive will override it.) This will allow the privileged instructions to be assembled. They still won't execute unless your program has the proper privilege level, which is assigned by the operating system.

If the program uses numeric coprocessor instructions, add the correct coprocessor instruction set directive. Because of the changes in the IEEE standard and enhancements to the processors, some instructions have been removed from the earlier numeric coprocessor instruction sets, other instructions have been added, and still others have changed their functions. Therefore, if you specify .287, some of the 8087 instructions will not assemble, while others might assemble differently. In particular, when you specify the .8087 directive, the assembler generates wait instructions before every coprocessor instruction. With the .287 and .387 directives, this doesn't happen.

The coprocessor instruction set directives do not affect the CPU instruction set, so you might also need to identify the CPU instruction set. For example, if the only instruction set directive you code in a module assembled by MASM is .287, the 8086/8088 instruction set will be assumed for the CPU instructions, but the '287 instruction set will be used for the coprocessor instructions.

To specify the instruction set, include the appropriate directives early in the program, before any instructions are assembled. It's particularly important to code the directive early in a 386 I ASM program, because the assembler assumes 32-bit addressing if you don't specify otherwise, and you can't change address size after the first instruction has been assembled. As a rule of thumb, include the instruction set directives with the beginning housekeeping directives on the first few lines of the module.

Listing Control

When requested, the assembler produces a listing showing the source program, the machine language translation, and perhaps other information. The listing can be used for debugging and eventually as part of the program documentation.

Figure 11-2 shows the first part of a MASM listing in its default format. The machine code is on the left in hexadecimal format. On the right is the source code. Some of the lines wrap around because the line length is only 60 characters. You can fix that with the **page** directive, explained shortly. If assembler errors are present, each error message appears directly underneath the line that caused it. The listing control directives shown in Figure 11-3 let you format the listing.

```
                              dosseg
                              .model  small
                              .286

03E8                          .stack 1000


0000                          .data
= 000D          cr            equ    0Dh         ; ASCII carriage
return
= 000A          lf            equ    0Ah         ; ASCII line feed

= 0001          std_device equ  1                ; monitor/keyboard
handle

0000  48 65 6C 70 21 20 49  help_msg     db      "Help! I'm being
held prisoner"
      27 6D 20 62 65 69 6E
      67 20 68 65 6C 64 20
      70 72 69 73 6F 6E 65
      72
001D  20 69 6E 20 79 6F 75               db      " in your microcom-
puter",cr,lf
      72 20 6D 69 63 72 6F
      63 6F 6D 70 75 74 65
      72 0D 0A


0035  0035          help_msg_len dw      $ - help_msg    ; length of
help_msg


0037  ????          bytes_out    dw      ?        ; needed by DosWrite


0000                              .code
                        extrn  DosWrite:far,DosExit:far
0000          begin:
0000  E8 000F R                  call   write_msg_proc
0003  E8 0006 R                  call   exit_proc

0006          exit_proc          proc   near
0006  6A 01                      push   1          ; to terminate
all threads
0008  6A 00                      push   0          ; return code
000A  9A 0000 ---- E             call   DosExit    ; terminates
program
```

Figure 11-2   Sample Assembler Listing in Default Format

title *text*   List a title at the top of each page.
subttl *text*   List a subtitle at the top of each page.

page [*length*][,*width*]
            Specify the length and width of a page.
page+   Advance section counter and force a page break.
page   Force a page break.

.list   List program statements.
.xlist   Don't list program statements.

.listi   List included statements.
.xlisti   Don't list included statements.

.lfcond   List false conditional blocks.
.sfcond   Suppress false conditional blocks.
.tfcond   Toggle false conditional blocks.

.lall   List complete macros.
.sall   Suppress macro expansion listings.
.xall   List only macro expansion lines that result in
                object code.

Figure 11-3   Listing Control Directives

Titles

The **title** and **subttl** directives assign a title and subtitle to the listing. The title labels the entire listing while the subtitle identifies sections within the listing. For example, for the listing shown in Figure 11-2, you might want to use the title "Help Program." The first subtitle might be "Program Code." Figure 11-4 shows the outcome. You can see the new directives on lines 1 and 2 of the source program. The title is printed at the top of the first page. Both the title and the subtitle are printed at the top of all subsequent pages.

Once a title is established, it cannot be changed. Only one **title** directive is permitted per module, but the subtitle can be changed as often as needed. Each **subttl** directive affects the subtitle at the top of the next page (which is why no subtitle appears on page 1).

```
Microsoft (R) Macro Assembler      3/29/89 13:58:33
Help Program                                        Page    1-1


                        title   Help Program
                        subttl  Program Code

                        dosseg
                        .model  small
                        .286


 0035  0035          help_msg_len dw    $ - help_msg      ; length of
help_msg
```

```
Microsoft (R) Macro Assembler      3/29/89 13:58:33
Help Program                                        Page    1-2
Program Code

 0000                        .code
                             extrn     DosWrite:far,DosExit:far
 0000              begin:
 0000  E8 000F R             call      write_msg_proc
 0003  E8 0006 R             call      exit_proc
```

Figure 11-4   Listing with Title and Subtitle

The first six characters of the program's title make up the program's name unless you specify another name with the **name** directive discussed later in this chapter.

Paging

There are several ways to control paging in the listing, all under the control of the **page** directives. If you specify a *length* and/or a *width*, the print area is adjusted accordingly. *Length* is specified in lines per page and must be between 10 and 255. *Width* is specified in characters per line and must be between 60 and 132. Figure 11-5 shows the **help** listing formatted at 132 characters per line. You can see the lines that were wrapped in Figure 11-2 now fit all on one line. (The line that defines **cr** is an example.) Placing 132 characters per line doesn't mean that your printer can print such long lines. If your printer can handle a maximum of 80 characters, then lines will be wrapped by your printer

```
Microsoft (R) Macro Assembler    3/29/89 11:49:14
Help Program                                    Page     1-1

                          page    ,132
                          title   Help Program
                          subttl  Program Code

                          dosseg
                          .model  small
                          .286

03E8                      .stack  1000

0000                      .data
= 000D          cr        equ     0Dh          ; ASCII carriage return
= 000A          lf        equ     0Ah          ; ASCII line feed


= 0001          std_device equ    1            ; monitor/kybd handle
```

Figure 11-5   Listing with 132 Characters per Line

when they exceed 80 characters. If you really want to print 132 characters per line, you might need to set your printer up for that line length
also. How you do that depends on your printer. It might involve changing to a wider paper, setting an external switch, and/or entering the
MODE command.

So to print 132-character lines, you have to do two things: tell the
assembler to issue 132-character lines and tell the printer to print
132-character lines.

The **page+** directive affects the page number starting with the next
page. Notice in Figure 11-5 that the page number has two parts, a
section number and a serial number. The **page+** directive increments
the section number, setting the serial number back to 1. It also forces a
page break. If **page+** appears on page 1-3, a new page is started and
numbered 2-1. You might use this feature if you are breaking your
program into sections with separate subtitles. At the end of a section,
enter the appropriate **subttl** directive for the next section, followed by
page+. Figure 11-6 shows the tops of two pages from a revised **help**
listing. You can see the effects of the **subttl** and **page+** directives.

The **page** directive (with no options) forces a page break. You might
use it to keep a subsection, such as a procedure block, from being split
over a page.

```
Microsoft (R) Macro Assembler   3/29/89 13:58:33
Help Program                                  Page     1-1


                     page    ,132

                     title   Help Program
                     subttl  Main Line

                     dosseg
```

```
Microsoft (R) Macro Assembler   3/29/89 13:58:33
Help Program                                  Page     2-1
Main Line

                     page+
0000                 .code
                     extrn  DosWrite:far,DosExit:far
0000            begin:
0000  E8 000F R          call   write_msg_proc
0003  E8 0006 R          call   exit_proc
```

Figure 11-6   Advancing the Section Number in a Listing

Contents

The remaining directives in Figure 11-3 control what is included in the program portion of the assembler listing.

Program Statements. Two directives control whether or not program statements are included in the listing file: .list and .xlist. .List turns on the listing of program statements. .Xlist turns it off. .List is the default. When you turn it off with .xlist, no more source or machine code is listed until a .list directive is encountered. You might use these directives to suppress the listing of such instructions as subttl and page+.

Included Statements. By default, the assembler lists all statements included from other files. You can suppress the listing of included statements with the .xlisti directive and turn it back on again with the .listi directive.

False Blocks. Unless you request otherwise, the assembler does not list conditional blocks that it does not assemble because the condition is false. The **.lfcond** directive causes false blocks to be listed, even though they are not assembled. The **.sfcond** directive suppresses false blocks again. The **.tfcond** directives toggles the current status.

Macro Expansions. By default, the assembler lists only those statements contained in a macro that generate object code. Equates and other statements that do not generate object code are not listed. If you want all statements from the macro definition listed, regardless of whether or not they generate object code, then use the **.lall** directive. (Macro comments are never listed.) To suppress all listing of macro expansion statements, use the **.sall** directive. In the resulting listing, the macro call is shown, but not the expansion lines themselves. To return to the default, use the **.xall** directive.

Figure 11-7 shows an example of all three forms of macro expansion. You can see a macro definition at the top of the page. (Listing of macro definitions is not affected by these directives; only the expansions are.) We have included a **local** directive, a macro comment, an equate, an **if...else...endif** structure, and some regular comments. Following the definition, you can see three different expansions of the macro, one for each listing option. The assembler lists a digit at the beginning of each line that results from a macro expansion showing the level of macro nesting.

Notice which lines were listed under the **.lall** directive. Even when all the lines are supposed to be listed, the **local** directive, the macro comment, and the false block are not listed. The false block is under the control of the **.sfcond** directive, not **.lall**. The assembler prints a comment semicolon to indicate where a macro comment was omitted.

Under the **.sall** directive, you can see that only the macro call itself is listed. Under the **.xall** directive, the equate, the **if** and **endif** statements, the regular comments, and the false block do not appear. **.Xall** gives a cleaner listing, but **.lall** is more informative.

Module Names

Every module has a name, which the assembler places in the header record of the object module. The link editor and some debuggers use this name to refer to the module (in error messages, for example). MASM and 386 I ASM use slightly different rules to determine the name.

```
                              amem      macro   dest,source
                                        local   okay
                              ;; adds two memory items
                              zero      =       0
                              if type dest eq type source
                                        mov     ax,source
                                        add     dest,ax
                                        jnc     okay
                              ; Zero result in case of overflow
                                        mov     dest,zero
                              okay:
                              else
                                ; note: expansion suppressed
                                ; operands not the same size
                                        endif
                                        endm

                                        .lall
                                        amem    profit,loss
                            1  ;
= 0000                      1  zero      =       0
                            1  if type profit eq type loss
0000  A1 003B R             1            mov     ax,loss
0003  01 06 0039 R          1            add     profit,ax
0007  73 06                 1            jnc     ??0000
                            1            ; Zero result in case of overflow
0009  C7 06 0039 R 0000     1            mov     profit,zero
000F                        1  ??0000:
                            1  endif
                                        .sall
                                        amem    profit,loss
                                        .xall
                                        amem    profit,loss
001E  A1 003B R             1            mov     ax,loss
0021  01 06 0039 R          1            add     profit,ax
0025  73 06                 1            jnc     ??0002
0027  C7 06 0039 R 0000     1            mov     profit,zero
002D                        1  ??0002:
```

Figure 11-7   Types of Macro Expansion

1. In MASM, if the **/zi** or **/zd** switch is specified on the assembler command, the name of the source file becomes the name of the module. These two switches set up the CodeView debugger and are discussed in Chapter 12. (These switches are not available with 386 l ASM.)
2. For 386 l ASM and for MASM when the debugging switches have not been set, the name included in the **name** directive is the name of the module.

name *text*   Names the module.

Figure 11-8   The Name Directive

3. If none of the above is specified, the **title** directive gives a name to the module. 386 I ASM uses the first six characters of the title, while MASM uses the first word (up to the first space).
4. If none of the above is specified, 386 I ASM uses the name of the source code file, while MASM assigns the name A.

If you find the default name unhelpful in messages, you can specify whatever name you want with the **name** directive, shown in Figure 11-8. In 386 I ASM, the name is limited to 132 characters. With MASM, the name must fit on one line. You can specify only one **name** directive per module.

Location Counter

The assembler uses a location counter to keep track of the current address when assembling a program. The location counter is 16 or 32 bits wide depending on the addressing mode. It starts at zero at the beginning of each segment and is incremented appropriately as each instruction is assembled. Some directives, such as the data definition directives, also cause the location counter to be incremented.

The value of the location counter when an instruction is assembled is the beginning address offset of that instruction. You can see what it is by inspecting the assembler listing.

Several directives let you adjust the location counter. The **org** directive lets you specify a new value for the location counter. The **even** directive forces the location counter to an even address. The **align** directive forces the location counter to the next specified boundary. Each of these directives is shown in Figure 11-9.

org *expression*   Reset the location counter to the value of *expression*.

even   Force next item to start on word boundary

align *expression*   Force alignment of next item to boundary represented by *expression*.

Figure 11-9   The Alignment Directives

Origin

The **org** directive lets you specify a new value for the location counter. It is used primarily to provide two or more definitions for the same data area. For example, you can define the same field as one double-word, then redefine it as four bytes. Here is a sample routine to do that:

```
dval        dd      ?
            org     dval
bval        db      4 dup (?)
```

The **org** directive resets the location counter to the address offset of **dval**. Therefore, **bval** is located at exactly the same address as **dval**. You can access the data stored at this address by either name. When you access it as **dval**, it will be processed as a doubleword. When you access it as **bval**, it will be processed as a byte. To reach the second byte, you would need to code **bval+1**, and so on.

This is obviously a dangerous yet extremely convenient facility, one that can get you into a lot of trouble if you don't know exactly what you are doing. Suppose you define initial values for both the variables defined above. The value of **bval** would overlay the value of **dval**. If you access **dval** expecting to get its defined value, you'll get **bval**'s value instead. Furthermore, bytes will be reversed when storing in and retrieving from **dval**, but they won't when storing to and retrieving from **bval**.

If you're desperate to save memory space in a program, the **org** directive can be used to overlay data blocks that are never needed at the same time. For example, suppose the program reads records from three different files, but processes only one at a time. You could save space by letting the three records share the same memory space. The three different definitions could be set to the same origin with **org**.

You can also use **org** to move the location counter ahead, but be careful not to leave a gap in the program. When the processor is executing code, it picks up instructions in sequence, not aware of any gaps. It will pick up leftover garbage from a gap and try to execute it. Hopefully, the outcome will be an invalid opcode exception. In the worst case, the garbage will be executable as an instruction, destroying the validity of the program and its data.

Alignment

Some earlier machines required instructions and data to be aligned on word or doubleword boundaries in memory. That is, the beginning address of each instruction and field had to be divisible by 2 (a word boundary) or 4 (a doubleword boundary). The 8086 family of processors does not require instructions or data to be aligned on any specific boundaries. An instruction or a data field can start at any address in the segment.

However, good data alignment can help to speed up a program because of the way that data is fetched from memory. Figure 11-10 illustrates the problem. Processors with 16-bit data buses always access a complete word of information aligned on a word boundary. To fetch or store a word that does not start on a word boundary requires two bus cycles, taking twice as long to fetch or store the information. The '386 fetches and stores by doublewords and must make two passes if a field straddles a doubleword boundary.

If the processor is waiting for the process to be completed, then the extra step costs time. You can avoid the wasted time and improve your program's efficiency by making sure that data and instructions don't straddle word boundaries (16-bit data buses) or doubleword boundaries (32-bit data buses).

When you define a segment, you specify the beginning alignment on the **segment** directive with the align type specifier, which is discussed later in this chapter. Then you can use one of the alignment directives (from Figure 11-9) to force a particular field to be aligned on a boundary within the segment. However, you can never force an alignment larger than the segment's *granularity*. The granularity is the largest alignment size the segment can handle, which is based on the initial alignment of the segment. That is, if the segment alignment is **byte**, then there's no way you can align a particular field on a word or larger boundary because the assembler has no knowledge of whether the initial address of the segment (determined when the program is loaded for execution) is even or odd. Similarly, the assembler can't find a doubleword boundary when the segment is byte or word aligned.

Even Alignment. The **even** directive forces the next statement to start on a word boundary, as long as the segment alignment is at least as large as **word**. Suppose you want to align **scores_array** starting on a word boundary. You could do it with these instructions:

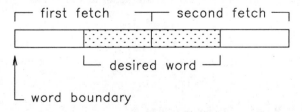

Figure 11-10   Fetching a Word that Straddles a Boundary

```
dseg          segment word ...
    ; any alignment larger than byte works
        ...                              ; other definitions
        even
scores_array dw    100 dup (?)
```

If the location counter is even when the **even** directive is executed, then no adjustment is made; **scores_array** will have an even beginning address naturally. However, if the location counter is odd, then the assembler inserts a **nop** instruction into the segment to take up one byte, forcing **scores_array** to start at an even address. Recall that **nop** is an instruction that does nothing except take up one byte in memory.

Larger Alignments. You'll need the **align** directive to align a field on a boundary larger than a word. The *expression* must evaluate to a legitimate boundary value; that is, it must evaluate to a power of 2. For doubleword alignment, it must be 4. You could use 4 as an immediate value, or you could use the reserved word **dword**, which has a value of 4. Suppose you want to force **scores_array** to start on a doubleword boundary. You could code these instructions:

```
dseg          segment   dword ...
    ; any alignment larger than word works
        ...                              ; other definitions
        align   dword
scores_array dd    100 dup (?)
```

The assembler will insert up to three **nop** instructions to make the field align correctly.

Assembler Messages

Figure 11-11 shows some directives you can use to display messages on the standard output device during the assembly process. Thus you can

%out *text*   Display message on monitor.

%out*n* *text*   Display monitor message on nth pass.

(386|ASM only)

Figure 11-11   Message Display Directives

send messages to yourself about true-false branches, procedures completing assembly, and so forth. Suppose you want to send a message to the monitor saying that the **sum_array_proc** procedure is being assembled. You could do it like this:

```
sum_array_proc proc  near

          %out   Sum_array_proc being assembled
```

This message would be displayed twice, once on each pass. With 386 I ASM, you could send different messages for pass 1 and pass 2 like this:

```
sum_array_proc proc  near

          %out1  First pass on sum_array_proc

          %out2  Second pass on sum_array_proc
```

You can accomplish the same thing with MASM using the **if1** or **if2** conditional assembly directives:

```
sum_array_proc proc  near

if1

          %out   First pass on sum_array_proc

else

          %out   Second pass on sum_array_proc

endif
```

Program and Segment Structure

In the rest of this chapter, you'll see in more detail than in previous chapters how to define the structure of the program and its segments, as well as how to work with programs that require multiple data and code segments. Here more than anywhere else, MASM and 386 I ASM differ. Figure 11-12 lists program and segment directives for MASM. The 386 I ASM directives are covered later.

Defining Program Structure (MASM Only)

In MASM you use the **.model** directive to specify the format. You get five models to choose from:

- **Small** model involves one data segment and one code segment. All code and data can be accessed as near.

```
.model model        Specifies whether the program is small, medium,
                    compact, large, or huge.

.stack [bytes]      Defines a stack segment.
.data               Defines an initialized near data segment.
.data?              Defines an uninitialized near data segment.
.fardata [name]     Defines an initialized far data segment.
.fardata? [name]    Defines an uninitialized far data segment.
.const              Defines a constant data segment.
.code [name]        Defines a code segment.

name segment [align] [combine] [use] ['class']
                    Marks the beginning of a segment and defines its
                    characteristics.
name ends           Marks the end of a segment definition.

.alpha              Specifies alphabetic segment order.
.seq                Specifies sequential segment order.

name group segment[,segment...]
                    Groups logical segments together into one
                    physical segment.

dosseg              Specifies the standard order of segments.
```

Figure 11-12   MASM Program and Segment Directives

- **Medium** model involves one data segment but multiple code segments. Therefore, all data references are near, but far calls and jumps are possible.

- **Compact** model involves one code segment but multiple data segments. Therefore, all calls and jumps are near (except calls to operating system services), but data references can be far.

- **Large** model involves multiple code segments and multiple data segments. References may be near or far.

- **Huge** model involves not only multiple code and data segments, but also permits data arrays to span segments. Thus, array references may be far.

The **.model** directive must precede any other segment directive in the program; otherwise, an assembler error will result. If you are using the shorthand segment definitions (**.data, .code,** and so on) with the '386 processor, then put the **.386** directive before the **.model** directive if you want 32-bit addressing, but put the **.model** directive before the **.386** directive if you want 16-bit addressing.

Always use the smallest possible model for your program, because far references are less efficient than near references. In stand-alone assembler programs—that is, programs that are not called as submodules from other languages—you can specify **near** and **far** for variable names, labels, and procedure names when you define them. This is the technique we have used throughout this book.

If you are writing assembler submodules to be called by programs written in higher-level languages, then you must follow the rules for those languages. Furthermore, not all models are supported by all higher-level languages. See your language manual for details.

Shorthand Segment Definitions

You've seen how to define stack, data, and code segments using the shorthand directives. Several other types of segments can also be created, as you'll see in this section.

Stack Segments. The **.stack** directive creates a stack segment. Every program must have at least one stack segment. If you are creating a program with only one module, that module must define at least one stack segment. If you are creating a program with multiple modules, then at least one of the modules must define a stack segment. If you are creating a module to be linked with modules created in a higher-level language, then the high-level language modules will automatically have stack segments (generated by the compiler or interpreter), and you do not need to define one. The **.stack** directive operand is optional, but at least one stack segment for a program must have some memory space in it.

Data Segments. Five different types of data segments can be created by shorthand directives. **.Data** creates an initialized near data segment. **.Data?** creates an uninitialized near data segment. **.Fardata** creates an initialized far data segment while **.fardata?** creates an uninitialized one. **.Const** creates a constant segment.

The difference between uninitialized and initialized data segments is important for some high-level languages, but if you are writing a stand-alone assembler program, you can place both kinds of definitions in one segment, as we have done throughout this book. And again, the

@segcur	Name of the current segment.
@filename	Name of the current source code file.
@farcode	Value 0 for models limited to one code segment and 1 for models permitting more than one code segment.
@fardata	Value 0 for models limited to one data segment, 1 for models permitting more than one data segment, and 2 for the huge model, which permits multi-segment arrays.

Figure 11-13   MASM Shorthand Segment Equates

difference between near and far data segments is more important in high-level languages than in stand-alone assembler programs.

A constant segment is a data segment containing only constant data—that is, data that can't be changed at run time. Some high-level languages keep constant data separate and protect it from being overwritten. If you are writing a module to be linked with modules created by such a language, then you might want to define your constant data in a separate segment. For stand-alone programs, you might as well place your constants in the **.data** segment.

For the small and compact models, you can specify only one code segment. If you place a name on the **.code** directive, it will be ignored. For the models that permit multiple code segments, each code segment must have a name so you can reference the different segments. Usually, one module has only one code segment. For the larger models, you combine modules to get more than one code segment.

Predefined Equates for MASM Shorthand Definitions. The MASM shorthand segment definitions include the definition of several equates, as listed in Figure 11-13. The **@segcur** symbol helps you supply the segment name when you don't know what it is. The shorthand segment directives assign names to each segment, which you'll see shortly, but if you want to refer to the current segment name without looking it up, you can use **@segcur** instead. You might also need **@segcur** to end a segment definition when you are mixing shorthand and full segment definitions, as in this example:

```
        .data

        ...

@segcur    ends
```

```
dseg        segment   ...
```

The **@filename** symbol is equated to the current file name (excluding the extension). If the source file being assembled is HELP.ASM, **@filename** equals **help**. Suppose you are creating a procedure to be included in many different source programs. You could individualize the procedure name for each source program this way:

```
@filename_formit  proc   near

        ...

@filename_formit  endp
```

You can use the **@farcode** and **@fardata** symbols in **if** directives to determine whether near or far references are required. Again, you would use these in situations where you don't know when you're writing the code what type of program it will be included in.

Full Segment Definitions (Both MASM and 386|ASM)

Now let's take a look at how to use the **segment** directive to do a full segment definition. 386 I ASM uses the same format as MASM for this directive, which is shown in Figure 11-12.

Segment Names. The segment name need not be unique. (Surprised?) The link editor combines all segments with the same name into one segment. Ordinarily, one module contains unique segment names, but several different modules might contribute sections to one data segment and one code segment. This helps to keep the model small.

Microsoft advises you always to use standard segment names, which are the same names assigned by the segment shortcut directives as well as all Microsoft high-level compilers. In this way, you can easily link a module into many different programs, some of which are created by high-level languages. Even if you're using the 386 I ASM or another non-Microsoft assembler, you might need to combine your segments with ones created by a Microsoft compiler, so it's a good idea to adopt this habit. Figure 11-14 shows the standard Microsoft segment names.

Align Type. The align type determines the type of boundary the segment starts on. Figure 11-15 shows the five options. If no align type is given, **para** is the default. The assembler uses the align type to determine alignment of addresses within the segment when one of the alignment directives is specified. The linker uses the align type to

Segment	Name
code segment	_text for small or compact models @filename&_text for medium and large models
data segment	_data for small and medium models @filename&_data for compact and large models
stack segment	stack
constant segment	const
uninitialized data segment	_bss
far data segment (uninitialized)	far_data
far data segment (initialized)	far_bss

Figure 11-14   Standard Segment Names

determine the alignment of the segment relative to the other segments. The actual beginning address is determined by the operating system when the program is executed.

Selecting an align type larger than necessary can waste memory space. If the linker has to skip 255 bytes to get to the next page boundary, for example, you can conserve space by selecting a smaller align type. For most purposes, **word** alignment is sufficient when 16-bit addressing is in use, **dword** alignment for 32-bit addressing. Keep in mind, however, that the align type determines the granularity of the segment. If you specify **word** alignment, the assembler cannot align fields on **dword** or larger boundaries.

Type	Segment Alignment
byte	Can start at any address.
word	Starting address must be even (divisible by 2).
dword	Starting address must be divisible by 4.
para	Starting address must be divisible by 16.
page	Starting address must be divisible by 256.
page4K	Starting address must be divisible by 4096.

Figure 11-15   Alignment Types

Type	Effect
public	Concatenate segments with the same name into one segment.
stack	Same as public except that the stack registers are initialized.
common	Overlay segments with the same name so that only one at a time appears in memory.
memory	Same as public.
private	Does not combine segments with the same name.
at address	Load the segment at the address specified. (Meant for PROM use only.)

Figure 11-16   Combine Types

Combine Type. You've seen that segments with the same name are combined into one segment. The combine type determines how they are combined. Figure 11-16 shows the six possible combine types. Ignoring the **at** option, which is meant for PROM use, you can either concatenate segments, overlay them, or not combine them at all.

The **public** combine type lets you concatenate segments from several different modules into one segment. For example, suppose you are linking together three different modules. Each module has one data segment named **_data** and one code segment named **_text**. To cause these segments to be concatenated into one data segment and one code segment, you could define them this way:

```
MODULE A
_data       segment     word public
dataword    dw      ?
_data       ends
_text       segment     byte public
begin:
            mov     dataword,0
_text       ends


MODULE B
_data       segment     word public
```

```
myword        dw      ?
_data         ends
_text         segment    byte public
              mov     myword,0
_text         ends


MODULE  C
_data         segment    word public
yourword      dw      ?
_data         ends
_text         segment    byte public
              mov     yourword,0
_text         ends
```

The linked program will have one **_data** segment and one **_text** segment, which will contain the translation of these statements:

```
_data         segment
dataword      dw      ?
myword        dw      ?
yourword      dw      ?
_data         ends
_text         segment
              mov     dataword,0
              mov     myword,0
              mov     yourword,0
_text         ends
```

Obviously, that's an extremely simplified example, but it should suffice to show you how a program segment is concatenated from module segments. The advantages should be obvious. You keep the program module as small as possible and use the much more efficient near references. The danger is in exceeding the segment limit. The linker will tell you if a segment exceeds the 64K segment limit of 16-bit addressing or the 4G limit of 32-bit addressing.

When public segments are combined, they must have the same attributes, or at least nonconflicting attributes. It's easier just to give them all the same attributes. In fact, it's easiest to just define the attributes in the main module and leave out everything but the combine type in the other modules.

Since public segments with the same name will end up as one segment, can the segment in module B refer to instructions and data from module A as if they were near references? The assembler will reject a reference to an undefined symbol. However, you can declare them as external symbols of type **near** and reference them. For example, Modules A and C above could be revised like this:

```
MODULE A

                public      begin
_data           segment     public
dataword        dw      ?
_data           ends
_text           segment     public
begin:
                mov     dataword,0
_text           ends


MODULE C

                extrn   begin:near
_text           segment     public
                ...
                jne     begin
_text           ends
```

By making **begin** a global symbol with a **near** type, any module in the program can reference it as long as the reference ends up in the same code segment as the label.

The **memory** combine type is the same as the **public** type and exists for compatibility with other systems. For new programs, use **public**.

Whenever you create an object module from several source modules, be sure that only one source module specifies the program entry point on the **end** directive. Every module needs an **end** directive, but only one should specify an entry point. If more than one entry point is encountered, an assembler error is issued.

The **stack** combine type is also the same as **public** with the addition that it causes the stack registers to be initialized. When the linker puts together a stack segment from one or more modules, it will cause SS to be initialized to the base address of this segment and (E)SP to be initialized to the end of the segment. If no segment in any module is identified with the **stack** combine type, then the stack registers are not initialized automatically and must be loaded by instructions in the program. The linker issues a warning message in this case.

The **common** combine type causes segments of the same name to overlay each other, meaning that only one is available at a time. This is an advanced technique for saving memory space that you probably will never need to use with virtual memory systems. Don't try to use it unless you know what you are doing.

The **private** combine type means that segments are not combined. It is the default combine type on the assumption that if you don't specify one of the **public** types, you probably didn't mean to combine the segments and the identical names were accidental.

Addressing Mode. When the target processor is the '386, then you can specify either 16- or 32-bit addressing with the *use* attribute on the **segment** directive. Simply specify either **use16** or **use32**. The default is **use32** for the '386 in protected mode, **use16** for everything else.

Ordering the Segments and Identifying the Code Segment. The final **segment** directive attribute is **class**, which identifies code segments and partially determines the final order of segments in the executable module. The linker does not necessarily place the combined segments in the same order as they appeared in the source code. Several factors determine the final order of segments:

- The assembler arranges the segments in sequential order (the order they appear in the source file). MASM will rearrange the segments into alphabetical order if the **.alpha** directive is used in the program or the **/a** switch is used in the assembler command.

- The linker places all segments having the same class name together. It does not combine them into one segment, but it does place them one after another in the order that it encounters them in the object modules.

- The linker then orders classes according to the sequence they were encountered in the object modules.

• The **dosseg** assembler directive (MASM) or the **–dosorder** command switch (386 l LINK) specifies that the segments should be in DOS segment order. This order places all segments whose class names end with **code** first. All segments not in the **dgroup** group are ordered second, in the sequence they are encountered. All segments in **dgroup** are ordered third: first **begdata** class, then all other classes, then **bss** class, and finally **stack** class. This is the sequence that Microsoft high-level compilers use automatically, but the assemblers and linkers will not use it unless told to do so.

To get the segments into the correct order for DOS or OS/2, it's easiest to specify the **dosseg** directive for a MASM program or the **–dosorder** switch when linking with 386 l LINK. Then be sure to give each segment the correct class name on the **segment** directive.

All code segments should be given the class name **'code'**. This class name identifies the segment as an executable code segment. Don't give a non-code segment the class name **'code'** or any class name that ends with **'code'**.

All other segments are probably a part of **dgroup** (which is discussed shortly). Unless you have some reason to do otherwise, you can probably assign all data segments to the class name **'data'** and all stack segments to the class name **'stack'**. This will cause all your data segments to be ordered immediately after the code segments, with the stack segments last.

Grouping Segments

A segment group is a collection of logically separate segments that are concatenated in memory so they have the same starting address and can use the same segment register. A segment group and combined segments differ in the type of references that can be used. Combined segments become one segment and can use near references throughout the combination. A segment group share the same segment register but is considered different segments so that a reference from one to the other must be a far reference. The advantage of grouping segments lies in not having to reload the segment register to access the different segments in the group. For a group of segments called **dgroup**, when the DS register is pointing at the beginning of the group, any data in any of the segments in the group can be accessed through DS. You don't need to resort to ES, FS, etc. The linker calculates all offsets from the beginning of the group.

A group and a class differ in how references are made. A class of segments is simply a collection of segments that are stored one after another in memory. Each segment must still have its own segment register in order to be referenced. For example, suppose that **dseg** and **eseg** are both in the 'data' class and are not part of the same group. **Dseg** is your main data segment; DS points to it at all times. To reference a variable in **eseg**, you must point one of the other data segment registers at **eseg** and use a segment override. Two steps are necessary because you can't load segment addresses directly into segment registers:

```
mov     ax,eseg

mov     es,ax              ; ES pointing at eseg

mov     ax,es:myword
```

However, if you group **dseg** and **eseg** together and point DS at the beginning of the group, then all references to data in both segments can go through DS.

The **dgroup** is an extremely important group in the world of DOS and OS/2. When there is a group of this name, the loader points DS at the beginning of the group automatically when the program is loaded. Therefore, you don't have to point DS yourself. For most of your programming situations, you will probably want to group all your non-code segments into **dgroup**. Then you don't have to fuss about the addressability of your data. However, there is a size limit on a group. Since offsets are calculated from the beginning of the group and continue throughout the group, a group cannot exceed the maximum possible offset size. That is, a group has the same size limitations that an (ungrouped) segment does: 64K for 16-bit addressing, 4G for 32-bit addressing.

Grouping segments does not specify their order in memory unless you are using DOS order, in which case **dgroup** is located together. If you are not using DOS order, then other segments might get placed in between segments that belong to a group. They are not addressable from the same segment register as the group, but, of course, their sizes must be accounted for in offsets within the group. Therefore, you must be able to predict the segment order and determine that the total size of a group plus all intervening segments does not exceed the maximum offset size. That's another good justification for using DOS order.

The assembler must know where the segment registers are pointing so that it can calculate offsets and segment overrides correctly. The **assume** directive tells the assembler where the registers are pointing. If you are using a group such as **dgroup**, you should use its name in the **assume** statement instead of an individual segment name, as in this example:

```
assume cs:_text,ds:dgroup,ss:dgroup
```

If you want to point a segment register at the beginning of a group, thus making the entire group addressable through the register, you can use the group name in the **mov** instruction:

```
mov     ax,extra_group

mov     es,ax
```

This points the ES register at a group named **extra_group**.

Shorthand Segment Assumption (MASM Only)

Now that you have seen how segments are defined in full, let's look at the assumptions that MASM makes when you use the shorthand seg-

segment	name	align	comb.	class	group
small					
.code	_text	byte	public	'code'	
.data	_data	word	public	'data'	dgroup
.stack	stack	para	stack	'stack'	dgroup
.const	const	word	public	'const'	dgroup
.data?	_bss	word	public	'bss'	dgroup
medium					
.code	*name*_text	byte	public	'code'	
.data	_data	word	public	'data'	dgroup
.stack	stack	para	stack	'stack'	dgroup
.const	const	word	public	'const'	dgroup
.data?	_bss	word	public	'bss'	dgroup
compact					
.code	_text	byte	public	'code'	
.data	_data	word	public	'data'	dgroup
.stack	stack	para	stack	'stack'	dgroup
.const	const	word	public	'const'	dgroup
.data?	_bss	word	public	'bss'	dgroup
.fardata	far_data	para	private	'far_data'	
.fardata?	far_bss	para	private	'far_bss'	
large					
.code	*name*_text	byte	public	'code'	
.data	_data	word	public	'data'	dgroup
.stack	stack	para	stack	'stack'	dgroup
.const	const	word	public	'const'	dgroup
.data?	_bss	word	public	'bss'	dgroup
.fardata	far_data	para	private	'far_data'	
.fardata?	far_bss	para	private	'far_bss'	

name is the source code file base name

Figure 11-17   Segment Attribute Assumptions for Shorthand Segment Definitions

ment definitions. Figure 11-17 lists them. The standard Microsoft segment names are used, as are the standard class names. All segments except code segments and far data segments are grouped in **dgroup**. All combine types are public or stack except for far data segments, which are private. This means that all segments defined with **.data** will be combined into one segment, all segments defined with **.stack** will be combined into one segment, and so forth. Notice, however, that code segments from different modules in medium and large models will not be combined because they will have different segment names.

Near data segments are aligned on word boundaries, far data and stack segments are aligned on paragraph boundaries, and code segments are aligned on byte boundaries. These boundaries might give you some problems if you need to align individual instructions or fields on word or doubleword boundaries. If you need better granularity than is presented here, you'll have to use the full segment definition.

Assembling

So far you've been assembling programs using all default values for the assembler options. In this chapter, you'll learn how to assemble several source files into one object module, control the output produced by the assembler, and define symbols for the **ifdef** and **ifndef** conditional directives, along with other options of the 386│ASM and MASM assemblers. You will also see how to use Microsoft's cross-reference facility, CREF.

Assembling with 386│ASM

Figure 12-1 shows the format of the assembly command for 386│ASM. You enter the word **386asm** followed by at least one filename and perhaps some switches. The filenames identify the files containing the source modules. If the extension is **.asm**, then you can omit it. To assemble the source code in **help.asm**, you would enter:

```
386asm help
```

You can specify a path with the filename, as in these examples:

```
386asm d:\help
```

```
386asm filename [filenames] [switches]
```

```
Switches:
```

```
-Object filename -NOObject -NODelete
-List filename -NOList -NOSym
-ErrorList filename
-Include dirname[,dirname...]
-8086 -80186 -80286 -80286P -80386 -80386P
-8087 -80287 -80387 -NO87
-TWOCase -ONECase
-Define symbol[=string]
-FULLWARN
```

Defaults are underlined. Abbreviations are shown in upper-case or large numbers.

Figure 12-1   The 386asm Command

```
386asm \asmdev\help
386asm a:help
```

You can also specify the extension, even if it is **.asm**:

```
386asm help.pl
386asm help.asm
```

All of the above jobs would produce an object file named **help.obj**, unless severe errors are encountered. A listing file named **help.lst** is also produced. Error messages are placed in the listing file and sent to the standard output device.

Assembling Multiple Files

If more than one input file is specified, all the input files are assembled into one object module, which takes its name from the first file listed in the command. The following command assembles three files:

```
386asm help1 help2 help3
```

The object module will be named **help1.obj**, and the listing file will be named **help1.lst**. Filenames can be separated by spaces or commas.

The assembler processes the input files in the order they are listed on the command line. Since that affects the order of the segments if sequential order is being used, be sure to list the files in the desired order. Only one **end** directive should specify an entry point for the program.

Switches

You can override the defaults and control other features with the **386asm** command switches. Every switch starts with a hyphen. (Don't start your filenames with hyphens or 386 ASM can't tell them from invalid switches.) Most of the switches can be abbreviated. You can specify the switches in any order, and you can intermix switches and filenames on the command line. If a switch takes an argument, it must immediately follow the switch name, separated only by spaces.

Overriding the Object File. If you don't want to use the default object file name, you can specify a different name with the **–object** switch. For example, the following command assembles three source files and produces an object file named **help.obj**:

```
386asm help1 help2 help3 -o help.obj
```

If you don't want an object file produced, use the **–noobject** switch. The following command causes a syntax check to be performed on the three source files:

```
386asm help1 help2 help3 -noo
```

By default, the assembler deletes the object file if any fatal errors are encountered. If you want an object file produced even if errors are found, use the **–nodelete** switch, as in this example:

```
386asm help -nod
```

Avoid using conflicting switches, such as **–noobject** and **–object**, in the same command. If the assembler encounters conflicting switches, it uses the rightmost one.

Controlling the Listing File. To specify the name of the listing file, use the **–list** switch. For example, the following command gives the listing file the default name but places it in a specific directory:

```
386asm help -l c:\asmdoc\help.lst
```

The **–nolist** switch suppresses the listing file, as in this example:

```
386asm help1 help2 help3 -nol
```

When a listing file is generated, a symbol table is printed at the end. You'll see an example shortly. You can suppress the symbol table listing with the **–nosym** switch. The following command generates a listing file without a symbol table at the end:

```
386asm help -nos
```

By default, errors are listed on the standard output device. They are also included in the listing file. If you would also like a separate error listing, use the **–errorlist** switch. You must specify a filename for the list; there is no default. The following command suppresses the usual listing file but requests an error listing.

```
386asm help -nol -el help.err
```

Specifying the Instruction Set. The instruction set switches are familiar to you, since you have already seen the instruction set directives. The switches serve the same function as the directives, with this exception: the directives in a program override the switches. Thus, if a source file contains no instruction set directive, you can specify the instruction sets with switches when you assemble the file. If neither directives nor switches are used, the default is the 80386 set (unprivileged) and no coprocessor set. The following command specifies that the unprivileged '286 and '287 instruction sets should be used:

```
386asm help -286 -287
```

Specifying Case Sensitivity. By default, the assembler is not case sensitive. That is, symbols, operands, reserved words, and so forth, can be specified in uppercase, lowercase, or a mixture of the two. You don't even need to be consistent about it. To make the assembler case sensitive, you can specify the **–twocase** switch. When **–twocase** is specified, the assembler will consider **Profit**, **profit**, and **PROFIT** to be three different symbols. The following command specifies case sensitivity for the **help** module:

```
386asm help -twoc
```

The **–onecase** switch is never needed because if you omit **–twocase**, **–onecase** is the default.

Defining Symbols on the Command Line. Defining symbols on the command line gives you the ability to control conditional assembly at assembly time. Suppose you want to assemble two versions of a program: a test version and a production version. The test version contains extra procedures to print out variable values at certain breakpoints; these procedures should be omitted from the production version. You can use the **ifdef** directive to mark the code to be conditionally assembled:

```
ifdef test

trace       proc   near

            . . .

trace       endp

endif
```

Make sure that no variable named **test** is defined anywhere in the program. Now, to assemble the test version, you would enter this command:

```
386asm help -d test
```

The switch defines the **test** symbol. (The fact that it doesn't have any type, size, or value is unimportant as long as you don't use it as an operand in the program.) The **ifdef** condition is true and the **trace** procedure gets assembled. To assemble the production version, don't include the **–define** switch on the command:

```
386asm help
```

Now **test** not defined; the **ifdef** condition is false, and the procedure is not assembled. This version would overlay the earlier version because the object file in both cases defaulted to **help.obj**. To keep both versions, you might enter commands similar to this:

```
386asm help -o helpt -d test

386asm help -o helpp
```

If you have more than one test situation, you can give the symbol a text value on the command line and test for various values in the conditional blocks with **ifidn** and **ifdif** directives. For example, suppose you want to assemble four different versions of a program: weekend, month-end, quarter-end, and year-end. The program itself contains different procedures for each of these four conditions:

```
ifidn <term>,<week>

week_end    proc   near
```

```
               . . .
week_end      endp
endif
ifidn <term>,<month>
month_end    proc    near
               . . .
month_end    endp
endif
ifidn <term>,<quarter>
quarter_end proc     near
               . . .
quarter_end endp
endif
ifidn <term>,<year>
year_end     proc    near
               . . .
year_end     endp
endif
```

You might also have a procedure that is assembled into every version but the **week_end** version:

```
ifdif <term>,<week>
summary_proc  procnear
               . . .
summary_proc          endp
endif
```

You might also include a conditional block near the beginning of the module that makes sure that at least one form of the symbol has been defined:

```
ifndef term
        %out   You forgot to define "term".
        %out   Fatal error. Object module is deleted.
        %out   You can cancel the assembly with Ctrl-C.
        .err
```

```
endif
```

To assemble the four different versions of the program, you would enter commands similar to these:

```
386asm help -o helpw -d term=week

386asm help -o helpm -d term=month

386asm help -o helpq -d term=quarter

386asm help -o helpy -d term=year
```

Requesting Extra Error Checking. The **–fullwarn** switch requests error checking beyond that which is normally done. The extra errors, which are at the warning level, fall into the following categories:

• A segment register is implied in an instruction but no instruction has ever loaded that register. For example, the string move instructions always imply the ES register for the destination. If no instruction loads ES prior to a string move, then a warning will be generated if **–fullwarn** is on.

• A **nop** instruction is placed in a jump instruction to fill in for a short jump.

Assembling with MASM

Figure 12-2 shows the format of the MASM assembly command. In its most basic form, it consists of the word **masm** followed by a filename and a semicolon. The semicolon indicates that default values should be taken for the other filenames (an object file is produced but the listing file and cross-reference file are suppressed). If you leave the extension off the source filename, **.asm** is assumed. The following command assembles a file named **help.asm**:

```
masm help;
```

You can specify a path with the filename, as in these examples:

```
masm d:\help;

masm \asmprac\help;

masm a:help;
```

You can also specify the extension, even if it is **.asm**:

```
masm help.p1;

masm help.asm;
```

masm [*options*] *source*[,*object*,*listing*,*cref*] [;]

Options:

/h	Display help list
/l	Create a listing file
/n	Suppress symbol tables
/x	Include false conditionals in listing
/d	Create a pass 1 listing
/c	Do a cross-reference listing
/a	Write segments in alphabetical order
/s	Write segments in sequential order
/d*symbol*[=*value*]	Define a symbol
/w*n*	Set error display level
/z	Display error lines on screen
/p	Check for impure code
/v	Display extra statistics
/t	Suppress successful assembly messages
/ml	Establish case sensitivity for all module names
/mx	Establish case sensitivity in external and public names
/mu	Establish case insensitivity (convert all names to uppercase)
/b*number*	Set buffer size
/i*path*	Set the include file search path
/zi	Prepare object file for CodeView
/zd	Put line number information in object file

Figure 12-2   The Masm Command

All of the above jobs would produce an object file named **help.obj**, unless fatal errors were encountered. Error messages are sent to the standard output device. No listing file or cross-reference file is produced.

Displaying Command Help

You can get a listing of the command line and its switches by entering this command:

```
masm /h
```

No other parameters should be entered with this command because you can't assemble modules at the same time that you request the help display. The output looks like this:

```
Usage: masm /options source(.asm),[out(.obj)] ,[list(.lst)]
       ,[cref(.crf)][;]

/a         Alphabetize segments
/b         Set I/O buffer size, 1-63 (in 1K blocks)
/c         Generate cross-reference
/d         Generate pass 1 listing
/Dsym[=val] Define symbol
/e         Emulate floating point instructions and use IEEE data
/Ipath     Search directory for include files (up to 10 paths)
/l         Generate listing
/M{lxu}    Preserve case of labels:l-All,x-Globals,u-Uppercase Globals
/n         Suppress symbol tables in listing
/p         Check for pure code
/s         Order segments sequentially
/t         Suppress messages for successful assembly
/v         Display extra source statistics
/w{012}    Set warning level: 0-None, 1-Serious, 2-Advisory
/X         List false conditionals
/z         Display source line for each error message
/Zi        Generate line-number and symbolic information for CodeView
/Zd        Generate line-number information
```

Overriding the Object File

If you don't want to use the default object file name, you can specify the object filename. For example, the following command assembles **help** and produces an object file named **try.obj**:

```
masm help,try;
```

You can omit the object filename extension because **.obj** is the default. The semicolon tells MASM to use default values for the rest of the files.

If you don't want an object file produced, use **nul** for the filename. The following command causes a syntax check to be performed on the source file:

```
masm help,nul;
```

If you want to code any of the filenames that follow the object file in the command format, then you must code either the object filename or its comma. The following command requests an object file using the default name and a listing file:

```
masm help,,doc.lst;
```

Controlling the Listing File

By default, no listing file is created. To create a listing file, specify its name in the command line. For example, the command shown below creates a listing file named **help.lst**:

```
masm help,,help;
```

When you don't specify an extension, **.lst** is assumed. You can use the default listing filename by coding a comma without entering a name:

```
masm help,,;
```

You can send the listing file directly to the printer by coding **prn** as the filename:

```
masm help,,prn;
```

You can also request a listing file with the default filename by including the **/l** switch. The default name is used. The following command requests both an object file and a listing file with default names:

```
masm /l help;
```

When a listing file is generated, a symbol table is printed at the end. You'll see an example shortly. You can suppress the symbol table listing with the **/n** switch. The following command generates a listing file without a symbol table at the end:

```
masm /n /l help;
```

You've already seen that MASM suppresses the listing of false conditionals by default. The **/x** switch can be used to cause false conditional blocks to be listed. However, this switch is overridden by the **.sfcond** and **.tfcond** directives.

If you want to add a pass 1 listing to the listing file, perhaps to track down a phase error, use the **/d** switch. This option also causes the assembler to display error messages for pass 1, whether or not a listing file is created.

Controlling the Cross-Reference Listing

MASM has a facility called CREF that creates a cross-reference listing of all symbols in a module, a handy debugging feature. If you would like to use CREF, you must start by creating a cross-reference listing file. You can do that by including a fourth filename on the command line or by specifying the /c switch. The following command creates a cross-reference listing file named **debug.crf**:

```
masm help,,,debug.crf
```

A semicolon is not needed after the fourth filename because no more filenames are omitted. The following commands have the same effect; they both specify a cross-reference file using the default name, which is the source filename with the extension **.crf**:

```
masm help,,,,
masm /c help;
```

The cross-reference file created by the assembler is not formatted for humans. The CREF program formats it so that you can read it. You'll see how to use CREF shortly.

Controlling Segment Order

The default segment order is sequential (the order the segments are encountered in the source modules). If you want to switch the segment order from sequential to alphabetic, use the /a switch.

Defining Symbols on the Command Line

Defining symbols on the command line gives you the ability to control conditional assembly at assembly time. Suppose you want to assemble two versions of a program: a test version and a production version. The test version contains extra procedures to print out variable values at certain breakpoints; these procedures should be omitted from the production version. You can use the **ifdef** directive to mark the code to be conditionally assembled:

```
ifdef test
trace      proc near
           ...
trace      endp
endif
```

Make sure that no variable named **test** is defined anywhere in the program. Now, to assemble the test version, you would enter this command:

```
masm /dtest help;
```

This indicates that the **test** symbol is defined. (The fact that it doesn't have any type, size, or value is unimportant.) The **ifdef** condition is true and the **trace** procedure gets assembled. To assemble the production version, don't include the **/d** switch on the command:

```
masm help;
```

Now **test** is undefined; the **ifdef** condition is false, and the procedure is not assembled. This version would overlay the test version because the object file in both cases defaulted to **help.obj**. To keep both versions, you might enter commands similar to this:

```
masm /dtest help,helpt;

masm help,helpp;
```

If you have more than two cases to test, you can give the symbol a text value on the command line and test for various values in the conditional blocks with **ifidn** and **ifdif** directives. For example, suppose you want to assemble four different versions of a program: weekend, month-end, quarter-end, and year-end. The program itself contains different procedures for each of these four conditions:

```
ifidn <term>,<week>

week_end    proc    near

              . . .

week_end    endp

endif

ifidn <term>,<month>

month_end   proc    near

              . . .

month_end   endp

endif

ifidn <term>,<quarter>

quarter_end proc    near

              . . .

quarter_end endp
```

```
endif

ifidn <term>,<year>
year_end     proc    near
             . . .
year_end     endp
endif
```

You might also have a procedure that is assembled into every version except the **week_end** version:

```
ifdif <term>,<week>
summary_proc proc near
             . . .
summary_proc endp
endif
```

You might also include a conditional block near the beginning of the module that makes sure that at least one form of the symbol has been defined:

```
ifndef term
        %out   You forgot to define "term".
        %out   Fatal error. Object module is deleted.
        %out   You can cancel the assembly with Ctrl-C.
        .err
endif
```

To assemble the four different versions of the program, you would enter commands similar to these:

```
masm /dterm=week help,helpw;
masm /dterm=month help,helpm;
masm /dterm=quarter help,helpq;
masm /dterm=year help,helpy;
```

Controlling the Message Display

Several options let you control what messages are issued during the assembly process. You can choose the severity of messages that should be issued. MASM can issue three levels of messages: 0-severe errors; 1-serious warnings; and 2-advisory warnings. Ordinarily, MASM issues messages for severe errors and serious warnings. Severe errors are errors that cause the object file to be deleted. Serious warnings result from code that threatens the integrity of the program, but may be intentional, such as extra characters on a line, missing **end** directive, and defining a symbol that is a reserved word. Advisory warnings result from possibly inefficient code such as **nop** instructions inserted to compensate for short jumps. You can revise the message level up or down with the /w switch. If you specify /w0, only severe errors are issued. If you specify /w2, all three levels are issued. The /z switch requests MASM to display the lines causing the errors along with the error messages.

When in protected mode, instructions that write in the current code section are suspect. However, they will be ignored by the assembler unless you set the /p option. Then any instruction that uses CS as an override to write data will cause an error.

By default, a message is issued to the standard output device at the end of the assembly that lists the amount of symbol space free and the number of warnings and errors. If you include the /v option on the command line, MASM also reports the number of lines and symbols processed.

The /t option suppresses all output messages unless errors are encountered. This provides a cleaner output for batch files.

Case Sensitivity

By default, MASM is not case sensitive. **Profit, profit,** and **PROFIT** are considered synonymous. To make MASM case sensitive for all names within the module, use the /ml switch. To make MASM case sensitive for external and public names only, use the /mx switch. The /mu switch makes the system case insensitive if you have changed the default to /ml or /mx.

Setting up the Assembly Environment

There are several steps you can take to set up the assembly environment. You can establish the buffer size, establish a search path for included files, and change the default switch settings.

The /b switch establishes the amount of memory space allocated to the source file, from 1K to 63K. The default is 32K. The more space you allocate, up to the size of the file, the faster the assembly job. To allocate the maximum size, you would use the following command:

```
masm /b63 help;
```

The /i switch sets up a search path for included files (files referenced by the **include** directive). You can specify one path name per /i switch, and you can include up to ten /i switches in one command. The order of the switches establishes the search order. For example, to search the root directories of C:, D:, and A:, in that order, you would enter this command:

```
masm /iC:\ /iD:\ /iA:\ help;
```

If an **include** directive in the source file contains a path, then the search path established by /i switches is overridden and only the specified path is searched for that particular file.

You can establish your own defaults for the MASM switches and the **include** search path with the DOS or OS/2 **set** command. **Set** stores a variable in the operating system environment. Whenever you execute MASM, it looks for two variables in the environment: **masm** and **include**. The **masm** variable controls the default values for all the MASM switches. If it's not stored in the environment, MASM uses its default values. But if a **masm** variable has been stored in the environment, it dictates the default settings. Suppose you want to establish /l (listing), /c (cross-reference), /w3 (error display level 3), /b63 (63K buffer), and /mx (external case sensitivity). You could enter the following command at your DOS or OS/2 system prompt. Be sure not to put spaces around the equal sign.

```
set masm=/l/c/w3/b63/mx
```

Now these switches are the default for all MASM jobs. You can override them on individual command lines. For example, to make MASM case insensitive for the current job, you could enter this command:

```
masm /mu help;
```

To set up a permanent include path for all future MASM jobs, you could enter the following command at the DOS or OS/2 prompt:

```
set include=c:\;d:\a:
```

You can still specify include switches on the MASM command line. MASM will look in those directories first, then in the current directory, then in the environmental include path.

Environmental variables remain in effect until they are replaced by another **set** command or until you reboot. To make the defaults permanent, put the **set** commands in your AUTOEXEC.BAT file (or its OS/2 equivalent).

Setting up Debugging Information

Two types of symbolic information can be written to the object file if needed: line number data and type data. The CodeView debugger needs both types of data. Other online debuggers might need only the line number data. You might also want line number data to show up in the linker map.

By default, neither type of information is written to the object file. (It takes up room and time.) The **/zi** option causes both types of information to be written. The **/zd** option causes only line number data to be written. To prepare a file for CodeView, you would use a command like this:

```
masm /zi help;
```

Using the Prompted Version of MASM

If you are uncomfortable with the MASM command line, you can use an interactive version to specify the names of the files. If you enter the **masm** command with file names missing, MASM prompts you for them with these four prompts:

```
Source filename [.ASM]:

Object filename [source.OBJ]:

Source listing [NUL.LST]:

Cross-reference [NUL.CRF]:
```

The defaults are shown in brackets. For the source file, there is a default extension but you are required to supply a filename. You can put switches anywhere. They will be read just as if they were entered on the command line.

You can also use a partially prompted version. If you include some of the filenames in the command but omit the final filename or semicolon, MASM prompts you for the missing filenames.

The Assembler Listing

Figure 12-3 shows an example of the first page of a 386 I ASM listing file. A MASM listing file is very similar. The top three lines appear on every page of the listing as a header. First comes the assembler name, the date, and the time. Next comes a line with the title, if any, and the page number. Underneath that is the subtitle, if any, which can change from page to page.

The statement lines start on the left with the offset, in hexadecimal. (MASM also prints a line number if you request a cross-reference

```
                        ;
                        ; HELLO.ASM - Hello world program for
386 protected mode
                        ;
                        ; This program is the [in]famous "Hel
lo world" program.  It illustrates
                        ; making MS-DOS system calls from 386
protected mode.
                        ;
                            assume  cs:_text,ds:_data
00000000                _text segment para public use32 'code'

                        public _start_

00000000                _start_ proc    near

00000000  B4 09             mov ah,09h

00000002  BA 00000000 R     mov edx,offset hellomsg        .

00000007  CD 21             int 21h

00000009  C3                ret

                        _start_ endp

0000000A                _text    ends

00000000                _data segment para public use32 'data'

00000000  48 65 6C 6C 6F 20 77 6F      hellomsg db'Hello
world!!!!!!!!!',0DH,0AH,'$'
          72 6C 64 21 21 21 21 21
          21 21 21 0D 0A 24

00000016                _data    ends

00000000                _stack segment byte stack use32 'stack'

00000000  00002000[ ?? ]        db  8192 dup (?)

00002000                _stack ends

                        end
```

Figure 12-3   Sample Assembler Listing

listing.) Then comes the object code, if any, in hexadecimal. For instructions, the machine translation is shown. For data declarations, the initial value is shown. The assembler prints word and doubleword values as single values, without reversing their bytes. This makes them easier to read and interpret. The source line appears on the right.

Several symbols are used in the listing. Symbols used with object code are listed in Figure 12-4. Symbols used with source code are listed in Figure 12-5. You can see some of the symbols in Figure 12-3. For example, at _text:00000002, the machine code is **BA 00000000** followed by the symbol **R**, meaning that the address for **hellomsg** will be determined by the linker or loader.

At _stack:00000000, the initialized value is listed as **00002000[??]**, meaning that 8192 uninitialized bytes have been defined.

Figure 12-6 shows the last page from a listing, showing some of the tables generated by the assembler. Seven tables are possible: groups and segments, structures, records, macros, procedures, variables and labels, and constants. (MASM generates groups and segments, structures and records, macros, and symbols.) Each table shows all the elements defined in the program that fit into its category and lists

value R	The *value* will be determined by the linker or loader.
---- R	The segment selector value will be determined when the program is loaded.
value E	The *value* is defined externally and will be resolved by the link editor.
= *value*	An equate has been defined.
xx:	The indicated segment override prefix has been output.
xx/	An instruction prefix (such as **rep**) has been output.
66|	A prefix overriding the default operand size has been output.
67|	A prefix overriding the default address size has been output.
count[*value*]	The **dup** operator has duplicated the *value*, *count* times.
??	An uninitialized byte has been defined.

Figure 12-4   Symbols Used in Object Code Listing

I	The source statement was included from another file. (386IASM)
C	The source statement was included from another file. (MASM)
n	Macro and repeat block expansion. The number indicates the nesting level.
+	Macro and repeat block nesting level is greater than 9.

Figure 12-5   Symbols Used in Source Language Listing

pertinent information about each element. You might find the tables handy for debugging, but they take time and space, so suppress them if you don't need them.

Using CREF (MASM Only)

Figure 12-7 shows an example of a cross-reference listing as prepared by CREF. This listing shows each symbol defined in the program and indicates which lines reference it. The line that defines it is indicated by the symbol #. Cross-reference information is often handy for debugging and maintaining a program.

```
      GROUPS AND SEGMENTS
Name                        Size      Use    Align Combine   Class

_data . . . . . . . . .00000016  USE32  PARA  PUBLIC    data
_stack . . . . . . . . .00020000  USE32  BYTE  STACK     stack
_text  . . . . . . . . .0000000A  USE32  PARA  PUBLIC    code

   PROCEDURES
Name                        Type      Offset    Scope    Segment

_start_  . . . . . . . .N PROC   00000000  Public  _text

   VARIABLES AND LABELS
Name                        Type      Offset    Scope    Segment

hellomsg . . . . . . . .BYTE     00000000  Prvate  _data

      5 Symbols
      0 Warning Errors
      0 Severe Errors
```

Figure 12-6   Sample Assembler Tables

```
Microsoft Cross-Reference                    Mon Apr 10 17:41:29 1989
Help Program

  Symbol Cross-Reference        (# is definition)             Cref-1
??0000 . . . . . . . . . . . . .    46      49#
??0001 . . . . . . . . . . . . .    53      53#
??0002 . . . . . . . . . . . . .    55      55#

AMEM . . . . . . . . . . . . . .    22      40        52        54

BEGIN. . . . . . . . . . . . . .    16#     101
BYTES_OUT. . . . . . . . . . . .    11#     97

CODE . . . . . . . . . . . . . .    14
CR . . . . . . . . . . . . . . .    11#     11

DATA . . . . . . . . . . . . . .    11
DOSEXIT. . . . . . . . . . . . .    15#     86
DOSWRITE . . . . . . . . . . . .    15#     98

EXIT_PROC. . . . . . . . . . . .    57      77#       87

HELP_MSG . . . . . . . . . . . .    11#     11        94
HELP_MSG_LEN . . . . . . . . . .    11#     95

LF . . . . . . . . . . . . . . .    11#     11
```

Figure 12-7   Sample CREF Listing

To obtain a cross-reference listing, you start by producing a cross-reference output file from the assembly process, either by specifying a filename or by using the **/c** switch. For example, this command specifies the filename:

```
masm help,,,debug.crf
```

The following uses the **/c** switch to let the default name (**help.crf**) be used:

```
masm /c help;
```

The assembler issues the cross-reference file in binary form. To convert it to ASCII, you process it with the CREF program. The format of the CREF command is:

```
cref source[,listing][;]
```

The source file is the cross-reference file that was generated by the assembler. The listing file will have the same name with a **.ref** extension if you don't specify a name. To prepare a reference listing from **debug.crf,** you could enter:

```
cref debug.crf;
```

You could leave off the **.crf** extension since it is the default. The listing file will be called **debug.ref** in this case. To specify a different name, you could code:

```
cref debug,my.ref
```

You could leave off the **.ref** extension. You can also specify a device name for the listing file:

```
cref debug,prn
```

```
cref debug,con
```

Like MASM, CREF will prompt you for filenames if you omit them.

Link Editing

Like the assembler, the link editor has many options that control its behavior and its outputs. This chapter shows you how to link multiple object modules together, control the contents of the listing file (called a map file), control the linking environment, and use libraries and definitions files. Both 386 | LINK and Microsoft LINK are covered.

Using 386|LINK

Figure 13-1 shows the format of the 386 | LINK command line, which has the same general format at the 386 | ASM command line. The switches, of course, are different. If you specify more than one source filename, all the modules will be linked into one program file. For example, to link **help.obj**, **helpsub.obj**, and **helpext.obj** together, you would enter this command:

```
386link help helpsub helpext
```

This job would produce a program file named **help.exp**, a map file (the linker listing file) called **help.map**, and various messages on the standard output device. The command switches let you control the

386link *filename* [*filenames*] [*switches*]

Switches:

Switch	Description
-Map *filename*	Produces the specified map file
-NOMap	Suppresses the map file
-SWitches	Lists command switches in map file
-NOSWitches	Doesn't list command switches in map file
-PUBList *option*	Controls the listing of public symbols
-FULLSEG	Breaks segments into constituent parts
-DUMP	Dumps object records in map file
-OneCase	Ignores case
-TwoCase	Pays attention to case
-Lib	Specifies a library file
-FULLWARN	Does extra error checking
-NOOutput	Suppresses the output file
-8086	Specifies 8086 or any other processor in real mode as the target CPU
-80386	Specifies 80386 in protected mode with 32-bit addressing as the target CPU
-Exe *filename*	Specifies .exe format for output file (.Exp for 80386 protected mode)
-RELEXE *filename*	Specifies .rex format for output file
-Hex *filename*	Specifies Intel 8086 Absolute Hex format for output file
-SRECord *filename*	Specifies Motorola hexadecimal format for output file
-PACK	Packs an .exp file
-NOPACK	Doesn't pack the .exp file
-SYMbols	Includes symbol table in executable file
-NOSYMbols	Doesn't include symbol table in executable file
-Stack *n*	Sets up a stack segment of *n* bytes
-DOSORDER	Orders segments in Microsoft order
-LOGORDER	Orders segments in standard order

Defaults are underscored. Uppercase letters and large numbers indicate abbreviations.

Figure 13-1   The 386link Command

format and contents of the output. 386 I LINK has standard defaults for all the various switch settings. However, you can create a version for your own installation that sets up the defaults the way you like them. In Figure 13-1, the standard defaults are underlined, but bear in mind that your installation might have different defaults. Several switches that you might need in less common situations are omitted from the figure. You can find the complete list in your 386 I LINK documentation.

Displaying a Command Summary

If you enter the command **386link** with no arguments, a help message is displayed, listing a summary of the switches.

Working with the Map File

Figure 13-2 shows an example of a map file produced by 386 I LINK in its default format. You can see:

* A heading showing information about the linker and the target CPU.

* A list of switches in effect for this link job.

* A list of the object files that were linked to produce the program, in the order they were read by the linker.

* A list of the segments that make up the program. Included are details about group, class, type, base address (relative to the program start), and size in bytes.

* A list of the public symbols that were resolved by the linker, the address value of the symbol, the object module where the symbol was defined, the segment in which the symbol resides, and its size if it is a common symbol.

If problems were encountered by the linker, the map also contains any error messages and a list of unresolved external symbols.

All this information can help in debugging a program. For example, if a program won't run, you might have linked it with the wrong switches or for the wrong target CPU. You might have missed a message that was displayed on the screen. You might have linked the object modules in the wrong order or forgotten to include one. The list of public symbols and their addresses can help you when using an

```
386|LINK: 2.0 — Copyright (C) 1986-88 Phar Lap Software, Inc.
Target CPU is 80386


Command line switches:

-switches -exe vr vrmain vrsub


Input module(s):

"vrmain.asm" from file "vrmain.obj".
"vrsub.asm" from file "vrsub.obj".


Segment map

  Name          Group        Class     Type   Offset      Size


 _DATA         DGROUP                   PUB    00000000    00000190
 _STACK        DGROUP                   STK    00000190    000007D0
 _TEXT                        CODE      PUB    00000960    00000033


Public symbols

  Name         Value      Module       Segment      Size


 ZEROLOOP     00000986   vrsub.asm     _TEXT
```

Figure 13-2   Sample 386|LINK Map

online debugger, where you have to know the address of an item in
order to examine its contents in memory. (The addresses of nonpublic
symbols are included in the assembler listing.)

Many of the switches in Figure 13-1 control the layout and content of
the map, as explained in the following sections.

Suppressing the Map File. The map file is produced unless **–nomap** is
specified. You can use the **–map** switch to specify a path or a nondefault name, or to override **–nomap** if it has been set up as the
default for your installation. **–Noswitches** suppresses the switches
list, which saves a little time and space. **–Switches** will override
–noswitches if that is the current default. The following command
specifies a nondefault name for the map file and suppresses the switch
list:

```
386link help -m a:help.doc -nos
```

Listing the Public Symbols. Several switches pertain to the list of public symbols. By default, they are listed in alphabetical order (**–publist byname**). Sometimes it's handy to sort them by their address values instead (**–publist byvalue**). Then it's easier to find out what's at a particular address. You can list them both ways with **–publist both** and suppress the list altogether with **–publist none**.

```
386|LINK: 2.0 — Copyright (C) 1986-88 Phar Lap Software, Inc.
Target CPU is 80386


Command line switches:

-switches -fullseg -exe vr vrmain vrsub


Input module(s):

"vrmain.asm" from file "vrmain.obj".
"vrsub.asm" from file "vrsub.obj".


Segment map
```

Name	Group	Class	Type	Offset	Size
_DATA	DGROUP		PUB	00000000	00000190
vrmain.asm	DGROUP		PUB	00000000	000000C8
vrsub.asm	DGROUP		PUB	000000C8	000000C8
_STACK	DGROUP		STK	00000190	000007D0
vrmain.asm	DGROUP		STK	00000190	000003E8
vrsub.asm	DGROUP		STK	00000578	000003E8
_TEXT		CODE	PUB	00000960	00000033
vrmain.asm		CODE	PUB	00000960	00000015
vrsub.asm		CODE	PUB	00000978	0000001B

```
Public symbols
```

Name	Value	Module	Segment	Size
ZEROLOOP	00000986	vrsub.asm	_TEXT	

Figure 13-3   **Sample Map with –Fullseg Listing**

Breaking Down the Segment List. The **–fullseg** switch causes the linker to break segments down into their constituent parts from the input modules. Figure 13-3 shows an example of a –fullseg listing. You can see how the different modules contributed portions to the final three segments.

Dumping the Object Records. If 386 I LINK tells you that an object file contains errors, and you can't track down the errors any other way, you can dump the object records into the map file with the **–dump** switch. Interpreting a hex dump of object code is beyond the scope of this book, but if you can deal with the dump, 386 I LINK can give it to you.

Controlling the Linker Environment

A few switches control the environment in which the linker operates. You can specify case sensitivity, library files, and extra error checking.

Case Sensitivity. By default, 386 I LINK ignores case in segment names, public symbols, and the other symbols that it deals with. To make it case sensitive, use the **–twocase** switch. If your installation has set **–twocase** as the default, you can override it for a particular job with the **–onecase** switch.

Linker Libraries. A linker library is a collection of object modules gathered into one file on disk. They usually contain generalized routines that can be linked into many programs. Most high-level compilers include one or more linker libraries full of hand routines you can reference as submodules. If you're working strictly in assembly language, you can create your own linker libraries using 386 I LIB, which is not covered in this book. 386 I LIB creates a library file in the correct format for 386 I LINK.

To use a routine from a link library, your program references it just like any other object module. On the 386 I LINK command, you specify not the name of the module but the name of the library. For example, suppose your source module contains these statements:

```
extrn   stdrepl:near
...
call    stdrepl
```

The module, **stdrep1**, is contained in a library named **stdforms.lib**. Your link command should look like this:

```
386link help -stdforms
```

386 I LINK will search the **stdforms.lib** file for the **stdrep1** module.

You can specify a path for the library filename. If you don't state the extension the default **.lib** is used. You can specify multiple libraries with multiple filenames in one **-lib** switch, with multiple **lib** switches, or both. 386 I LINK searches libraries in the order listed, so if more than one library contains a **stdrep1.obj** module, the first one encountered is the one used.

Extra Warnings. When you specify the **-fullwarn** switch, 386 I LINK issues a warning message if it encounters either of two specific situations.

Suppose two or more segments with the same name and **common** combine type initialize data areas with different values. Since **common** segments overlay each other, one segment's initial values overlay the other's. Initial values from the last module processed go into the program file. This may or may not be what the programmer wanted.

Suppose the **org** directive backs up the location counter, causing two areas to share the same memory space. This could be a mistake, or it could be intentional on the programmer's part.

By default, the linker does not warn you of these situations. If you would like to be warned, specify the **-fullwarn** switch.

Controlling the Program File

Most of the 386 I LINK switches give you control over the executable program module produced by the linker. You can control the target CPU, the format, and some of the contents of this file. To suppress the executable file completely, specify the **-nooutput** switch. You'll still get the map file and the error and warning messages, which can help in debugging the program before attempting to produce an executable module.

Selecting Target CPU and Program Format.

386 I LINK lets you prepare programs for two target CPU's in a variety of formats. By default, programs are prepared in .EXP format (which is a variation on the standard .EXE format) for the '386 running in protected mode under the DOS-Extender. To select the 8086, or any processor running in real

mode, use the **–8086** switch. To select the '386 if that is not the default
at your installation, use the **–80386** switch.

The default program format is **–exe**, which produces an .EXE file if
the target CPU is **–8086** and an .EXP file if the target CPU is **–80386**.
If you are working with the appropriate system, you can also choose
the **–relexe** (relocatable exe) format, the **–hex** (Intel absolute hexadecimal) format, or the **–srecord** (Motorola absolute hexadecimal)
format. If you want to use the default format, you can still specify the
switch to override the default directory or filename.

Packing an .EXP File. .EXP files can be compressed (packed) to save
disk space and loading time. To pack a program, specify **–pack** on the
command line. You can do this only if the program format is .EXP,
which means the target CPU must be the '386.

Packing involves replacing multiple occurrences of a character with
a single occurrence followed by a value indicating how many times the
character is repeated. Therefore, packing produces the greatest savings when the program contains large fields of uninitialized data or
data initialized to the same value. You can try linking a program both
ways and checking the file sizes in the directory to see if packing
reduces the size significantly.

The standard default is **–nopack**. To pack a file, specify **–pack**.

Controlling the Segment Order. By default, 386 I LINK orders segments
in its own order, which is basically sequential order. To use Microsoft's
standard order, specify the **–dosorder** switch. If **–dosorder** has been
made the default, you can override it with the **–logorder** switch.

Including a Symbol Table. Normally, symbols have disappeared from the
program by the time it is an executable file. This makes it a little more
difficult to use an online debugger. Instead of asking for the value of
profit, for example, you have to ask for the value at DS:0014. But
some debuggers, called symbolic debuggers, can relate symbols to addresses and their contents if you include a symbol table in the executable module with the **–symbols** switch. Phar Lap's Minibug, which
is discussed in the next chapter, is not a symbolic debugger. But if you
have a symbolic debugger, then use the **–symbols** switch when you
link a program that needs debugging. The default switch, **–nosym-
bols**, can be used if your environment has established **–symbols** as
the default.

Specifying the Stack Size. The –stack switch can be used to specify a stack segment size if none of the modules create a stack segment. The switch overrides any stack segment definition within the program. However, if the –stack switch decreases the size of the stack segment, an error results.

Streamlining 386|LINK Commands

You can save yourself a lot of work on individual 386 l LINK commands by setting up as much in advance as possible. You can revise the default switches to reflect your most frequent needs, and you can simplify command repetition by placing the arguments for a particular command in an indirect command file.

Revising the Default Switches. There are two ways to revise the default switches. The first is to revise 386LINK.EXE itself to set up whatever default switches you want. This requires the use of the CFIG386 program, which we are not covering in this book. See your Phar Lap documentation for details if you are interested in pursuing this path.

The other way is to set the **386link** variable in your operating system environment. For DOS and OS/2, you do this with the **set** command. To set **–switches, –nomap,** and **–twocase** as the defaults for all future 386 l LINK jobs, you would enter this command at the system prompts:

```
set 386link=-switches -nomap -twocase
```

Notice that no spaces surround the equal sign. 386 l LINK always checks the operating system environment for a **386link** variable at the beginning of each link job. Once you have set up default switches this way, you can still override them with switches included in individual commands.

Using Indirect Command Files. An indirect command file is a file containing the arguments for a 386 l LINK job. You can include filenames and switches. Several lines can be used, so you can create much longer commands than are possible with the normal command line. You can also include comments, each preceded by an exclamation point (!). Suppose you are currently debugging a program named **vr.exp**, which is linked by this command:

```
386link vrmain vrsub -exe vr -fullwarn -fullseg -dosorder
-pack
```

You could create the following indirect command file (using any ASCII editor):

```
! Creates vr.exp from vrmain.obj and vrsub.obj
vrmain
vrsub
-exe vr      ! specifies the name of the output file
-fullwarn    ! for ORG
-fullseg     ! details segments in maps
-dosorder    ! Microsoft segment order
-pack        ! packs the .EXP file
```

To reference an indirect command file, precede its name with an at sign (@) on the command line. If the command file is named **vrjob.lnk**, then you would use it in a 386|LINK command like this:

```
386link @vrjob
```

.Lnk is assumed when you don't specify an extension.

Using Microsoft LINK

If you are preparing a program to run under DOS or OS/2 and have assembled it with MASM (or any assembler that produces object files in Microsoft Relocatable Object Module Format (OMF), then you can link it with Microsoft's LINK. The possible outputs are an .EXE (executable) file, a map file, and error and warning messages.

LINK Command Format

Figure 13-4 shows the format of the **link** command, which is similar to the **masm** format. The arguments and options, of course, are different from those in the **masm** command. This chapter discusses only the more commonly used options; for information about the other options, see your Microsoft reference manual.

You can specify the full name for a switch or any abbreviation that makes it identifiable from other switches. For example, if you enter /pa, LINK can't identify whether you want /PackCode, /PadCode, /PadData, or /Pause. If you enter /pac, then the only possible option is /PackCode. All the options are shown in Figure 13-4, including the less commonly used ones, so that you can decide how to abbreviate the ones you want to use.

```
link [options] object-files[,executable-file,map-file,library-
    files,definition-file] [:]
```

Options discussed in chapter:

```
/Help                   Display help list
/CodeView               Include symbolic information for CodeView
/ExePack                Pack executable file
/PackCode[:n]           Pack segment groups
/NoPackCode             Don't pack segment groups
/FarCallTranslation     Translate far calls into near calls
/NoFarCallTranslation   Don't translate far calls
/Stack:n                Create stack of n bytes
/Dosseg                 Use standard Microsoft segment order
/Map[:n]                List global symbols in map
/LineNumbers            Include line numbers in map
/Batch                  Don't prompt for library specs
/NoDefaultLibrarySearch    Don't search default libraries
/Information            Display progress information
/WarnFixup              Warn about segment/group offset problems
/NoIgnoreCase           Pay attention to case
```

Other options:

```
/Align:n                Set segment sector alignment
/CParmaxAlloc           Allocate extra memory to program
/DSAlloc                Locate data at high end of segment
/High                   Locate program in high memory
/Incremental            Produce sym and ilk files for ILINK
/NoExtDictionary        Ignore extended library dictionary
/NoGroupAssociation     Ignore groups
/NoNullsDosseg          Same as /Dosseg without initial nulls
/OverlayInterrupt       Control overlay interrupts
/PadCode:n              Pad code segment for ILINK
/PadData:n              Pad data segment for ILINK
/Pause                  Pause to change diskettes
/Segments:n             Specify maximum number of segments
```

Figure 13-4   The Link Command

Since the option names are so long, it is common to print the complex ones in upper- and lowercase as shown in the figure. **/NoIgnore-Case** is easier to read than **/noignorecase**. LINK always ignores the case of options even when it is case sensitive for module names and external names. Therefore, you can use any mixture of case you like when typing the options on the command line.

To get an online display of the **link** switches, enter this command:

```
link /he
```

Unless you are using the **/help** switch, you must specify at least one object file. You can also specify the path and name for the .EXE file, the path and name for the .MAP file, paths and names for library files, and the path and name for a definition file. To take the defaults for the remaining files on the command line, terminate the command with a semicolon. The following command specifies one object file as input and takes the defaults for the .EXE file, the map file, the library files, and the definition file:

```
link help;
```

This command results in an executable program file named **help.exe** and no map file. No input library files or definition files are used. The following command specifies the input object file name and the output .EXE file name, but takes the default values for the map file and the library files:

```
link help,a:help1;
```

If you need to specify a later file name, you must code the intervening commas. For example, to use **doscalls.lib** and **help.def** for a job, you could code:

```
link help,,,doscalls.lib,help.def
```

This command doesn't need a semicolon since no file names are omitted after **help.def**. Unlike the preceding jobs, this job will produce a map file named **help.map**, since the map file default changes from no to yes when you code a comma rather than a semicolon.

Using the Prompted Command

If you omit one or more file names on the command line, LINK will prompt you for the missing file names with these prompts:

```
Object Modules [.OBJ]:

Run File [name.EXE]:

List File [NUL.MAP]:

Libraries [.LIB]:

Definitions File [NUL.DEF]:
```

After you supply one or more object file names, the linker will fill in the default name of the run file. You can fill in any line just as if you were entering that argument on the command line. You can leave it blank to take the default (except for the object module) or fill in file names, with or without paths. You can add options to any line. To take defaults for all the remaining values, you can enter a semicolon on any line.

Using a Response File

Another way to provide arguments for the **link** command is with a response file. To create a response file, imagine you are filling out the answers to the prompted version of the command. Create one line per prompt line. For example, to link **help.obj**, produce an output file named **try.exe**, and a map file name **help.map**, you could create this file:

```
help

try

help;
```

To use the response file, use its file name preceded by @ in the **link** command. For example, if the above file was named **help.lnk**, you could enter this command:

```
link @help.lnk
```

Response files are handy when you must repeat the same job many times and when your command arguments are longer than the command line. You can continue a response file line by coding a plus sign as the final character on the line.

Specifying the Object Files

At least one object file must be specified in the **link** command. The default path is the current path and the default extension is **.obj**. To specify more than one object file, connect them with spaces or plus signs, as in this example:

```
link help+helpsub1+helpsub2;
```

This could also be entered as:

```
link help helpsub1 helpsub2;
```

LINK processes the object files in the order specified, so if you are concerned about the sequential order of the segments, be sure to put them in the desired order. In most cases, you'll put the main module first.

Specifying the Run File

The executable program file is the major output of the link process. By default, its name is the root name of the first object module plus the .EXE extension. If you give it another name, be sure to use the .EXE extension in order to run it under DOS or OS/2. The default directory is the current directory, regardless of the directories of any of the object files.

Several switches pertain to the executable file. You can include debugging information in the file, save space by packing the file, translate far calls into near calls, and generally manipulate the segments.

Including CodeView Information. For symbolic debuggers such as Code-View to operate, symbolic debugging information must be included in the file. By default, it is not. To include it, specify the /**CodeView** switch on the command line. The debugging information is ignored when the file is executed outside of a debugging environment, but it makes the file longer so you might want to relink the program without the /**co** switch when you are ready to put it into production.

Packing the Program File. .EXE files can be compressed (packed) to save disk space and loading time. To pack a program, specify /**exepack** on the command line. Packing involves replacing multiple occurrences of a character with a single occurrence followed by a value indicating how many times the character is repeated. It produces the greatest savings when the program contains large fields of uninitialized data or data initialized to a single value. You can try linking a program both ways and checking the file sizes in the directory to see if packing has any significant effect.

You can also pack a file by combining contiguous logical code segments into a single physical code segment, much like combining segments. Only segments in the same group can be packed this way. For this type of packing, specify the /**PackCode** switch. You can specify a numeric parameter indicating the maximum size of the resulting physical segment. The default is 65536 bytes—the maximum size in 16-bit addressing. If /**PackCode** has been set up as the default at your installation, you can override it with /**NoPackCode**.

Translating Far Calls. If a label has **far** type, then all calls to it must be far calls, even if they appear in the same segment. The /**FarCall-Translation** switch translates far calls into near calls whenever possible. Near calls take much less time. (No space can be saved since the assembler has already set aside the space for the far call.) You can override far call translation with the **/NoFarCallTranslation** switch if it is the default for your installation.

Manipulating the Segments. You can specify a stack segment for the program with the **/stack** switch. Include a parameter indicating the size of the segment in bytes (maximum 65535). This overrides any stack segment specifications from within the modules. Be careful not to make the stack segment smaller than needed.

You can specify the standard Microsoft order for the segments with the **/dosseg** switch. This order is standard if you are linking to a module created by one of the Microsoft high-level compilers, but if you are linking a stand-alone assembly language program, then you might need to use this switch to override sequential order.

By default, LINK sets a maximum of 128 segments per program. If your program uses more segments, then you need to raise the limit with the **/segments** switch. You can specify up to 1024 segments.

Manipulating the Map File

The map file is the output listing of the linker. Figure 13-5 shows an example of a map file produced by LINK in its default format. You can see:

```
Start   Stop    Length  Name            Class
00000H  0005FH  00060H  _TEXT           CODE
00060H  0009CH  0003DH  _DATA           DATA
000A0H  00487H  003E8H  STACK           STACK

Origin  Group
0006:0  DGROUP

Program entry point at 0000:0010

Unresolved externals:

DOSWRITE in file(s):
 HELP1.OBJ(\wp50\masmbook\help1.ASM)
DOSEXIT in file(s):
 HELP1.OBJ(\wp50\masmbook\help1.ASM)
```

Figure 13-5   Sample LINK Map File

- A list of the segments that make up the program. Included are details about the start address, the ending address, the size, the name, and the class.

- A list of the segment groups.

- The program entry point.

- A list of external symbols that were never resolved.

All this information can help in debugging and documenting a program.

No map file is issued if you code a semicolon on the command line, or in the prompted or response file setup, before the map file name argument. If you code the comma for the map file but do not enter a name, then a map file is generated and given the same base filename as the executable file with the extension **.map**.

```
Start  Stop    Length  Name              Class
00000H 0005FH  00060H  _TEXT             CODE
00060H 0009CH  0003DH  _DATA             DATA
000A0H 00487H  003E8H  STACK             STACK

Origin      Group
0006:0      DGROUP

Address              Publics by Name
0006:0040              _bend
0000:0000 Abs          _edata


Address              Publics by Value
0000:0000 Abs          _edata
0006:0040              _bend

Program entry point at 0000:0010

Unresolved externals:


DOSWRITE in file(s):
     PROGS\HELP1.OBJ(\wp50\masmbook\help1.asm)
DOSEXIT in file(s):
     PROGS\HELP1.OBJ(\wp50\masmbook\help1.asm)
```

Figure 13-6   Map Including Public Symbols Lists

Including Public Symbols. You can include a listing of all public symbols in the map with the **/map** switch. Figure 13-6 shows an example of a map that includes two public symbols lists. The first is sorted by name, the second by address. If you are working with an online debugger that cannot respond to symbol names, then you'll need the public symbols list to find out the addresses of items you want to look up. (The addresses of nonpublic symbols are included in the assembler listing.)

If you include an operand with **/map**, it suppresses the alphabetic listing and specifies the maximum number of symbols to be sorted by address. The default is 2048.

The **/map** option is ignored if the main body of the command does not call for a map file to be generated.

Including Line Numbers in Maps. Debugging can be easier if line numbers from the original source program are carried through to the map. Figure 13-7 shows an example of a map with line numbers. Each entry shows a line number from the source program followed by the segment:offset address of the object code generated by the line. Only code section lines that resulted in object code are included in the list. The **/LineNumbers** option requests the line number list, but only if the

```
Start   Stop    Length  Name            Class
00000H  0003CH  0003DH  _TEXT           CODE
0003EH  0007CH  0003FH  _DATA           DATA
00080H  00467H  003E8H  STACK           STACK

Origin    Group
0003:0    DGROUP

Line numbers for HELP2.OBJ(\wp50\masmbook\help2.ASM) segment _TEXT

   20 0000:0010    21 0000:0010    22 0000:0013    25 0000:0016
   26 0000:001A    27 0000:001E    31 0000:0023    32 0000:0027
   33 0000:0028    34 0000:002C    35 0000:002D    36 0000:0031
   37 0000:0032    38 0000:0036    39 0000:0037    40 0000:003C

Program entry point at 0000:0010

Unresolved externals:


DOSWRITE in file(s):
    HELP2.OBJ(\wp50\masmbook\help2.ASM)
DOSEXIT in file(s):
    HELP2.OBJ(\wp50\masmbook\help2.ASM)
```

Figure 13-7   Sample Map with Line Numbers

object modules contain the line number information. To cause that to happen, include the /zd switch when you assemble the module.

Using Libraries

An object module library is a collection of object modules gathered into one file on disk. They usually contain generalized routines that can be linked into many programs. Most high-level compilers include one or more object module libraries full of handy routines you can reference as submodules. If you're working strictly in assembly language, you can create your own libraries using LIB, which is not covered in this book. LIB creates a library file in the correct format for access by LINK.

To use a routine from a library, your program references it just like any other object module. On the LINK command, you specify not the name of the module but the name of the library. For example, suppose your source module contains these statements:

```
extrn   stdrep1:near

. . .

call                     stdrep1
```

The public symbol, **stdrep1**, is defined in a module contained in a library named **stdforms.lib**. Your **link** command should look like this:

```
link help,,,stdforms;
```

LINK will search the **stdforms.lib** file for the module that defines the **stdrep1** symbol.

You can specify an extension if the default .lib is not correct. You can specify multiple libraries by connecting library names with plus signs. LINK searches libraries in the order listed, so if more than one library contains a **stdrep1.obj** module, the first one encountered is the one used. The following command specifies four different libraries:

```
link help,,,stdforms+os2+jnfmath+duolib;
```

If you are linking with modules prepared by a high-level compiler, then a default library name will be built into the object module. You can specify additional library names on the **link** command. These libraries are searched before the default library is searched.

You can include a path for an individual library. Or you can code a path with no file name, in which case LINK includes that path in the library search path. You can set up a default search path by assigning a value to the **lib** environment variable with the **set** command at the

DOS or OS/2 prompt. For example, the following command sets up a search path of three directories:

```
set lib=d:\os2\lib;c:\os2\lib;a:\
```

Be sure there are no spaces around the equal sign.
LINK looks for a particular library in this order:
1. If the library name is prefixed with a path name, then only that directory is searched.
2. If no path name is attached to a library name, then LINK looks first in the current directory.
3. If not found in the current directory, LINK looks in all paths specified in the **link** command.
4. If not found in those directories, LINK looks in the default search path specified by the **lib** environment variable.

Suppose you want to search the root directories of all four drives for every library in the job. You could specify a command like this:

```
link help,,,c:\+d:\+a:\+b:;
```

When searching for a particular library, LINK would look in the current directory first, those four root directories second, and then whatever directories are specified in the **lib** search path variable.

If LINK can't find a library in any of the search paths, it prompts you for the correct name/path with this prompt:

```
LINK : warning L4051: library-name : cannot find library
Enter new file spec:
```

This gives you a chance to correct the library specification without having to reenter the job. However, if you want to suppress this service, then include the **/batch** option in the **link** command. Instead of prompting you for the correct filespec, the job will terminate with a fatal error message if the desired library can't be found. Although option switches can usually appear in any position on the command line, this one must precede the file names in order to work. The following command does not suppress the library error prompt:

```
link help,,,os2+mylib; /b
```

But the following command does suppress the prompt:

```
link /b help,,,os2+mylib;
```

The **/batch** option doesn't suppress any other prompts unless you leave the name of the object module itself out of the job. Usually, LINK will prompt for the name of the object module when none is included on the command line. But with the **/batch** switch, the job terminates with a fatal error message.

To suppress whatever default library is indicated in the object module, specify the **/NoDefaultLibrarySearch** option. You could use this option to override a compiler-supplied library with one of your own. If you use the **/nod** option and end up with unresolved external references in the job, then you'll have to fix your library or go back to using the default one.

Using Definition Files

One of the inputs to LINK is an OS/2 definition file. This file defines the module and the segments beyond what you can do in assembler **segment** statements. Figure 13-8 shows the format of the statements in a definition file for an application module. (Other statements and options are used for drivers and dynamic link libraries.) You can see that many of the segment attributes can be defined here. If you don't include a module definition file, then all the defaults are taken.

The creation of a definition file is beyond the scope of this book. If you would like to include a definition file in your link job, include its name as the last argument on the **link** command line.

Controlling the Job

Some switches affect the way LINK performs its job. You can control what information is displayed and case sensitivity.

Displaying Extra Messages. The **/Information** option causes LINK to display progress information as it works on the file. For long link jobs, you might appreciate the progress reports. The **/WarnFixup** switch causes LINK to display warning messages when an offset is relative to a segment base that is not the group base.

Establishing Case Sensitivity. Ordinarily, LINK is insensitive to the differences between uppercase and lowercase. To make it sensitive, specify the **/NoIgnoreCase** switch.

Fixup Error Messages

One of the most frequent error messages from the link editor is a fixup error message. After the linker has combined and grouped the segments, it goes back and "fixes up" all the addresses. It not only finalizes the external references that the assembler left unresolved, it also overwrites assembler-supplied offsets that have changed because of

```
NAME  [modulename]                    ; specify an application program
   [WINDOWAPI | WINDOWCOMPAT | NOTWINDOWCOMPAT]
                                      ; compatibility  with Presentation
                                      ; Manager

DESCRIPTION 'string'                  ; embed string in EXE file

PROTMODE | REALMODE                   ; specify mode (if only one)

EXETYPE                               ; host operating system
   [OS2 | WINDOWS | DOS4]

CODE                                  ; characteristics of class 'code'
                                      ; segments
   [PRELOAD | LOADONCALL]             ; when to load
   [EXECUTEONLY | EXECUTEREAD]        ; protection from reading
   [IOPL | NOIOPL]                    ; i/o privilege
   [CONFORMING | NONCONFORMING]       ; access by other segments

DATA                                  ; characteristics of non-'code'
                                      ; class segments
   [PRELOAD | LOADONCALL]             ; when to load
   [READONLY | READWRITE]             ; permitted operations
   [NONE | SINGLE | MULTIPLE]         ; how DGROUP is shared
   [SHARED | NONSHARED]               ; how segment is shared
   [IOPL | NOIOPL]                    ; access by other segments

SEGMENTS                              ; override CODE and DATA state-
                                      ; ments for specific segments
   name [CLASS['classname']]          ; identify segment or class being
                                      ; described
   [PRELOAD | LOADONCALL]
   [READONLY | READWRITE]
   [EXECUTEONLY | EXECUTEREAD]
   [IOPL | NOIOPL]
   [CONFORMING | NONCONFORMING]
   [SHARED | NONSHARED]

EXPORTS                               ; functions available to other
                                      ; programs
   exportname [stackparams]

IMPORTS                               ; functions to be imported from
                                      ; other modules
   [internalname=]modulename.entryname | modulename.number

STUB 'filename.EXE'                   ; stub program for DOS execution
```

Defaults are underlined. Key words must be in uppercase.

Figure 13-8   Definition File Format

segment rearrangements. If the amount of space left by the assembler for an address is too small to hold the finalized address, then a fixup error occurs. This can happen if the source code specified or implied that the reference was short or near, but it turned out to be larger than that, or if a segment group turned out to be larger than the maximum allowable size. You can fix these and try again.

Introduction to Online Debuggers

An online debugger can be an invaluable tool in locating and correcting a subtle logic error in a program. The debugger lets you execute the program being debugged, which we call the *target program* in this chapter, on an instruction-by-instruction basis. After each instruction, you can examine values in the registers and memory (including the stack). With more advanced debuggers, you can keep fields on the screen and watch them change as the program executes. You can even insert values into memory and the registers and insert new instructions into the program.

This chapter introduces the two debuggers that come with the program development packages we have been using throughout this book: Phar Lap's MINIBUG and Microsoft's CodeView. MINIBUG is a basic debugger, accomplishing the essentials, while CodeView is highly advanced. However, in both cases, we can do little more in this book than introduce you to the most basic facilities and briefly acquaint you with what else is available. You can learn enough in this chapter to get started with your debugger and do some simple manipulation. You'll also be aware of some more advanced facilities that you might want to look up in the debugger reference manual when you're ready to progress beyond the basics.

Introduction to MINIBUG

MINIBUG is the debugger that comes with the 386 I ASM package. It's not as fully featured as some other debuggers—in particular, it cannot relate source program line numbers and symbols to their actual address values—but you can still debug effectively with it. MINIBUG works with programs in .EXE and .EXP formats. It can also handle a program that has been bound with the 386 I DOS-Extender.

Sample Program

Figure 14-1 shows complete listing for the sample program used to explain MINIBUG. It consists of two modules: an error message module and a stub. The error message module is being developed to serve many programs in a large system. When the module receives an error message number in the stack, it displays the requested error message on the monitor, then returns control to the calling program. At this time, which is early in the development of the entire system, only seven error messages are available, but the module is set up to accommodate as many as are needed.

The stub program is simply a calling module created to test out the error message module. All it does is place a value in the stack, call the error message module, then terminate.

Notice that the program refers to a variable that it neither defines nor declares as an external variable: **msg_num**. It is set up to define **msg_num** from the command line when the program is assembled. That way, we can try out several different error message numbers with a minimum of fuss. The command we use to assemble the module with an error message number of 5 is:

```
386asm -d msg_num=5 stub
```

Figure 14-1 shows the assembler listings for both **errmsg** and **stub** and the linker map for the combined module. You'll find it useful to refer back to this listing throughout the MINIBUG discussion.

Getting Ready to Use MINIBUG

You need no special preparation to run MINIBUG. Simply assemble and link the program as you would for normal execution. You might want to print the assembler listing and linker map so you have a list of address offsets handy. If the program contains combined segments,

```
Phar Lap Macro Assembler   Version 2.0      Thu Jul 06 17:50:19 1989
stub                                                  Page     1-1


                                title    stub
                                page     ,132
                                .386
                                assume   cs:_text,ds:_data,ss:stack

                                extrn    err_msg_proc:near

00000000                        stack    segment stack byte use32 'stack'
00000000   000003E8[ ?? ]       db       1000 dup (?)
000003E8                        stack    ends

00000000                        _data    segment dword public use32 'data'
00000000                        _data    ends

00000000                        text     segment dword public use32 'code'
00000000                        begin:
00000000   6A 05                push     msg_num
00000002   E8 00000000 E        call     err_msg_proc
00000007   B4 4C                mov      ah,4ch
00000009   CD 21                int      21h
0000000B                        _text    ends
                                end      begin


Phar Lap Macro Assembler   Version 2.0      Thu Jul 06 17:50:19 1989
stub                                                  Symbols-1

    GROUPS AND SEGMENTS
Name                         Size       Use     Align   Combine Class
_data . . . . . . . . . .    00000000   USE32   DWORD   PUBLIC  Data
_text . . . . . . . . .      0000000B   USE32   DWORD   PUBLIC  code
stack . . . . . . . .        000003E8   USE32   BYTE    STACK   stack

    VARIABLES AND LABELS
Name                         Type       Offset      Scope   Segment
begin . . . . . . . . .      N LABEL    00000000    Prvate  text
err_msg_proc . . . . . .     N LABEL                Extern

    CONSTANTS
Name                         Type   Value
msg_num . . . . . . .        Text   5


        6 Symbols
        0 Warning Errors
        0 Severe Errors
```

Figure 14-1   Program Documentation (part 1 of 5)

```
Phar Lap Macro Assembler   Version 2.0      Thu Jul 06 17:50:21 1989
errmsg                                                    Page    1-1


                                            title    errmsg
                                            page     ,132
                                            .386
                                            public   err_msg_proc
                                setebp      macro
                                            push     ebp
                                            mov      ebp,esp
                                            add      ebp,8
                                            endm

00000000                        stack       segment stack
00000000  000003E8[ ?? ]                    db       1000 dup (?)
000003E8                        stack       ends

00000000                        _data       segment public
= 00000005                      num_len     equ     5
= 00000037                      msg_len     equ     55
= 00000009                      write_code  equ     9
= 00000001                      min_msg     equ     1
= 00000007                      max_msg     equ     7

00000000  45 52 52 4F 52 20     err_start   db       'ERROR '
00000006  30 30 30 30 30        err_num     db       '00000'
0000000B  3A 20                             db       ': '
0000000D  00000037[ ?? ]        err_msg     db       msg_len dup (?)
00000044                        _data       ends

00000044                        _data       segment public
00000044  30 30 30 30 31        message_table db     '00001'
00000049  46 69 6C 65 20 6E 6F 74           db       'File not found$'
          20 66 6F 75 6E 64 24
00000058  00000023[ ?? ]                    db       35 dup (?)
0000007B  30 30 30 30 32                    db       '00002'
00000080  46 69 6C 65 20 77 72 69           db       'File write protect
ed$'
          74 65 20 70 72 6F 74 65
          63 74 65 64 24
00000095  0000001D[ ?? ]                    db       29 dup (?)
000000B2  30 30 30 30 33                    db       '00003'
000000B7  46 69 6C 65 20 65 6D 70           db       'File empty$'
          74 79 24
000000C2  00000027[ ?? ]                    db       39 dup (?)
000000E9  30 30 30 30 34                    db       '00004'
000000EE  46 69 6C 65 20 6E 6F 74           db       'File not readable$'
          20 72 65 61 64 61 62 6C
          65 24
```

Figure 14-1   Program Documentation (part 2 of 5)

```
00000100  00000020[ ?? ]                       db      32 dup (?)
00000120  30 30 30 30 35                        db      '00005'
00000125  46 69 6C 65 20 69 6E 20               db      'File in use$'
          75 73 65 24
00000131  00000026[ ?? ]                        db      38 dup (?)
00000157  30 30 30 30 36                        db      '00006'
0000015C  44 72 69 76 65 20 6E 6F               db      'Drive not respondi
ng$'
          74 20 72 65 73 70 6F 6E
          64 69 6E 67 24
```

Phar Lap Macro Assembler Version 2.0   Thu Jul 06 17:50:21 1989
errmsg   Page   1-2

```
00000171  0000001D[ ?? ]                       db      29 dup (?)
0000018E  39 39 39 39 39                        db      '99999'
00000193  55 6E 73 70 65 63 69 66               db      'Unspecified error$'
          69 65 64 20 65 72 72 6F
          72 24
000001A5  00000020[ ?? ]                        db      32 dup (?)
000001C5                           _data        ends

00000000                           _text        segment public
                                                assume cs:_text,ds:_data,s
s:stack,es:_data
00000000                           err_msg_proc proc    near
                                                setebp
00000000  55                    1               push    ebp
00000001  8B EC                 1               move    bp,esp
00000003  83 C5 08              1               add     ebp,8
00000006  57                                    push    edi
00000007  56                                    push    esi
00000008  51                                    push    ecx
00000009  66| 83 7D 00 01                       cmp     word ptr [ebp],min_
msg
0000000E  0F 8D 0000000A                        jnl     min_ok
00000014  E8 00000055                           call    bad_input_proc
00000019  E9 00000010                           jmp     max_ok
0000001E               min_ok:
0000001E  66| 83 7D 00 07                       cmp     word ptr [ebp],max_
msg
00000023  0F 8E 00000005                        jng     max_ok
00000029  E8 00000040                           call    bad_input_proc
0000002E               max_ok:
0000002E  8D 35 00000044 R                      lea     esi,message_table
00000034  B8 00000037                           mov     eax,msg_len
00000039  66| FF 4D 00                          dec     word ptr [ebp]
0000003D  66| F7 65 00                          mul     word ptr [ebp]
```

Figure 14-1   Program Documentation (part 3 of 5)

```
00000041  03 F0                          add     esi,eax
00000043  8D 3D 00000006 R               lea     edi,err_num
00000049  B9 00000005                    mov     ecx,num_len
0000004E  F3/ A4                         rep movsb
00000050  8D 3D 0000000D R               lea     edi,err_msg
00000056  B9 00000037                    mov     ecx,msg_len
0000005B  F3/ A4                         rep movsb
0000005D  8D 15 00000000 R               lea     edx,err_start
00000063  B4 09                          mov     ah,write_code
00000065  CD 21                          int     21h
00000067  59                             pop     ecx
00000068  5E                             pop     esi
00000069  5F                             pop     edi
0000006A  5D                             pop     ebp
0000006B  C2 0002                        ret     2
                             err_msg_proc endp

0000006E                     bad_input_proc proc near
0000006E  66| C7 45 00 0007              mov     word ptr [ebp],7
00000074  C3                             ret
                             bad_input_proc endp
00000075                     _text       ends
                                         end
Phar Lap Macro Assembler  Version 2.0      Thu Jul 06 17:50:21 1989
errmsg                                                   Symbols-1
```

```
      GROUPS AND SEGMENTS
Name                          Size      Use     Align Combine  Class
_data . . . . . . . . . .  .000001C5   USE32   PARA  PUBLIC
_text . . . . . . . . . .  .00000075   USE32   PARA  PUBLIC
stack . . . . . . . . . .  .000003E8   USE32   PARA  STACK

      MACROS
Name                          # Params  # Lines
setebp . . . . . . . . .      0         3

      PROCEDURES
Name                          Type      Offset    Scope    Segment

bad_input_proc . . . . . .    N PROC    0000006E  Prvate   _text
err_msg_proc . . . . . . .    N PROC    00000000  Public   _text

      VARIABLES AND LABELS
Name                          Type      Offset    Scope    Segment

err_msg . . . . . . . . .     BYTE      0000000D  Prvate   _data
err_num . . . . . . . . .     BYTE      00000006  Prvate   _data
err_start . . . . . . . .     BYTE      00000000  Prvate   _data
max_ok . . . . . . . . . .    N LABEL   0000002E  Prvate   _text
```

Figure 14-1   Program Documentation (part 4 of 5)

```
message_table  . . . . . .  BYTE      00000044  Prvate  _data
min_ok . . . . . . . . . .  N LABEL   0000001E  Prvate  _text

    CONSTANTS
Name                        Type      Value
max_msg  . . . . . . . . .  Integer   00000007
min_msg  . . . . . . . . .  Integer   00000001
msg_len  . . . . . . . . .  Integer   00000037
num_len  . . . . . . . . .  Integer   00000005
write_code . . . . . . . .  Integer   00000009


    17 Symbols
     0 Warning Errors
     0 Severe Errors


386|LINK: 2.0 — Copyright (C) 1986-88 Phar Lap Software, Inc.
Target CPU is 80386


Command line switches:

-fullseg \ws5\stub \ws5\errmsg


Input module(s):

"stub" from file "\ws5\stub.obj".
"errmsg" from file "\ws5\errmsg.obj".


Segment map
Name          Group       Class     Type  Offset      Size

STACK                     STACK     STK   00000000    000007D8
  stub                    STACK     STK   00000000    000003E8
  errmsg                            STK   000003F0    000003E8
_DATA                     DATA      PUB   000007D8    000001CD
  errmsg                            PUB   000007E0    000001C5
_TEXT                     CODE      PUB   000009A8    0000008D
  stub                    CODE      PUB   000009A8    0000000B
  errmsg                            PUB   000009C0    00000075

Public symbols

Name          Value       Module        Segment     Size

ERR_MSG_PROC 000009C0     errmsg        _TEXT
```

Figure 14-1   Program Documentation (part 5 of 5)

you can use the **–fullseg** switch with the linker to see the beginning offset of each segment in the map.

You start MINIBUG by entering the **minibug** command. Figure 14-2 shows the complete format of this command. Most switches are the same ones you can use with RUN I 386 when you execute the program in its real environment; we aren't covering them here. The arguments are used only if the program expects arguments from the command line. Most of the time, you can probably start up MINIBUG with just the program name, as in this example:

```
minibug stub
```

MINIBUG looks for an .EXP file first, then an .EXE file, and finally an .REX file. So if you have all three versions in the directory, the .EXP

```
minibug [switches] program-name [arguments]


Switches:
-com1 -com2         Redirect I/O to COM1: or COM2:
-baud speed         Set speed of port to which I/O is
                    redirected

-small (default)    Specify program model
-compact
-medium
-large

386|DOS-Extender Switches:
-minreal n          Specify real mode memory
-maxreal n
-realbreak n

-callbufs n         Specify buffer space
-minibuf n
-maxibuf n
-nistack
-istksize n

-1167 on|off|auto   Set up 1167 numeric coprocessor

-hwivec n           Set up interrupt vectors
-privecn

-extlow n           Set up extended memory
-exthigh n

-nobim              Do not use Compaq built-in memory
```

Figure 14-2   The Minibug Command

version prevails. If you want to run another version, specify the extension, as in this example:

```
minibug stub.rex
```

You can also specify a path.

MINIBUG starts up with a header message, a mode indicator, and a command prompt, which is simply a hyphen. A typical startup display looks like this:

```
386 MiniBug: 2.0 -- Copyright (C) 1986-88 Phar Lap Software Inc.
Serial Number xxxxx
[80386 protected mode]
-
```

Some Basic MINIBUG Commands

Figure 14-3 lists the commands you'll use to control MINIBUG after it has started up. This section shows you how to use the first set of commands, identified in the figure as the "Basic Commands." For details on the remaining commands, see your MINIBUG reference manual.

Displaying Registers. You might start by displaying the registers, because that also displays the current instruction. The **r** (registers) command brings up a display similar to this:

```
Basic Commands:

r [reg] [val]          Display register(s) or insert value
                       in register

t [=addr] [count]      Trace count instructions

p [=addr] [count]      Procedure trace (step over calls)

g [=addr] [addr]       Go (execute instructions) until
                       stopped

h val val              Do hexadecimal arithmetic

d [range]              Display memory
da [range]
db [range]
dw [range]
dd [range]

q                      Quit
```

Figure 14-3   MINIBUG Debugging Commands (part 1 of 2)

Other Commands:

c *range addr*	Compare memory areas
com1|com2|con	Redirect I/O
dg [*range*] di [*range*] dl [*range*]	Display system tables (GDT, IDT, and LDT)
e *addr val(s)* eb *addr val(s)* ew *addr val(s)* ed *addr val(s)*	Enter value(s) in memory at address
f *range val(s)*	Fill memory range with value(s)
i *port*	Input value from port
m *range addr*	Move (copy) data from range to address
mc|ml|mm|ms	Select memory model (small is default)
m?	Display current memory model
o *port vals*	Output values to port
pd [*range*]	Display system page directory
pt *table* [*range*]	Display system page table
rx	Display extended registers
s *range vals*	Search memory
u|u16|u32 [*range*]	Unassemble instructions

Figure 14-3   MINIBUG Debugging Commands (part 2 of 2)

```
-r
EAX=00000000  EBX=00000000  ECX=00000000  EDX=00000000
ESI=00000000  EDI=00000000  EBP=00000000  ESP=000007D0
DS=0014  SS=0014  ES=0014  FS=0014  GS=0014
CS:EIP=000C:000009A8  EFLAGS=00000202  NV  UP  EI  PL  NZ  NA  PO  NC
000C:000009A8  6A05                    PUSH Dword Ptr 5
```

In the first line, you can see the command prompt and the **r** command. The next five lines are the output from the command. You can see each of the eight general registers, which have all been initialized to zero except ESP, which points to the top of the stack. You can see each of the data segment registers, which are always initialized to 14h for RUN I 386 programs. CS:EIP is always initialized to 000C plus the starting offset of the program. You can see the hexadecimal value in EFLAGS, but the flags are also interpreted as VM (virtual 8086 mode), which does not show in the above example since virtual mode is not in effect; NV (not overflow) or OV (overflow); UP (not direction—"up") or DN (direction—"down"); DI (not interrupts—"disable interrupts") or EI (interrupts—"enable interrupts"); PL (not sign—"plus") or NG (sign—"negative"); NZ (not zero) or ZR (zero); NA (not auxiliary) or AC (auxiliary—"auxiliary carry"); PO (not parity—"parity odd") or PE (parity—"parity even"); and NC (not carry) or CY (carry).

The final line of the display shows the address, hexadecimal contents, and assembly language version of the current instruction. The assembly language version may not exactly match your original source line, especially if a symbolic operand or expression was used, because MINIBUG cannot reach back to the source code file for the original instruction. It disassembles the machine language instruction to determine the assembly language version.

The instruction shown on the final line has not been executed yet. It is the instruction that is currently awaiting execution.

Executing Instructions. MINIBUG has three ways to execute instructions. The **t** (trace) and **p** (procedure trace) commands each execute a specific number of instructions, while the **g** (go) command executes until something stops it. The difference between **t** and **p** lies in how they react to **call** and **int** instructions. **T** steps through the instructions in the called routine, while **p** counts the entire called routine as one instruction, thus giving precedence to the current procedure. If you are looking for a bug in the current procedure and are confident that the subroutines it calls work properly, use **p**. If you're not sure where the bug is, use **t**.

If you use **t** or **p** with no operands, one instruction is executed and the registers are displayed automatically. To execute the first instruction of the **stub** program, you could enter the following command and receive the output shown:

```
-t
Step to 000C:000009AA
EAX=00000000   EBX=00000000   ECX=00000000   EDX=00000000
ESI=00000000   EDI=00000000   EBP=00000000   ESP=000007CC
DS=0014  SS=0014  ES=0014 FS=0014  GS=0014
CS:EIP=000C:000009AA  EFLAGS=00000202     NV  UP  EI  PL  NZ  NA  PO  NC
000C:000009AA E811000000            CALL        000009C0
```

Compare this output to the preceding register display and you can see the change to ESP brought about by the **push** instruction. You can also see the change to CS:EIP and the current instruction. The current instruction is now a **call** instruction. The address shown is the address offset of the **err_msg_proc** procedure.

You can specify a *count* operand with either **t** or **p**, indicating how many steps you want to trace. An * causes MINIBUG to trace until either the program ends or an interrupt occurs. The registers are displayed after each instruction, so what you get on your screen is a scrolling display of instructions and register values, which you can pause with Ctrl-S, restart with any key, and kill with Ctrl-C. Suppose you are trying to find the instruction that is setting the sign flag. Enter either **t** * or **p** *, depending on whether or not you want to check out subroutines, and keep your eye on the PL flag. When it changes to NG, press Ctrl-C. You should be able to see the instruction that set the flag in the register display above the one where the flag first shows as NG.

You can also specify a starting address for a trace command. For example, suppose you want to repeat the procedure, starting at offset 000009C0 again. You could execute the first five instructions with this command:

```
-t =9C0 5
```

Keep in mind when you do this that the setup of registers, flags, memory variables, and the stack might not be the same as when the instruction is encountered in normal execution.

The **g** command executes instructions until some condition occurs. Conditions that terminate the **g** command are:

• An exception occurs,

• The program terminates,

• You press Ctrl-C, or

• A breakpoint is encountered.

The secret of the **g** command is in the breakpoints, which are addresses of instructions. Suppose you want to execute up to the **mov** instruction at address offset 19Ah. You could use this command:

```
-g 19A
```

MINIBUG automatically displays the registers upon completion of the **g** command, so you can see the setup for the breakpoint instruction. Unlike the trace commands, which display the registers after every instruction, **g** displays them only at the termination of the command.

If you are not sure what path the program will take, you can specify up to four breakpoints. **G** terminates if any one of them is reached. Once the command terminates, the breakpoints are forgotten. To execute another **g** command with the same breakpoints, you must enter them again. You can also enter a starting address for **g**, preceded by an equal sign to distinguish it from a breakpoint, just as with **t** and **p**.

Once the program terminates, you can no longer use **t**, **p**, or **g** to execute instructions unless you specify a start address. You can also quit MINIBUG with the **q** (quit) instruction and restart it. This has the advantage of reinitializing the registers and memory fields.

Determining Addresses. You will often need to specify an address with a command, as you have seen for **t**, **p**, and **g**. If you code an incorrect address for these three instructions, they will not work. For example, if you code a breakpoint address that falls in the middle of an instruction instead of the beginning, MINIBUG will execute right past the breakpoint without recognizing it.

There are a couple of ways to determine the addresses you need. You can trace through the program one step at a time, copying down the addresses you need as they appear. The addresses of symbolic variables appear in instructions that reference those variables.

The other way is to calculate the desired offset from the assembler listing and the linker map. Suppose you want to determine the address of the **mov** instruction near the middle of **err_msg_proc** in the **errmsg** module. (It's two lines down from the **max_ok** label.) Figure 14-4 shows the relevant portions of the assembler listing and linker map. (The map was created with the **–fullseg** switch so you can see the offsets of the original portions of the segments.) From the assembler listing, you can see that the offset from the beginning of the **_text** segment is 34h. The linker listing shows that the segment starts at offset 9C0h. A little hexadecimal arithmetic shows that the **mov** instruction starts at address 9F4h. If you're uncomfortable with hexadecimal arithmetic, you can get MINIBUG to do it for you with the **h** command like this:

```
-h 9C0 34
```

MINIBUG displays both the sum and the difference of the two numbers, like this:

```
000009C0 + 00000034 = 000009F4
000009C0 - 00000034 = 0000098C
```

```
0000002E                          max_ok:
0000002E  8D 35 00000044 R                 lea     esi,message_table
00000034  B8 00000037                      mov     eax,msg_len
00000039  66| FF 4D 00                     dec     word ptr [ebp]
```

Segment map

Name	Group	Class	Type	Offset	Size
STACK		STACK	STK	00000000	000007D8
stub		STACK	STK	00000000	000003E8
errmsg			STK	000003F0	000003E8
_DATA		DATA	PUB	000007D8	000001CD
errmsg			PUB	000007E0	000001C5
_TEXT		CODE	PUB	000009A8	0000008D
stub		CODE	PUB	000009A8	0000000B
errmsg			PUB	000009C0	00000075

Figure 14-4   Locating the Address of an Instruction

To find the address of a symbol, you can start with the symbols table from the assembler listing. Suppose you need the address of the variable named **err_msg**. Figure 14-5 shows the relevant portions of the listings. The variable is offset 0Dh bytes from the beginning of its segment, and its segment starts at 7E0h, so the variable's address

VARIABLES AND LABELS

Name	Type	Offset	Scope	Segment
err_msg	BYTE	0000000D	Prvate	_data
err_num	BYTE	00000006	Prvate	_data
err_start	BYTE	00000000	Prvate	_data
max_ok	N LABEL	0000002E	Prvate	_text
message_table	BYTE	00000044	Prvate	_data
min_ok	N LABEL	0000001E	Prvate	_text

Segment map

Name	Group	Class	Type	Offset	Size
STACK		STACK	STK	00000000	000007D8
stub		STACK	STK	00000000	000003E8
errmsg			STK	000003F0	000003E8
_DATA		DATA	PUB	000007D8	000001CD
errmsg			PUB	000007E0	000001C5
_TEXT		CODE	PUB	000009A8	0000008D
stub			CODE	PUB	000009A8	0000000B
errmsg			PUB	000009C0	00000075

Figure 14-5   Locating the Address of a Variable

offset is 7EDh. (If you have a symbolic debugger, you don't have to go through this.)

Displaying Memory. To examine data in memory, including the stack, you use one of the **d** commands: **da** (display ASCII), **db** (display bytes), **dw** (display words), **dd** (display doublewords), or **d** (display the previous type again). You can specify a start address and an end address. If you specify no start address, the address following the last displayed address is used. 128 bytes are displayed if you don't include an end address.

The **db** command is the most basic. It causes the information to be separated into individual bytes. Both the hex form and the ASCII form are shown. Dots represent unprintable characters in the ASCII display. Suppose you want to examine 64 bytes starting at DS:892. (DS is assumed with the **d** commands.)

```
-db 892 8D1
0014:00000892       30 30 30 30 33 46-69 6C 65 20 65 6D 70 74  ..00003File empt
0014:000008A0  79 24 00 00 00 00 00 00-00 00 00 00 00 00 00 00  y$..............
0014:000008B0  00 00 00 00 00 00 00 00-00 00 00 00 00 00 00 00  ................
0014:000008C0  00 00 00 00 00 00 00 00-00 30 30 30 30 34 46 69  .........00004Fi
0014:000008D0  6C 65                                            le
```

At the left, you can see the address of the first byte of each line. The first line of the display starts at the third byte, since we asked for 892 instead of 890. The hex representation of each byte appears in the middle—eight bytes on the left, a hyphen, and eight bytes on the right. At the far right, the ASCII interpretation appears. The area of memory displayed contains an error message, some uninitialized bytes, and the start of the next message.

When you display individual bytes, non-ASCII values appear in their reversed form. It's easier to interpret non-ASCII values if you display fields in their defined sizes, where MINIBUG straightens the values out for you. For example, suppose you want to examine the word at 823:

```
-dw 823 824
0014:00000823 3000
```

The word contains 3000h. To examine the doubleword starting at 400, use this command:

```
-dd 400 403
0014:00000400 39FF2D10
```

There are no commands for examining quadwords or tenbytes directly. You have to display them as bytes, words, or doublewords and figure out for yourself how to interpret the values you see.

If you want to examine the ASCII values of a field, you can use **da**, which behaves similarly to **db** but displays only the address and ASCII columns.

Interpreting the Stack. If you specify a register instead of an address with the **d** commands, MINIBUG uses the register as an indirect address. Thus, to see the current value in the stack, you can use SS:ESP as the start address. The display will look something like this:

```
-dd ss:esp
0014:000007C4   00000000 000009AF 00000005 00000000
0014:000007D4   00000000 00000000 00000000 4F524245
0014:000007E4   30302052 3A303030 00000020 00000000
0014:000007F4   00000000 00000000 00000000 00000000
0014:00000804   00000000 00000000 00000000 00000000
0014:00000814   00000000 00000000 00000000 00000000
0014:00000824   30303030 6C694631 6F6E2065 6F662074
0014:00000834   24646E75 00000000 00000000 00000000
```

Remembering that the stack is built upside down in memory, you can see several stack entries when you display the stack like this. The first doubleword is the most recent doubleword pushed. Following it is the penultimate doubleword. In our example, these instructions have already been executed:

```
push    dword ptr 5

call    err_msg_proc

push    ebp
```

The first doubleword shows the value of EBP, which was 0 when it was pushed. The next doubleword shows the value of EIP that was pushed by the **call**. It was 9AF. The next doubleword shows the 5 that was pushed as an immediate doubleword. That is the bottom of the stack. The area beyond it, from address 7D0 on, belongs to the _data segment.

Other MINIBUG Commands

The few commands we have detailed in this chapter should get you started with MINIBUG. As you can see in Figure 14-3, there are many more commands. You can manipulate memory areas in various ways, comparing, filling, copying, searching, and entering data into them. You can enter data into registers and display an extended set of registers. You can also display various system areas from memory: the system tables, the page directory, and page tables. I/O can be redirected to one of the communications ports, and you can input from and output directly to ports. You can specify the memory model if the program does not have the small model. And you can unassemble instructions, much like the **r** instruction does. After you have used MINIBUG a few times with just the basic commands, you might want to try some of these more advanced facilities. Your MINIBUG reference manual can help you with the details.

If you are not interested in CodeView, you are finished with this chapter and the book.

Introduction to CodeView

Microsoft's CodeView is a fully featured symbolic debugger that can run under DOS, Windows, or OS/2. With CodeView, you can see your source code on the screen while you debug. You can ask to see the current value of a memory area by its symbolic name. You can even ask CodeView to display the value of a memory area and keep the value up to date while the program executes. And you can ask the debugger to execute code until a condition becomes true.

CodeView can handle .EXE files created by Microsoft LINK. It cannot handle memory-resident programs and also has restrictions on included code, macros, packed files, and .COM files. If you need to debug any of these types of programs, see your CodeView manual for more details.

Preparing for CodeView

To use CodeView in its full form, in which you can see and work with the source code and refer to symbolic names, the symbolic information must be carried through from the source program to the executable module. Use the **/zi** switch with MASM and the **/co** switch with LINK. These two switches cause the necessary information to be copied into the object and executable files.

Use the standard Microsoft segment definitions when you create the source file. Before trying to start CodeView, make sure all the following files are available: CV.EXE, CV.HLP (for online help), the target program file, the target program's source code files, and the target program's I/O files.

Starting CodeView

Figure 14-6 shows the format of the CodeView command, including all the options. More information about the options is included in your CodeView reference manual. The *arguments* pertain to the target program. If it needs command line arguments, include them in the Code-View command in whatever form the target program requires. Code-View passes them to the target program.

Depending on what system you have, CodeView starts up either in window mode or sequential mode. Sequential mode looks something like this:

```
CodeView (TM) Version x.xx

(C) Copyright Microsoft Corporation years

>
```

When in this mode, you communicate with CodeView with commands and CodeView responds by displaying whatever data you request. Previous interactions scroll off the top of the screen as you work.

Window mode has many more features. Figure 14-7 shows a typical window-mode display. The names of several pull-down menus appear

```
cv [options] program-name [arguments]
```

```
Options:
/w | /t              Select window mode or sequential
                     (text) mode

/b                   Display in black-and-white (or
                     monochrome)

/s | /f              Select screen swapping or flipping

/d                   ?

/d | /i              Disable or enable function maskable
                     interrupts (including break function)

/e                   Enable expanded memory

/m                   Ignore mouse

/43                  Use 43 line display

/2                   Use two monitors
```

Figure 14-6   The CodeView Command

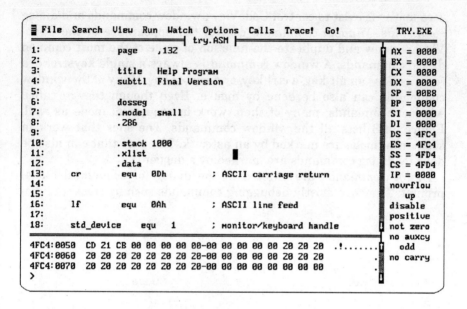

Figure 14-7   The CodeView Window Display

on the top line. The program display area fills most of the screen, between the two sets of double lines. In the example, the source code file is currently being displayed. Beneath the bottom double line is the dialog area, which is much like sequential mode described previously. The right edge of the screen shows a display of the general registers and the flags.

If your system starts out in sequential mode, try the /w switch with the CodeView command. If that doesn't bring up window mode, your system is probably not capable of it. You can still accomplish the same functions, but the display won't be as convenient. Since any IBM-compatible system should be able to handle it, the rest of this chapter assumes you are working with window mode.

Getting Online Help

CodeView includes an online help system when the CV.HLP file is present. To enter the help system, press F1. A tree-structured set of menus lets you select the topics you need help with.

Controlling CodeView

Two methods exist to control CodeView: window commands and dialog commands. *Window commands* control the appearance of the Code-View window and duplicate the function of some of the most common dialog commands. A window command is always a single keystroke: a function key, an alt-key, a ctrl-key, or a cursor key. Many of the window commands can also be done by mouse. Even though they're called window commands, many of them work in sequential mode as well. Figure 14-8 lists all the window commands. The ones that work in sequential mode are marked by an asterisk. The ones that can also be done by dialog commands are marked by a dagger (†).

Dialog commands are entered at the dialog (or sequential mode) prompt. They are mostly debugging commands such as trace and dis-

Key	Effect	Mouse
F1*	Help	
F2*†	Toggle register window on/off	
F3*†	Switch display window mode: source, assembly, mixed	
F4*†	Show output screen	
F5*†	Go to next breakpoint	Click (either button) on Go!
F6	Move cursor between display and dialog windows	
F7†	Go to highlighted line	Click right on desired line
F8*†	Trace one line	Click left on Trace!
F9*†	Set or clear breakpoint	Click left on desired line
F10*†	Step one line	Click right on Trace!
	Complement flag†	Click on flag in register window

Figure 14-8   CodeView Window Commands (part 1 of 2)

^U	Move the display/dialog window separator up one line	
^D	Move the display/dialog window separator down one line	
^C	Interrupt program execution	
?	Move the cursor up one line	Click left on up icon
?	Move the cursor down one line	Click left on down icon
PgUp	Scroll up one page	Click right on up icon
PgDn	Scroll down one page	Click right on down icon
Home	Scroll to beginning of file or command buffer	Click both on up icon
End	Scroll to end of file or command buffer	Click both on down icon

*Works in sequential mode (perhaps differently)

†Can also be done by a dialog command

Figure 14-8   CodeView Window Commands (part 2 of 2)

play bytes. They frequently take arguments such as register names, symbolic addresses, and counts.

Figure 14-9 lists all the dialog commands. The first group of commands, identified in the figure as "Basic Commands," are covered in detail in this chapter. For more information about the remaining commands, see your CodeView reference manual.

Executing Code. CodeView lets you execute one or more lines of code. The **trace** and **program step** commands each execute a specific number of instructions, while the go command executes until something stops it. The difference between **trace** and **program step** lies in how they react to **call** and **int** instructions. **Trace** enters the called routine and steps through the instructions there also, while **program step** counts the entire called routine as one instruction, thus giving precedence to the current procedure. If you are looking for a bug in the

Basic Commands:

t [count]	Execute *count* instructions (trace into calls)
p [*count*]	Execute *count* instructions (step over calls)
g [*breakpoint*]	Execute until stopped
d[*type*] [*addr*|*range*]	Dump memory
bp [*addr* [*count*]["*com-mands*"]]	Set a breakpoint
bc *list*|*	Clear a breakpoint
bl	List breakpoints
w[type] *range*	Watch memory
wp? *exp*[,*format*]	Set watchpoint
tp[*type*] *range*	Set memory tracepoint
y *number*|*	Delete watch statement(s)

Other Commands:

e	Slow motion execute until stopped
l [*arguments*]	Restart current program
? *expression* [,*format*]	Display value of expression
x* or x? [*module*!][*routine.*] [*symbol*] [*]	Display symbols@FIG COL1 = bd *list*|*
c *range addr*	Compare memory fields
s *range list*	Search memory
i *port*	Input from port
r	Display registers
7	Display coprocessor registers
	Disable breakpoint
be *list*|*	Enable breakpoint
w? *exp*[,*format*]	Watch expression

Figure 14-9   CodeView Dialog Commands (part 1 of 2)

tp? *exp*[,*format*]	Set memory tracepoint from expression
w	List watch statements
s[+ | - | &]	Set display mode
u [*addr*|*range*]	Unassemble code
v [*exp*]	View source code lines
v [.[*filename*:] *linenumber*]	View source code lines
.	Display current line
k	Display calls currently in effect
a [*addr*]	Assemble new instructions
e[*type*] *addr* [*list-of-values*]	Enter data into memory
f *range list-of-values*	Fill memory with *values*
m *source-range dest-addr*	Move data in memory
o *port byte*	Output *byte* to *port*
r [*register-name*[[=]*exp*]]	Change value in register
h	Enter help system
q	Quit CodeView
n [*radix*]	Set the input radix
@	Redraw the screen
\	Exchange screens
/ [*exp*]	Search for expression in source file
! [*command*]	Go to shell
# *n*	Set tab size for display screen
< *device*	Redirect CodeView input
[t]>[>] *device*	Redirect CodeView output
= *device*	Redirect CodeView input and output

Figure 14-9   CodeView Dialog Commands (part 2 of 2)

current procedure and are confident that the subroutines it calls work properly, use **program step**. If you're not sure where the bug is, use **trace**.

If you use **trace** or **program step** with no operands, one instruction is executed. If you use the dialog command, you can specify a *count* operand with either **trace** or **program step**, indicating how many steps you want to **trace**. An * causes CodeView to **trace** until either the program ends or an interrupt occurs. Suppose you are trying to find the instruction that is setting the sign flag. Enter either **t** * or **p** *, depending on whether or not you want to check out called routines, and keep your eye on the **positive** flag. When it changes to **negative**, press Ctrl-C. You should be able to see the instruction that set the flag in the program display.

The **go** command executes instructions until some condition occurs. Conditions that terminate the **go** command are:

• An exception occurs,

• The program terminates,

• You press Ctrl-C, or

• A breakpoint, watchpoint, or tracepoint is encountered.

Using Breakpoints, Watchpoints, and Tracepoints. The key to the **go** command is in the breakpoints, watchpoints, and tracepoints, which are used to halt program execution at specified points in the program. A breakpoint is an instruction address in the code segment; **go** executes until it reaches the instruction at that address. A watchpoint is an expression such as **errnum < 5**; **go** executes until the expression becomes true. A tracepoint is a memory area; **go** executes until there is any change to the value of the memory area.

Breakpoints are used to execute up to a certain point in the program. For example, to execute up to **bad_input_proc**, you could enter this command (or its window equivalent):

```
>g bad_input_proc
```

This command sets up **bad_input_proc** as a temporary breakpoint, pertaining only to this command. You can also create up to 20 permanent breakpoints, which interrupt all future **go** commands until you clear or disable them. You set a permanent breakpoint with the breakpoint command. To set up **bad_input_proc** as a permanent breakpoint, you could enter the following command (or its window equivalent):

```
>bp bad_input_proc
```

You can see breakpoints on your window display. All breakpoint lines are highlighted and marked with the notation **bp***n*. You can list your current breakpoints with the breakpoint list command. You can clear one or more breakpoints with the breakpoint clear command.

You set and delete watchpoints in a manner similar to breakpoints. A watchpoint continues to operate until you clear it. When you set the first watchpoint, a watch window appears on the window display, underneath the menu bar and above the display window. Figure 14-10 shows a sample display with three watchpoints set. Any expression that evaluates to a zero (false) or nonzero (true) value can be used as a watchpoint. The current evaluation is shown in the window after the colon. In the example in Figure 14-10, all three watchpoints are currently false.

When debugging an assembly language program, you must use C format expressions. Unfortunately, this differs somewhat from the assembly language expression formats you have learned in this book. If you stick to simple expressions involving the plus sign (+), minus sign (–), greater than sign (>), and less than sign (<), you should be all right. You must use two equal signs for equality, as in this expression:

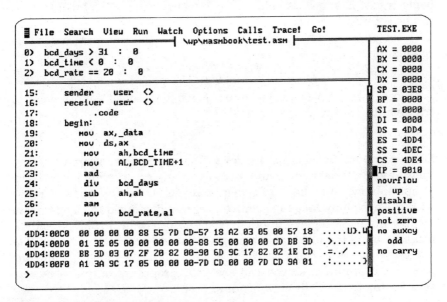

Figure 14-10   The Watch Window

```
filter==5
```

For more complex expressions, check your CodeView documentation. Suppose you want to execute your program until **filter** reaches 256. You could set the watchpoint with this command:

```
>wp? filter==256
```

Then issue a **go** command. You can also ask CodeView to watch fields or expressions without making them into watchpoints, using the **watch** command. You can attach a type specifier to the command: **wb** displays bytes, **ww** displays words, and so forth. For example, suppose you want to keep an eye on **filter** while you trace some steps, but you don't want to use **filter** as a watchpoint. You could enter this command:

```
>wd filter
```

Then enter your **trace** command. The value of **filter**, expressed as a doubleword, will be displayed in the watch window and constantly updated. You can delete a watch statement or watchpoint with the **y** command.

Execution is slowed dramatically by watches; several watches can cause a routine to take several minutes instead of several microseconds. Tracepoints are nearly as effective as watchpoints and don't take so much time. A tracepoint halts execution whenever the item being traced changes its value. Only memory ranges (up to 128 bytes) can be set up as tracepoints.

To set up a tracepoint whenever **filter** changes in value, enter this command:

```
>tpd filter
```

Tracepoints are also displayed in the watch window. You can delete a tracepoint with the **y** command.

Flipping to Other Screens and Windows. When you first start up Code-View, if you are debugging an assembly language program on an IBM-compatible system, the first screen you see is the CodeView window with the assembly-language source program displayed in the program display area. F3 toggles to other forms of program display, based on disassembling the machine language. F4 shows the output screen. You use F4 to switch to the screen that would normally appear when your program is running, so you can see your program's output. Any key returns you to the CodeView window.

Examining Data. You can dump memory onto the monitor screen with the dump commands. The type suffix indicates the format of the display. For example, you can dump 50 bytes from **err_msg** in the byte format with the following command:

```
db err_msg L 50
```

The command shows how you can express a length in a range operand. Without the L, CodeView would interpret the 50 as the ending address of the range. The L 50 tells CodeView to dump from **err_msg** for a length of 50 bytes. If you specify no length or ending address, 128 bytes are assumed for every format except real numbers, and one number is displayed if the type indicates a real number.

The **db** command is the most basic. It causes the information to be separated into individual bytes. Both the hex form and the ASCII form are shown. Dots represent unprintable characters in the ASCII display. Suppose you want to examine 64 bytes starting at DS:892. (DS is assumed with the dump commands.) CodeView assumes all constants are in decimal unless you specify otherwise. The easiest way to handle hexadecimal addresses is to prefix the address with 0x (zero-x), as in the instruction below.

```
>db 0x892 L 64
483C:0890          30 30 30 30 33 46-69 6C 65 20 65 6D 70 74  ..00003File empt
483C:08A0   79 24 00 00 00 00 00 00-00 00 00 00 00 00 00 00  y$..............
483C:08B0   00 00 00 00 00 00 00 00-00 00 00 00 00 00 00 00  ................
483C:08C0   00 00 00 00 00 00 00 00-00 30 30 30 30 34 46 69  .........00004Fi
483C:08D0   6C 65                                            le
```

At the left, you can see the address of the first byte of each line. The first line starts at the third byte, since we asked for 892 instead of 890. The hex representation of each byte appears in the middle—eight bytes on the left, a hyphen, and eight bytes on the right. At the far right, the ASCII interpretation appears. The area of memory we have displayed contains an error message, some uninitialized bytes, and the start of the next message.

When you display individual bytes, non-ASCII values appear in their reversed form. It's easier to interpret non-ASCII values if you display fields in their defined sizes, because CodeView straightens the values out for you. For example, suppose you want to examine the word at 823:

```
>dw 0x823 L 1
483C:0823 09A4
```

The word contains 09A4h.

If you want to examine just the ASCII values of a field, you can use **da,** which behaves similarly to **db** but displays only the address and ASCII columns.

You can dump signed integers with **di** and real numbers with **ds** (dump short real), **dl** (dump long real), and **dt** (dump real tenbyte). CodeView displays the hex form of the value and interprets it in decimal.

Interpreting the Stack. If you specify a register instead of an address with the dump commands, CodeView uses the register as an indirect address. Thus, to see the current value in the stack, you can use SS:ESP as the start address. The display will look something like this:

```
>dd ss:sp
483C:03E0   0000 096B 0005 0000 0000 0000 0000 0000
483C:03F0   0000 0000 0000 0000 0000 0000 0000 0000
483C:0400   0000 0000 0000 0000 0000 0000 0000 0000
483C:0410   0000 0000 0000 0000 0000 0000 0000 0000
483C:0420   0000 0000 0000 0000 0000 0000 0000 0000
483C:0430   0000 0000 0000 0000 0000 0000 0000 0000
483C:0440   0000 0000 0000 0000 0000 0000 0000 0000
483C:0450   0000 0000 0000 0000 0000 0000 0000 0000
```

Remembering that the stack is built upside down in memory, you can see several stack entries when you display the stack like this. The first word is the most recent word pushed. Following it is the penultimate word. In our example, these instructions have already been executed:

```
push       5
call   err_msg_proc
push   bp
```

The first word shows the value of EBP, which was 0 when it was pushed. The next word shows the value of EIP that was pushed by the **call.** It was 96B. The next word shows the 5 that was pushed as an immediate word. That is the bottom of the stack. The area beyond it, from address 3E6 on, belongs to the **_data** segment.

Other CodeView Commands

Even though this introduction to CodeView has been brief, you can probably solve most of your debugging problems with the commands we have presented here. But occasionally you'll need every trick in the book to locate and correct a bug. You can use the command lists in Figures 14-8 and 14-9 as a guide to other functions that are available. Your CodeView reference manual contains the details.

Appendix A
Instruction Reference

(Status flags in parentheses are undefined.)

Instruction	Status Flags	Notes
MOVING DATA		
mov *dest, source* Copy value from *dest* to *source*.	none	1. *Dest* can be register or memory. 2. *Source* can be register, memory, or immediate. 3. *Dest* and *source* must be the same size. 4. *Dest* and *source* cannot both be memory fields.
xchg *dest1, dest2* Exchange values in *dest1* and *dest2*.	none	1. Each operand can be register or memory. 2. Operands cannot both be memory fields.
LOADING REGISTERS		
lea *dest, source* Load address offset of *source* into *dest*.	none	1. *Dest* must be a register. 2. *Source* must be a memory field.
lds *dest, source* **les** *dest, source* **lfs** *dest, source*	none	1. *Dest* must be a register. 2. *Source* must be a memory field.

lgs *dest,source*
lss *dest,source*

Load segment portion
of *source* address
into segment register
indicated by opcode.
Load offset portion
of *source* address
into *dest* register.

lahf   none

Load staus flags
into AH register.

STORING REGISTERS

sahf   SF,ZF,AF
                            PF,CF
Store bits 0, 2, 4,
6, and 7 from AH in-
to FLAGS.

PUSHING

push *source*   none   1. *Source* can be register, memory,
                                            or immediate.
Decrement (E)SP by   2. In '286, *source* must be a word.
number of bytes in   3. In '386, *source* can be a word
source. Copy *source*   or dword.
to [SS:(E)SP].

pusha   none   1. Pusha pushes 16-bit registers.
pushad   2. Pushad pushes 32-bit registers.
                                        3. Order of registers pushed:
Push all general   (E)AX, (E)CX, (E)DX, (E)BX,
registers.   original value of (E)SP, (E)BP,
                                            (E)SI, (E)DI.

pushf   none   1. Pushf pushes FLAGS.
pushfd   2. Pushfd pushes EFLAGS.

Push (E)FLAGS.

POPPING

pop *dest*   none   1. *Dest* can be memory or register.
                                        2. In '286, *dest* must be a word.
Copy [SS:(E)SP] to   3. In '386, *dest* can be a word or
dest. Increment (E)SP   dword.

by number of bytes in
dest.

popf   SF,ZF,AF,
popfd   PF,CF,OF

Pop (E)FLAGS.

1. Popf pops one word into FLAGS.
2. Popfd ('386 only) pops a dword into EFLAGS.
3. Popfd never affects VM and RF. IOPL and IF are changed only if the task's privilege level is high enough.

4. *Dest* cannot be CS.

popa   none
popad

Pop all general registers, but discard value for (E)SP.

1. Popa pops the 16-bit general registers.
2. Popad pops the 32-bit general registers.
3. Registers are popped in this order: (E)DI, (E)SI, (E)BP, the next value is discarded, (E)BX, (E)DX, (E)CX, (E)AX.

CONVERSIONS

movsx *dest,source*   none

Copy value from *source* to *dest*, extending the sign bit to fill dest.

1. '386 only.
2. *Dest* must be a register.
3. *Source* can be register or memory.
4. Converts signed value to a larger size.
5. If *source* is a byte, *dest* can be a word or dword.
6. If *source* is a word, *dest* must be a dword.

movzx *dest,source*   none

Copy value from *source* to *dest*, filling upper bits of *dest* with zeros.

1. '386 only.
2. *Dest* must be a register.
3. *Source* can be register or memory.
4. Converts unsigned value to a larger size.
5. If *source* is a byte, *dest* can be a word or dword.
6. If *source* is a word, *dest* must be a dword.

cbw   none

Extend sign bit of AL through AH.

cwd   none

Extend sign bit of AX through DX.

cwde	none	1. '386 only.

Extend sign bit of AX
through upper word of
EAX.

cdq	none	1. '386 only.

Extend sign bit of
EAX through EDX.

xlat *source*   none
xlatb

Copy value from
source-seg:[(E)BX][AL]
to AL.

1. Translates value in AL to corresponding value from translation table.
2. (E)BX should contain base address of translation table.
3. With xlatb, DS indicates source-seg.
4. With xlat, segment of *source* is source-seg.

STRING MOVES

movs *dest, source*   none
movsb
movsw
movsd

Copy element from
[source-seg:(E)SI]
to [ES:EDI]. Advance
(E)SI and (E)DI by
the number of bytes
in element.

1. *Source* and *dest* must be memory fields.
2. *Source* indicates source-seg and size of element only. Address of *source* is always [source-seg:(E)SI].
3. *Dest* indicates size of element only. Address of destination is always [ES:(E)DI].
4. *Source* and *dest* must be the same size.
5. In '286, *source* and *dest* can be bytes or words.
6. In '386, *source* and *dest* can be bytes, words, or dwords.
7. With movsb, movsw, and movsd, source-seg is DS.
8. Movsd is '386 only.
9. Can be prefixed by rep.
10. DF indicates whether indexes are incremented or decremented.

lods *source*   none
lodsb
lodsw
lodsd

Copy element from
[source-seg:(E)SI]
to AL, AX, or EAX.

1. *Source* must be a memory field.
2. *Source* indicates source-seg and size of element only. Address of source is always [source-seg:(E)SI].
3. In '286, *source* can be a byte or word.
4. In '386, *source* can be a byte,

Advance (E)SI.

```
stos dest        none
stosb
stosw
stosd

Copy element from
from AL, AX, or EAX
to [DS:(E)DI].
Advance (E)SI.
```

word, or dword.
5. With movsb, movsdw and movsd,
   source-seg is DS.
6. Lodsd is '386 only.
7. Can be prefixed by rep.
8. DF indicates whether (E)SI is
   incremented or decremented.

1. *Dest* must be a memory field.
2. *Dest* indicates size of element
   only. Address of destination
   is always [ES:(E)DI].
3. In '286, *source* can be a byte
   or word.
4. In '386, *dest* can be a byte,
   word, or dword.
6. Stosd is '386 only.
7. Can be prefixed by rep.
8. DF indicates whether (E)SI is
   incremented or decremented.

JUMPS

```
jmp target       none

If target is a near
label, replace (E)IP
with indicated ad-
dress. If target is
a far label, replace
CS:(E)IP with indi-
cated address. If
target is a gate re-
quiring a task switch
or a TSS, switch to
the indicated task.
```

1. *Target* can be near or far
   label, a gate, or a TSS.
2. *Target* can be an indirect
   address, in which case the
   real target is obtained from
   the indicated register or
   data field.

```
jcond target     none

If cond is true,
transfer execution
control to target
address.
```

1. *Target* must be a near label
   only.
2. In the '286, *target* must be
   short.
3. In the '386, *target* can be
   short or near.

CALLS AND RETURNS

```
call target      none

If target is a near
label, push (E)IP
and transfer execution
```

1. *Target* can be an indirect address, in which case the real
   target address is taken from
   the indicated register or data
   field.

control to *target*. If
target is a far label
or a gate that doesn't
require a task switch,
push CS:(E)IP and
transfer execution
control to *target*. If
target is a gate re-
quiring a task switch
or a TSS, preserve the
current task's status
in its TSS and switch
to the indicated task.

ret [*value*]   none
retf [*value*]
retn [*value*]

Pop (E)IP (near re-
turns or CX:(E)IP (far
returns). Advance
(E)SP by *value*.

1. Ret without f or n suffix can
   appear only inside a proc.
   Type of proc determines type
   of return.
2. With 16-bit addressing, (E)SP
   is advanced by *value* bytes.
3. With 32-bit addressing, (E)IP
   is advanced by *value* words.

iret   none

Return from interrupt
procedure or task.

CREATE AND ELIMINATE STACK FRAME

enter *parms, level*   none

Create stack frame
with room for *parms*
parameters. If *level*
is greater than 0,
store display of
nested (E)BP pointers
in stack frame. Point
(E)BP at first ele-
ment in stack frame.

leave   none

Eliminate current
stack frame by copy-
ing (E)BP to (E)SP.

COMPARISONS

cmp *dest, source*   all

Set status flags as
if *source* were sub-
tracted from *dest*.

1. *Source* can be register, memory, or immediate.
2. *Dest* can be register or memory.
3. In the '286, *source* and *dest*
   can be bytes or words.
4. In the '386, *source* and *dest*
   can be bytes, words, or dwords.
5. *Source* and *dest* must be the
   same size unless *source* is
   immediate.
6. An immediate *source* can be
   shorter than *dest;* its value
   is sign-extended for the comparison.

cmps *dest, source*   all
cmpsb
cmpsw
cmpsd

Set status flags as
if [source-seg:(E)SI]
were subtracted from
[ES:(E)DI]. Advance
(E)SI and (E)DI by
size of *source* and
dest.

1. *Source* and *dest* must be memory
   fields of the same size.
2. In the '286, *source* and *dest*
   can be bytes or words.
3. In the '386, *source* and *dest*
   can be bytes, words, or dwords.
4. *Source* determines source-seg
   and size of source only. The
   actual address of source is
   always [source-seg:(E)SI].
5. *Dest* determines the size of
   the destination only. The
   actual address of the destination is always [ES:(E)DI].
6. In cmpsb, cmpsw, and cmpsd,
   source-seg is DS.
7. Cmpsd is '386 only.
8. DF determines whether indexes
   are incremented or decremented.
9. Can be prefixed by repe or
   repne.

scas *dest*   all
scasb
scasw
scasd

Set flags as if ele-
ment at [ES:(E)DI]
were subtracted from
AL, AX, or EAX. Ad-
vance (E)DI by size
of element.

1. *Dest* must be a memory field.
2. In the '286, *dest* can be a
   byte or word.
3. In the '386, *dest* can be a
   byte, word, or dword.
4. *Dest* determines the size of
   element only. The actual address is always [ES:(E)DI].
5. Scasd is '386 only.
6. DF determines whether (E)DI is
   incremented or decremented.
7. Can be prefixed by repe or
   repne.

set*cond* **dest**   none   1. *Dest* can be register or memory.
                                         2. *Dest* must be one byte.
If condition is true,
move 1 to *dest*. Else
move 0 to *dest*.

LOOPS

loop **target**   none   1. *Target* must be short address.

Decrement (E)CX. If
(E)CX is not 0,
transfer execution
control to *target*.

loope **target**   none   1. *Target* must be short address.
loopz **target**   2. Loope and loopz are synonyms.

Decrement (E)CX. If
(E)CX is not 0 and
zero flag is set,
jump to *target*.

loopne **target**   none   1. *Target* must be short address.
loopnz **target**   2. Loopne and loopnz are synonyms.

Decrement (E)CX. If
(E)CX is not 0 and
zero flag is clear,
jump to *target*.

rep *instruction*   none   1. *Instruction* can be movs*x* or
                                             stos*x*.
If (E)CX is not 0,
execute *instruction*,
then decrement (E)CX
and repeat from the
beginning.

repe *instruction*   none   1. *Instruction* can be cmps*x* or
repz *instruction*   scas*x*.
                                         2. Repe and repz are synonyms.
If (E)CX is not 0,
execute *instruction*,
then decrement (E)CX.
If zero flag is set,
repeat from the be-
ginning.

repne *instruction*   none   1. *Instruction* can be cmps*x* or
repnz *instruction*   scas*x*.
                                         2. Repne and repnz are synonyms.
If (E)CX is not 0,

execute *instruction*,
then decrement (E)CX.
If zero flag is clear,
repeat from the be-
ginning.

INTERRUPTS

int *n*   none

Activate interrupt
service routine *n*.

into   none

If overflow flag is
set, activate inter-
rupt service routine
4.

bound *reg,mem*   none

If *reg* < first ele-
ment of *mem* or if
reg > second element
of *mem*, activate
interrupt service
routine 5.

1. Interrupts if table address is
   not within table bounds.
2. *Reg* should contain table address to be checked.
3. Two words or dwords should be
   stored in memory starting at
   mem. The first should contain
   the lowest table address and
   the second should contain the
   highest table address.
4. With 16-bit addressing, *reg*
   and *mem* must be words. *Reg* is
   compared to *mem* and *mem*+2.
2. With 32-bit addressing, *reg*
   and *mem* must be dwords. *Reg* is
   compared to *mem* and *mem*+4.

ADDITION AND SUBTRACTION

inc *dest*   OF,SF,ZF,
                              AF,PF
Add 1 to *dest*.

1. *Dest* can be register or memory.
2. In the '286, *dest* can be a
   byte or word.
3. In the '386, *dest* can be a
   byte, word, or dword.

dec *dest*   OF,SF,ZF,
                              AF,PF
Subtract 1 from
dest.

1. *Dest* can be register or memory.
2. In the '286, *dest* can be a
   byte or word.
3. In the '386, *dest* can be a
   byte, word, or dword.

add *dest, source*   all

Add *source* to
dest, replacing
dest with result.

1. *Source* can be register, memory,
   or immediate.
2. *Dest* can be register or memory.
3. In the '286, *source* and *dest*
   can be bytes or words.
4. In the '386, *source* and *dest*
   can be bytes, words, or dwords.
5. *Source* and *dest* must be the
   same size unless *source* is
   immediate.
6. If immediate *source* is smaller
   than *dest*, its value is sign-
   extended to size of *dest*.

sub *dest, source*   all

Subtract *source*
from *dest*, replac-
ing *dest* with re-
sult.

1. *Source* can be register, memory,
   or immediate.
2. *Dest* can be register or memory.
3. In the '286, *source* and *dest*
   can be bytes or words.
4. In the '386, *source* and *dest*
   can be bytes, words, or dwords.
5. *Source* and *dest* must be the
   same size unless *source* is
   immediate.
6. If immediate *source* is smaller
   than *dest*, its value is sign-
   extended to size of *dest*.

adc *dest, source*   all

Add *source* and
carry flag to
dest, replacing
dest with result.

1. *Source* can be register, memory,
   or immediate.
2. *Dest* can be register or memory.
3. In the '286, *source* and *dest*
   can be bytes or words.
4. In the '386, *source* and *dest*
   can be bytes, words, or dwords.
5. *Source* and *dest* must be the
   same size unless *source* is
   immediate.
6. If immediate *source* is smaller
   than *dest*, its value is sign-
   extended to size of *dest*.

sbb *dest, source*   all

Subtract source
and carry flag
from *dest*, replac-
ing *dest* with re-
sult.

1. *Source* can be register, memory,
   or immediate.
2. *Dest* can be register or memory.
3. In the '286, *source* and *dest*
   can be bytes or words.
4. In the '386, *source* and *dest*
   can be bytes, words, or dwords.

5. *Source* and *dest* must be same size unless *source* immediate.
6. If immediate *source* is smaller than *dest*, its value is sign-extended to size of *dest*.

MULTIPLICATION

mul *source*   OF,CF
                         (SF,ZF,
If *source* is a byte,   AF,PF)
multiply AL by *source*
and replace AX with
result. If *source* is
a word, multiply AX
by *source* and replace
DX:AX with the result.
('386 only) If *source*
is a dword, multiply
EAX by *source* and re-
place EDX:EAX with
the result.

1. *Source* can be register or mem-ory.
2. In '286, *source* can be byte or word.
3. In '386, *source* can be byte, word, or dword.
4. Both multipliers are treated as unsigned values.
5. If the extended portion of the result is 0, OF and CF are cleared; otherwise they are set.

imul *source*   OF,CF
                         (SF,ZF
If *source* is byte,   AF,PF)
multiply AL by *source*
and replace AX with
the result. If *source*
is word, multiply AX
by *source* and replace
DX:AX with the result.
('386 only) If *source*
is a dword, multiply
EAX by *source* and re-
place EDX:EAX with
the result.

1. *Source* can be register or mem-ory.
2. In the '286, *source* can be byte or word.
3. In the '386, *source* can be byte, word, or dword.
4. Both multipliers are treated as signed numbers.
5. CF and OF are set if no sig-nificant digits appear in ex-tended portion of result; they are cleared otherwise.

imul *dest,source*   OF,CF
                         (SF,ZF,
Multiply *dest* by   AF,PF)
source and replace
dest with the result.

1. *Source* can be register, memory, or immediate.
2. *Dest* can be register or memory.
3. *Source* and *dest* must be the same size unless *source* is immediate.
4. If immediate *source* is smaller than *dest*, value in *source* is sign-extended to match size of dest.
5. In the '286, *source* can be byte or word.
5. In the '386, *source* can be byte, word, or dword.
7. Both multipliers are treated

as signed numbers.
8. CF and OF are set if the result does not fit in dest.

imul *dest, s1, s2*   OF,CF   1. *S1* can be register or memory.
                           (SF,ZF,   *S2* must be immediate.
Multiply *s1* by *s2*   AF,PF)   2. *Dest* can be register or memory.
and replace *dest*   3. *S1* and *dest* must be the
with the result.   same size. *S2* can be smaller.
                                     4. If *s2* is smaller than *s1* and
                                        dest, value in s*2* is sign-
                                        extended to match size of *s1*
                                        and *dest.*
                                     5. In the '286, *s1* and d*est* can
                                        be bytes or words.
                                     5. In the '386, *s1* and d*est* can
                                        be bytes, words, or dwords.
                                     7. Both multipliers are treated
                                        as signed numbers.
                                     8. CF and OF are set if the re-
                                        sult does not fit in *dest.*

DIVISION

div *divisor*   (all)   1. *Divisor* can be register or
idiv *divisor*   memory.
If divisor is a byte,   2. In the '286, *divisor* can be a
divide AX by divi-   byte or word.
sor, place the quo-   3. In the '386, *divisor* can be a
tient in AL and the   byte, word, or dword.
remainder in AH. If   4. With div, all values are
divisor is a word,   treated as unsigned numbers.
divide DX:AX by divi-   5. With idiv, all values are
sor, place the quo-   treated as signed numbers.
tient in AX and the   6. If quotient won't fit destina-
remainder in DX.   tion register, interrupt 0 is
('386 only) If divi-   activated.
sor is a dword, di-
vide EDX:EAX by divi-
sor, place the quo-
tient in EAX and the
remainder in EDX.

BCD ADJUSTMENTS

daa   all   1. Daa adjusts after addition.
das   2. Das adjusts after subtraction.

Adjust packed BCD
nibbles in AL.

---

aaa
aad

Adjust unpacked BCD byte in AL.

AF,CF
(OF,SF
ZF,PF)

1. Aaa adjusts after addition.
2. Aad adjusts after subtraction.

aam

Adjust byte in AL, yielding two unpacked BCD bytes. Place the high-order byte in AH and the low-order byte in AL.

SF,ZF,PF
(OF,AF,CF)

1. Aam adjusts after multiplication.

aad

Convert two unpacked BCD bytes in AH and AL into a binary value in AX.

SF,ZF,PF
(OF,AF,CF)

1. Aad adjusts unpacked BCD digits before division.

LOGICAL OPERATIONS

not *dest*

Complement each bit in *dest*.

1. *Dest* can be register or memory.
2. In the '286, *dest* can be a byte or word.
3. In the '386, *dest* can be a byte, word, or dword.

and *dest, source*

Set *dest* bit if both *source* bit and *dest* bit are set; clear *dest* bit otherwise.

OF,SF,ZF,
PF,CF

1. *Dest* can be register or memory.
2. *Source* can be register, memory, or immediate.
3. *Source* and *dest* must be the same size unless *source* is immediate.
4. In the '286, *source* and *dest* can be bytes or words.
5. In the '386, *source* and *dest* can be bytes, words, or dwords.
6. If immediate *source* is smaller than *dest*, value of *source* is sign-extended to size of *dest*.
7. OF and CF are always cleared.

or *dest, source*

Set *dest* bit if either *source* bit or *dest* bit are set; clear *dest* bit other-

OF,SF,ZF,
PF,CF
(AF)

1. *Dest* can be register or memory.
2. *Source* can be register, memory, or immediate.
3. *Source* and *dest* must be the same size unless *source* is immediate.

wise.

4. In the '286, *source* and *dest*
can be bytes or words.
5. In the '386, *source* and *dest*
can be bytes, words, or dwords.
6. If immediate *source* is smaller
than *dest*, value of *source* is
sign-extended to size of *dest*.
7. OF and CF are always cleared.

xor *dest, source*

Set *dest* bit if
either *source* bit
or *dest* bit, but not
both, are set; clear
dest bit otherwise.

OF,SF,ZF,
PF,CF
(AF)

1. *Dest* can be register or memory.
2. *Source* can be register, memory,
or immediate.
3. *Source* and *dest* must be the
same size unless *source* is
immediate.
4. In the '286, *source* and *dest*
can be bytes or words.
5. In the '386, *source* and *dest*
can be bytes, words, or dwords.
6. If immediate *source* is smaller
than *dest*, value of *source* is
sign-extended to size of *dest*.
7. OF and CF are always cleared.

test *dest, source*

Set flags as if
source were anded
with *dest*.

OF,SF,ZF,
PF,CF

1. *Dest* can be register or memory.
2. *Source* can be register, memory,
or immediate.
3. *Source* and *dest* must be the
same size unless *source* is
immediate.
4. In the '286, *source* and *dest*
can be bytes or words.
5. In the '386, *source* and *dest*
can be bytes, words, or dwords.
6. If immediate *source* is smaller
than *dest*, value of *source* is
sign-extended to size of *dest*.
7. OF and CF are always cleared.

neg *dest*

Negate *dest*.

OF,SF,ZF,
PF,CF

1. *Dest* can be register or memory.
2. In the '286, *dest* can be byte
or word.
3. In the '386, *dest* can be byte,
word, or dword.
4. CF is cleared if *dest* is 0;
set otherwise.

SHIFTS

sal *dest, count*   OF,SF,ZF,   1.   *Dest* can be register or memory.
shl *dest, count*   PF,CF   2.   *Count* can be immediate byte or
                      (OF)   CL. Maximum is 31.
Shift bits in *dest*   3.   In the '286, *dest* can be byte
count positions to   or word.
the left. Shift 0's   4.   In the '386, *dest* can be byte,
in on the right.   word, or dword.
                                         5.   If *count* is 1, OF is set if
                                            the new sign bit is different
                                            from the previous sign bit; it
                                            is cleared if the sign did not
                                            change.
                                         6.   If *count* > 1, OF is undefined.
                                         7.   Sal and shl are synonyms.

sar *dest, count*   OF,SF,ZF,   1.   *Dest* can be register or memory.
shr *dest, count*   PF,CF   2.   *Count* can be immediate byte or
                      (OF)   CL. Maximum is 31.
Shift bits in *dest*   3.   In the '286, *dest* can be byte
count positions to   or word.
the right. With shr,   4.   In the '386, *dest* can be byte,
shift 0's in on the   word, or dword.
left. With sar, dup-   5.   If *count* is 1, OF is always
licate the sign bit   cleared for sar. For shr, it
on the left.   is set to the original sign
                                            bit.
                                         6.   If *count* > 1, OF is undefined.

ROTATES

rcl *dest, count*   OF,CF (OF)   1.   *Dest* can be register or memory.
rol *dest, count*   2.   *Count* can be immediate byte or
                                            CL. Maximum is 31.
Rotate bits in *dest*   3.   In the '286, *dest* can be byte
count positions to   or word.
the left. With rcl,   4.   In the '386, *dest* can be byte,
rotate through the   word, or dword.
carry flag. With rol,   5.   If *count* is 1, OF is set if
rotate from high-   the rotate changed the sign
order bit to low-   of dest.
order bit, but copy   6.   If *count* > 1, OF is undefined.
high-order bit to CF.

rcr *dest, count*   OF,CF (OF)   1.   *Dest* can be register or memory.
ror *dest, count*   2.   *Count* can be immediate byte or
                                            CL. Maximum is 31.
Rotate bits in *dest*   3.   In the '286, *dest* can be byte
count positions to   or word.
the right. With rcr,   4.   In the '386, *dest* can be byte,
rotate through the   word, or dword.
carry flag. With ror,   5.   If *count* is 1, OF is set if

rotate from low-
order bit to high-
order bit, but copy
low-order bit to CF.

the rotate changed the sign
of dest.
6. If *count* > 1, OF is undefined.

BIT TESTS

bt *dest,position*   CF
bts *dest,position*
btr *dest,position*
btc *dest,position*

Copy bit from indi-
cated *position* in
dest to carry flag.
With bts, set the
indicated bit in
dest. With btr,
clear the indicated
bit in *dest*. With
btc, complement the
indicated bit in
dest.

1. '386 only.
2. *Dest* can be register or memory.
3. *Dest* can be byte, word, or
   dword.
4. *Position* can be an immediate
   byte or register.
5. If *position* is a register, it
   must be the same size as *dest*.
6. Maximum *position* is 31.

BIT SCANS

bsf *dest, source*   ZF
bsr *dest, source*

Scan *source* for first
nonzero bit. Place
position of first
nonzero bit in *dest*.
With bsf, scan *source*
from right to left.
With bsr, scan *source*
from left to right.

1. '386 only.
2. *Source* can be register or
   memory.
3. *Dest* can be register only.
4. Source and dest must be the
   same size.
5. *Source* and *dest* can be words
   or dwords.
6. If *source* is 0, ZF is set and
   result in *dest* is undefined.
7. If *source* is not 0, ZF is
   cleared and result is placed
   in *dest*.

SETTING AND CLEARING FLAGS

stc   CF

Set carry flag.

clc   CF

Clear carry flag.

cmc   CF

Complement CF.

std   DF

Set direction
flag.

cld   DF

Clear direction
flag.

Appendix B
System Instructions

Instruction	Status Flags	Notes
arpl *dest,source*	ZF	1. *Source* must be a word register.
If requested privilege level (RPL) of *dest* < RPL of *source*, set ZF and copy RPL of *source* to RPL of *dest*. Else, clear ZF.		2. D*est* must be a word register or memory field containing a segment selector. 3. The RPL is in bits 0 and 1 of the segment selector.
clts	none	
Clear task-switched flag.		
cli	none	
Clear interrupt flag.		
hlt		
Stop instruction execution and place processor in halt state. (An enabled interrupt or NMI will resume execution at next instruction.)		

in *dest,port*   none   1. *Dest* must be AL, AX, or EAX.
                                          2. Port can be immediate port ad-
Input value from   dress or DX.
port to *dest*.

ins *dest,*DX   none   1. Dest can be a memory byte,
insb   word, or dword.
insw   2. DF determines whether (E)DI is
insd   incremented or decremented.

Input element from
port addressed by
[DX] to (E)DI. Then
advance (E)DI. If
dest is given, it
determines segment
and size of dest.

lar *dest,source*   ZF   1. *Source* can be a register or
                                             memory.
If segment selector   2. *Dest* must be a register.
for *source* is visible
and a valid descrip-
tor type, copy the
access rights byte
from *source* to *dest*
and set ZF. Other-
wise, clear ZF.

lgdt *source*   none   1. *Source* must be a memory field.
lidt *source*

Load the global des-
criptor table or inter-
rupt descriptor table
from *source*.

lldt *source*   none   1. *Source* can be a register or
                                             memory word.
Load local descrip-
tor table register
from *source*.

lmsw *source*   none   1. *Source* can be a register or
                                             memory word.
Load machine status
word register from
source.

lock *instruction*   none   1. *Instruction* can be a bit test,
                                             xchg, addition, subtraction,
Assert LOCK# signal   or logical operation.
for *instruction*.

(Prevent other
processes from
accessing memory
operand of instruc-
tion.)

lsl *dest, source*   ZF   1. Source can be register or mem-
                                        ory field.
If segment selector   2. Dest must be a register.
of *source* is visible
and valid, copy seg-
ment limit from
source to *dest* and
set ZF. Otherwise,
clear ZF.

ltr *source*   none   1. Source can be a word register
                                        or memory field.
Load task register
from *source* and mark
task as busy.

out *dest, source*   none   1. *Source* can be register or mem-
outs *dest, source*   ory.
outsb   2. *Dest* must be DX.
outsw   3. DF determines whether (E)SI is
outsd   incremented or decremented.

Output element at
(E)SI to [DX]. Then
advance (E)SI. If
specified, source
indicates segment
and size of source
element.

sgdt *dest*   none   1. *Dest* must be a memory field.
sidt *dest*

Store global descrip-
tor table or inter-
rupt descriptor table
to *dest*.

sldt *dest*   none   1. *Dest* can be a register or mem-
                                        ory word.
Store local descrip-
tor table register
to *dest*.

smsw *dest*   none   1. *Dest* can be a register or mem-
                                        ory word.
Store machine status
word to *dest*.

sti   none

Set interrupt flag.

str *dest*   none   1. *Dest* can be a register or mem-
                                            ory word.
Store task register
to *dest*.

verr *source*   ZF   1. Source can be a register or
verw *source*   memory word containing a seg-
                                            ment selector.
If source segment
is reachable from
current privilege
level and is read-
able (verr) or
writable (verw),
set ZF. Otherwise,
clear ZF.

Appendix C
Coprocessor Instruction
Reference

Instruction   **Notes**

DATA TRANSFER

fld *source*   1. *Source* can be a stack register
                                             or real memory field.
Decrement stack pointer.
Convert real value from *source*
to extended-precision format
and place result in ST.

fild *source*   1. *Source* must be a word, short,
                                             or long integer in memory.
Decrement stack pointer.
Convert integer value from
source to extended-precision
format and place result in ST.

fbld *source*   1. *Source* must be a BCD tenbyte
                                             in memory.
Decrement stack pointer.
Convert BCD value from *source*
to extended-precision format
and place result in ST.

fst *dest*
fstp *dest*

Convert value from ST to real
format of *dest* as appropriate
and place result in *dest*. With
fstp, mark ST as empty and
increment stack pointer.

1. With fst, *dest* can be a stack
   register or a single- or
   double-precision real value
   in memory.
2. With fstp, *dest* can also be
   an extended-precision real
   value in memory.

fist *dest*
fistp *dest*

Convert value from ST to integer
format of *dest* as appropriate
and place result in *dest*. With
fistp, mark ST as empty and
increment stack pointer.

1. With fist, *dest* can be a word
   or short integer in memory.
2. With fistp, *dest* can also be a
   long integer in memory.

fbstp *dest*

Convert value from ST to BCD
format of *dest* and place result in *dest*. Mark ST as empty
and increment stack pointer.

1. *Dest* must be a memory tenbyte.

fxch [dest]

Exchange values of ST and *dest*.
If *dest* is omitted, exchange
values of ST and ST(1).

1. *Dest* must be a stack register.

NONTRANSCENDENTALS

fadd

Add ST to ST(1). Pop ST.

fadd *source*

Convert value from *source*
to extended-precision
format if necessary. Add result to ST.

1. *Source* must be a memory field.
2. *Source* must be in real format.

fadd *dest, source*
faddp *dest, source*

Add *source* to *dest*. With
faddp, pop ST.

1. *Source* and *dest* must both be
   register stack names.
2. Either *source* or *dest* must be
   ST.

fiadd *source*

Convert value from *source*

1. *Source* must be a memory field.
2. *Source* must be in integer
   format.

to extended-precision
format and add the result to
ST.

fsub

Subtract ST from ST(1). Pop
ST.

fsub *source*

Convert value from *source*
to extended-precision format
if necessary. Subtract result from ST.

1. *Source* must be a memory field.
2. S*ource* must be in real format.

fsub *dest, source*
fsubp *dest, source*

Subtract *source* from *dest*.
With fsubp, pop ST.

1. *Source* and *dest* must both be
   register stack names.
2. Either s*ource* or *dest* must be
   ST.

fisub *source*

Convert value from *source*
to extended-precision
format and subtract the result from ST.

1. *Source* must be a memory field.
2. *Source* must be in integer
   format.

fsubr

Subtract ST(1) from ST. Store
the result at ST(1). Pop ST.

fsubr *source*

Convert value from *source*
to extended-precision format
if necessary. Subtract ST
from the *source*. Store result at ST.

1. *Source* must be a memory field.
2. S*ource* must be in real format.

fsubr *dest, source*
fsubrp *dest, source*

Subtract *dest* from *source*.
Store result at *dest*. With
fsubrp, pop ST.

1. *Source* and *dest* must both be
   register stack names.
2. Either s*ource* or *dest* must be
   ST.

fisubr *source*

Convert value from *source*
to extended-precision
format and subtract ST from

1. *Source* must be a memory field.
2. *Source* must be in integer
   format.

it. Store the result at ST.

fmul

Multiply ST(1) by ST. Pop ST.

fmul *source*	1. *Source* must be a memory field.
	2. *Source* must be in real format.

Convert value from *source*
to extended-precision
format if necessary. Multiply
ST by result.

fmul *dest, source*	1. *Source* and *dest* must both be
fmulp *dest, source*	register stack names.
	2. Either s*ource* or d*est* must be
Multiply *dest* by *source*. With	ST.
fmulp, pop ST.	

fimul *source*	1. *Source* must be a memory field.
	2. S*ource* must be in integer
Convert value from *source*	format.
to extended-precision	
format. Multiply ST by the	
result.	

fdiv

Divide ST(1) by ST. Pop ST.

fdiv *source*	1. *Source* must be a memory field.
	2. *Source* must be in real format.

Convert value from *source*
to extended-precision
format if necessary. Divide
ST by result.

fdiv *dest, source*	1. *Source* and *dest* must both be
fdivp *dest, source*	register stack names.
	2. Either s*ource* or d*est* must be
Divide *dest* by *source*. With	ST.
fdivp, pop ST.	

fidiv *source*	1. *Source* must be a memory field.
	2. S*ource* must be in integer
Convert value from *source*	format.
to extended-precision	
format. Divide ST by the	
result.	

fdivr *source*	1. *Source* must be a memory field.
	2. S*ource* must be in real format.

Convert value from *source*
to extended-precision format

if necessary. Divide *source*
by ST. Store result at ST.

fdivr *dest, source*
fdivrp *dest, source*

Divide *source* by *dest*.
Store result at *dest*. With
fdivrp, pop ST.

1. *Source* and *dest* must both be
   register stack names.
2. Either s*ource* or *dest* must be
   ST.

fidivr *source*

Convert value from *source*
to extended-precision
format and divide it by ST.
Store the result at ST.

1. *Source* must be a memory field.
2. *Source* must be in integer
   format.

fsqrt

Replace ST with the square
root of ST.

fscale

Add ST(1) to exponent of ST.

1. With the '287, ST(1) should be
   an integer in the range -2^{15}
   to $+2^{15}$.

fprem
fprem1

Divide ST by ST(1). Discard
the quotient and leave the
remainder in ST. Limited to
a maximum reduction of 264
in one operation. Set C2 if
ST is not completely reduced
by the operation. Set C3, C1,
and C0 to the least-significant
three bits of the quotient.
Fprem1 produces the remainder
according to the final IEEE
standard.

1. Fprem1 is '387 only.

frndint

Round ST to an integer according
to the rounding control bits in
the control word register.

fxtract

Extract exponent and significand
from ST. Replace ST with exponent
and push significand onto stack.

fabs

Replace ST with its absolute
value.

fchs

Reverse sign of ST.

COMPARISONS

fcom [*source*]
fcomp [*source*]
fcompp [*source*]

Set condition codes as if
source were subtracted from
ST. If *source* is not given,
ST(1) is assumed. With fcomp,
ST is popped after comparison.
With fcompp, both ST and ST(1)
are popped.

1. *Source* can be a stack register
    or single- or double-precision
    memory field.

ficom *source*
ficomp *source*

Convert *source* to extended-
precision real format. Set
condition codes as if *source*
were subtracted from ST. With
ficomp, ST is popped after comparison.

1. *Source* can be a word or short
    integer memory field.

ftst

Set condition codes as if 0
were subtracted from ST.

fucom [*source*]
fucomp [*source*]
fucompp [*source*]

Just like fcom, fcomp, and
fcompp except does not cause
an exception if either operand
is a NaN.

1. '386 only.

fxam

Set condition codes to indicate

type of value in ST.

TRANSCENDENTALS

fcos

Replace value in ST with its co-sine. Set C2 and don't change ST if ST is out of range.

1. '386 only.
2. ST should be $< 2^{63}$.

fsin

Replace value in ST with its sine. Set C2 and don't change ST if ST is out of range.

1. '386 only.
2. ST should be $< 2^{63}$.

fsincos

Replace value in ST with its sine. Push cos(ST) onto the stack. Set C2 and don't change ST if ST is out of range.

1. '386 only.
2. ST should be $< 2^{63}$.

fptan

Replace ST with TAN(ST). Push 1 onto the stack.

fpatan

Replace ST(1) with ARCTAN(ST(1)/ST). Pop ST.

f2xm1

Replace ST with $2^{ST} - 1$.

1. ST must be in the range of -1 to +1.

fyl2x

Replace ST with (ST(1))(LOG₂ST).

1. ST must be positive.

fyl2xp1

Replace ST with (ST(1))(LOG₂(ST+1)).

1. ST must be in the range of $-(1-SQRT(2)/2)$ to $1-SQRT(2)/2$.

CONSTANTS

fldz

Push +0.0 onto stack.

fld1

Push +1.0 onto stack.

fldpi

Push pi onto stack.

fldl2t

Push $LOG_2 10$ onto stack.

fldl2e

Push $LOG_2 e$ onto stack.

fldlg2

Push $LOG_{10} 2$ onto stack.

fldln2

Push $LOG_e 2$ onto stack.

PROCESSOR CONTROL

finit
fninit

Initialize processor. With
fninit, fwait is not implied.

fldcw *source*	1. *Source* must be a memory word.

Load *source* into control word.

fstcw *dest*	1. *Dest* must be a memory word.

Store control word in *dest*.

fstsw *dest*	1. *Dest* must be a memory word.
fnstsw *dest*	
fstsw *ax*	
fnstsw *ax*	

Store status word at *dest*. With
fnstsw, fwait is not implied.
With fstsw ax and fnstsw ax, the
destination is ax.

fclex
fnclex

Clear exception flags in status
word register. With fnclex, fwait
is not implied.

fsave *dest*
fnsave *dest*

1. With 16-bit addressing, state
occupies 47 words. With 32-bit
addressing, state occupies 54
words.

Save entire coprocessor state
(all registers) at *dest*. With
fnsave, fwait is not implied.

frstor *source*

1. With 16-bit addressing, state
occupies 47 words. With 32-bit
addressing, state occupies 54
words.

Load coprocessor state (all
registers) from *source*.

fstenv *dest*
fnstenv *dest*

1. With 16-bit addressing, environment occupies 7 words. With
32-bit addressing, environment
occupies 14 words.

Store coprocessor environment
registers (control word, status
word, tag word, and pointers) to
dest. With fnstenv, fwait is not
implied.

fldenv *source*

1. With 16-bit addressing, environment occupies 7 words. With
32-bit addressing, environment
occupies 14 words.

Load coprocessor environment
from *source*.

fincstp

Increment stack pointer.

fdecstp

Decrement stack pointer.

ffree *dest*

1. *Dest* must be a stack register.

Change *dest* register's tag
to empty.

fnop

No operation.

fwait
wait

Wait for coprocessor to complete
current operation.

fsetpm   1. '287 only.

Set 80287 to protected mode.

Index

A

aaa, 139-140
aad, 141-142
aam, 141-142
aas, 139-140
adc, 120-123
add, 119-120
addition, 118-124, 137-139
address, 2, 13, 21, 22, 329-331
AF (auxiliary flag), 14, 137-140
affine closure, *see* infinity
AH (*see also* AX, EAX), 62, 133, 141,
AL (*see also* AX, EAX)
  with BCD adjustment instructions, 138, 139-140, 141
  with conversion instructions, 70, 71
  with load and store string instructions, 77
  with multiplication and division instructions, 126, 129, 133
  with scan string instructions, 103
alias, 201-202
align, 258
alignment, 43, 256-258, 263-264
and
  expression operator, 197
  instructions, 176-177

API (application program interface), 31
arccosine, 167
arcsine, 167
arctangent, 166-167
ASCII adjustments, 137, 139-143
ASCII values
  as immediate operands, 20
  carriage return and line feed, 32-33
  converting to and from BCD, 177, 178
  displaying with online debuggers, 331, 332, 343-344
  in data declarations, 195-196
  translation from EBCDIC, 71
assembler, 35-36
assembler listing, 247-255, 275-276, 282, 288-291
assembler messages, 258-259, 285-286
assume, 42, 270
AX, 11
  with BCD adjustment instructions, 141
  with conversion instructions, 70
  with load and store string instructions, 77
  with multiplication and division instructions, 126, 129, 133

About the Authors

Judi N. Fernandez and Ruth Ashley are copresidents of DuoTech, Inc. and authors of more than two dozen books on various aspects of micro-computers.